# TWO WORLDS IN THE TENNESSEE MOUNTAINS

Winner of the 1996 Appalachian Studies Award

# TWO WORLDS
# IN THE
# TENNESSEE
# MOUNTAINS

Exploring the Origins
of Appalachian
Stereotypes

DAVID C. HSIUNG

THE UNIVERSITY PRESS OF KENTUCKY

Publication of this volume was made possible in part
by a grant from the National Endowment for the Humanities

Scholarly publisher for the Commonwealth,
serving Bellarmine College, Berea College, Centre
College of Kentucky, Eastern Kentucky University,
The Filson Club Historical Society, Georgetown College,
Kentucky Historical Society, Kentucky State University,
Morehead State University, Murray State University,
Northern Kentucky University, Transylvania University,
University of Kentucky, University of Louisville,
and Western Kentucky University.

*Editorial and Sales Offices:* The University Press of Kentucky
663 South Limestone Street, Lexington, Kentucky 40508-4008

01  00  99  98  97      5  4  3  2  1

Hsiung, David C., 1961–
    Two worlds in the Tennessee mountains : exploring the origins of
  Appalachian stereotypes / David C. Hsiung.
        p.     cm.
    Includes bibliographical references and index.
    ISBN 0–8131–2001–2 (cloth : alk. paper)
    1. Tennessee, East—Social conditions.   2. Tennessee, East—
  Geography.   3. Tennessee, East—Economic conditions.   4. Social
  isolation—Tennessee, East—History.   5. Stereotype (Psychology)
  —Tennessee, East—History.   I. Title.
  HN79.T22E35   1997
  306'.09768—dc20                                          96–42954

This book is printed on acid-free recycled paper meeting
the requirements of the American National Standard
for Permanence of Paper for Printed Library Materials.
∞ ⊛

Manufactured in the United States of America

FOR RACHEL AND BENJAMIN

O no, it is an ever-fixed mark
That looks on tempests and is never shaken.
—William Shakespeare, from Sonnet CXVI

# Contents

# Figures, Maps, and Tables

TABLES

# Preface

AMERICANS HAVE a persistent fascination with Appalachia. In 1989, Dan Rather of the CBS news program *Forty-eight Hours* invited viewers to join him on "a disturbing journey to a separate world close to home," to Floyd County in eastern Kentucky. "What is it that keeps them [the residents] tied to a place that seems like something out of another century? Come along with us now for 48 hours to the isolated beauty of Appalachia, to hills and hollers most Americans have never seen and a life most Americans will never experience."[1] Even more frequently, Americans see the Appalachian mountaineer depicted in popular culture. The outlets for such images range from the recent movie *The Beverly Hillbillies* to Robert Schenkkan's Pulitzer Prize–winning play, *The Kentucky Cycle*. Ever since the 1930s, hundreds of daily newspapers have spread the image of what John Solomon Otto calls the "ill-kempt, ill-educated, and poverty-stricken farmers-cum-moonshiners who lived a static and unchanging life in the isolated Appalachian Mountains"[2] through the comic strips of Al Capp's "Li'l Abner" and Billy De Beck's "Barney Google and Snuffy Smith."

Harry Caudill's 1962 book *Night Comes to the Cumberlands* focused national attention on the mountain region in a different way. This best-seller not only helped spark national legislation for Appalachia but also reinforced images of the region and its inhabitants in the popular imagination. "Consider then these forces in synopsis: The illiterate son of illiterate ancestors, cast loose in an immense wilderness without basic mechanical or agricultural skills, without the refining, comforting and disciplining influence of an organized religious order, in a vast land wholly unrestrained by social organization or effective laws, compelled to acquire skills quickly in order to survive, and with a Stone Age savage as his principal teacher. From these forces emerged the mountaineer as he is to an astonishing degree even to this day" (p. 31). Caudill noted that although these women and men found rich natural resources in the mountains, the land, "intricately compartmented by its numberless valleys, afforded isolation for decades, and the illusion of isolation for more than a century. It remained an island of frontier life and circumstances far behind the real frontier and time forgot and ignored it for a hundred years" (p. 19). Caudill told Americans that physical isolation played a crucial role in shaping the mountaineers. Not surprisingly, federal aid for Appalachia in the 1960s funded thousands of miles of roads in the mountains.

The present book explains how society developed in the mountains and how such images of Appalachia first arose. In the process I analyze the ill-defined and overused term "isolation" and identify the different ways in which the inhabitants of Tennessee's northeastern tip were connected to (or were separated from) other peoples and places at the same time. During the revolutionary and antebellum eras, some residents of upper East Tennessee saw themselves as isolated from the rest of the United States, even though they were increasingly integrated into its larger society. Nevertheless, they strove to establish further connections with a railroad, faced opposition and apathy from some of their neighbors, and described these neighbors as backward. The evolution of such a self-image fostered Appalachian characterizations *within* the mountain region; when writers from outside the region tapped into this self-image, they obtained the raw material for best-selling short stories and novels that shaped the popular image of Appalachia for well over a century. In a letter to her publisher in 1882, Mary Noailles Murfree described the characters in her short stories as "a little known people in a wild and secluded region." These stories, collected in the best-selling volume *In the Tennessee Mountains*, presented readers with a distorted view of an isolated Appalachian world. While some mountaineers lived in relative isolation, others established a host of broader connections extending beyond the immediate locale. Therefore, two worlds existed in the Tennessee mountains, and the interplay between them produced a distinctive image of the region and its inhabitants.

The elusive nature of self-perceptions and images, as well as the different ways such views have been tied to notions of isolation, warrant the use of several different methodological approaches. One of my chapters will examine at times an area encompassing thousands of square miles and at other times only certain portions of a single county. One chapter focuses on the geographical development of the road system; others address war, the economy, and population migration. When these different approaches are united by a steady chronological progression from the 1780s to the 1880s, they permit a more complex understanding of Appalachian images than would be afforded by any single methodology. Because the Appalachian images under consideration pertain to white mountaineers, this book focuses on people of European rather than African or Native American descent. The approach taken to the interpretation of these images, however, can readily be applied to other peoples living in other environments. I address primarily the eighty years preceding the Civil War but pay little attention to the sectional crisis itself. Instead, I examine a people and a place at once strangely familiar and hopelessly foreign to readers at the end of the twentieth century. By understanding the images that inform our view of Appalachia, we can begin to understand this region's grip on our imagination even today.

I have received an astonishing amount of help and encouragement while working on this project. The reason, some might say, is that I took so long to finish the thing, but time is only a small part of the story. Many individuals and institutions, acknowledged here, have nourished my work for these many years.

At the University of Michigan, Shaw Livermore, Jr., Kenneth Lockridge, John Kolars, and especially John Shy and Gerald Linderman provided the guidance I greatly needed. Their example has influenced me in areas far beyond just my approach to the study and teaching of history. The staffs at the Map Room in the Harlan Hatcher Graduate Library and at the William L. Clements Library provided essential assistance. Similarly, those at the Hoskins Library, University of Tennessee, and the Lawson-Mc-Ghee Library (both in Knoxville) and at the Tennessee State Library and Archives in Nashville helped me at the beginning of this research. Most important, the staff at the Archives of Appalachia,

Sherrod Library, East Tennessee State University—Georgia Greer, Ned Irwin, Scott Schwartz (now at the Smithsonian), Ed Speer, Marie Tedesco, and Norma Myers—welcomed me to the region and did all that any researcher could ask for (even offering me housing!) to help make my work productive and enjoyable. Over the years, I have come to value their friendship far more than I treasure the collection for my research. Through them I also met Lucy Gump, a cheerful and enthusiastic historian who has always supported my interest in the region with words of encouragement, access to her research, and gracious hospitality.

Many other colleagues have encouraged me and analyzed my work critically. Through the Appalachian Studies Association, I met Tyler Blethen, Durwood Dunn, Barbara Howe, Benita Howell, Nancy Joyner, Ronald Lewis, Ken Noe, Mary Beth Pudup, Paul Salstrom, Jean Haskell Speer, Altina Waller, Jerry Williamson, Curtis Wood, and many others who provided much support and advice. When I presented my first paper before this organization, I had the great fortune of sharing the session with John Inscoe and Gordon McKinney. In the eight years since then, each has given vigorous support, made perceptive comments, and patiently read more drafts of chapters than I can count. No young scholar could have received more valuable assistance. Dwight Billings, Martin Crawford, and Ralph Mann also read the entire manuscript and provided clear analyses and a broad perspective that helped me to see the topic with fresh eyes. The organizers and participants at a number of conferences, especially Richard Brooks, Robert Calhoon, David Crass, Warren Hofstra, Kenneth Koons, Robert D. Mitchell, and Michael Puglisi, urged me to look beyond the Appalachian region and the discipline of history. Considerations of space, not a lack of gratitude, prevent me from naming others. For all who helped me grapple with a conceptual understanding of Appalachia and the southern backcountry, I hope this volume provides some return for your efforts.

Still others guided this work through the publication process. The staff of the University Press of Kentucky buoyed me with their enthusiasm and professionalism. David Barnes, under the direction of David Di Biase at Deasy GeoGraphics Laboratory, Pennsylvania State University, produced the remarkable maps included in this volume. They make clear what I express only clum-

sily in the text. My colleague Peter Goldstein saved me from
mixed metaphors, and my copyeditor, Marcia Brubeck, rescued me
from even worse writing. Louise Goldstein labored over the index
as if the book were her own.

Like the mountaineers of whom I write, I have been supported
by overlapping and reinforcing "bonds of mutuality" that energize
the communities in which I live. Juniata College has provided
generous institutional support for my work, while colleagues and
friends here—especially Betty Ann Cherry, Celia Cook-Huffman,
Dave Drews, Peter Goldstein, Klaus Kipphan, Keith Mann, Peter
Peregrine (now at Lawrence University), Ruth Reed, Dave
Reingold, Karen Rosell, Russ Shelley, Philbrook Smith, David
Sowell, Mary Taylor (now at Loyola University), Henry Thurston-
Griswold, Donna Weimer, and their families—have reminded me
that rigorous scholarship, passionate teaching, and close friend-
ships reinforce one another. Old friends (especially Jody Brown,
the Kabinses, Mary Lacey, and the late John Todd) and recent
ones (like the Gembinskis and Dot Mizzi) have helped more than
they probably realize. The most important support and encouragement have come from my family, both extended (all those
Hsiungs, Oakleys, Beebes, Wendts, Goulds, and Lockwoods) and
immediate (I include in this category long talks with big cousin
Nancy after Christmas and gourmet cooking from brother Bob
and sister-in-law Ingrid at especially desperate times). I am especially grateful for the love and support of my parents, who always
wanted me to try new things (I did) and to be happy (I am). I dedi-
cate this book to Rachel and Benjamin, the two brightest lights in
my life. They made the effort to complete this project not only
possible but worthwhile.

INTRODUCTION

# The Framework
# for Connectedness

THE WORD "APPALACHIA" evokes a host of images and stereotypes involving feuds, individualism, moonshine, subsistence
farming, quilting bees, illiteracy, dueling banjos, and many other
things. Both complimentary and derogatory images generally arise
from two important concepts, namely those of isolation and community. According to John Fox, Jr., a popular American novelist
at the turn of the twentieth century, "In the march of civilization
westward, the Southern mountaineer has been left in an isolation
almost beyond belief. He was shut off by mountains that have
blocked and still block the commerce of a century, and there for a
century he has stayed." As a result, the mountaineer "has lived in
the cabin in which his grandfather was born, and in life, habit, and
thought he has been merely his grandfather born over again." As
for the mountaineer's social world, Fox wrote, "His interest centered in himself, his family, his distant neighbor, his grist mill, his
country store, [and] his county town" rather than his state, region,
or nation.[1] Ever since Will Wallace Harney identified Appalachia
as "A Strange Land and Peculiar People" in 1873, Americans have
attributed the local characteristics in large part to tightly knit communities far removed from the mainstream of American society.[2]

Many scholars have studied popular perceptions of Appalachia.
Most recently, Allen Batteau has claimed that the image of Appalachia "is a creature of the urban imagination," invented to serve
the "economic opportunism, political creativity, or passing fancy
of urban elites." While Batteau analyzes the motives behind the
creation of these images—such as the urge to indict "the [Southern]

plantocracy and the decadent economy it constructed" during the antebellum period—he pays more attention to the persistence of such images over the past century than to the exact process by which the images were formed.[3] Batteau avoids distinguishing "myth" from "reality" in Appalachian images, but Henry Shapiro argues that local color writers like John Fox, Jr., and northern home missionaries wanted to persuade Americans that such images were accurate. Such individuals sought to sell more stories or to inaugurate benevolence programs and through their efforts "dominated public discussion of the nature of mountain life between 1870 and 1890." Shapiro declares, "The idea that Appalachia was a discrete region of the nation became a convention of the American consciousness by 1890."[4]

Once the region's distinctiveness had been established, according to Shapiro, it conflicted with "contemporary conceptions of America as a unified and homogeneous national entity." Shapiro claims that the dissonance generated by Appalachia's existence in modern America led in part to a flurry of explanations that "sought to integrate the fact of Appalachian otherness into the conceptual schemes by which American civilization was defined."[5] After 1890, the explanations fell into two categories, the first seeing the environment as a determinant of culture, which in turn distinguishes the mountains from other regions, and the second viewing the mountain residents as descendants of paupers and criminals ("poor white trash") who made the mountain population distinctive. Both explanations, however, drew on the notion of isolation. Shapiro observes that since 1870, "isolation has been the single characteristic which all descriptions of the region note, and about which all commentators upon the nature and implications of Appalachian otherness have had something to say. . . . By isolation has been meant a state of mind, an undesirable provincialism resulting from the lack of contact between the mountaineers and outsiders."[6]

Shapiro never claims that the writers and home missionaries accurately described the situation in the mountains, for "their discussions of the nature and meaning of Appalachian otherness were rarely made with reference to the real conditions of mountain life or the normal complexity of social and economic conditions which prevailed in the mountains as in every other section of the nation." Although there was "fundamental agreement on the importance of isolation as a cause of Appalachia's existence as a discrete region and as the principal characteristic by which Appalachian otherness was defined, there was no real agreement on the manner in which isolation affected the quality of mountain life." Shapiro was not concerned with the accuracy of such impressions, for "where these notions came from and how they became a convention of the American consciousness after the Civil War is the subject of a different book than this one."[7] These issues, however, lie at the heart of my book.

In order to understand Appalachia and the origins of its accompanying stereotypes, we must look critically at the notions of isolation and community. How are such terms defined? What physical and social forces unite or fragment a community? In what ways can a region be isolated from surrounding areas and integrated with them? Such questions, and the search for origins, push us back from the twentieth and nineteenth centuries to the beginnings of permanent white settlement. After all, isolation can make the recent mountaineer "the pioneer of the Revolution, the living ancestor of the Modern West," only if it existed from the time of the first settlement.[8] The detail required by these questions encourages us to focus on a specific Appalachian locale rather than to survey the region as a whole.

Upper East Tennessee (which includes the northeastern tip of the state), for example, contains some of the most mountainous terrain found east of the Mississippi River. The Unaka Range, which forms the border between Tennessee and North Carolina, contains many steep and high mountains; nearly twenty have elevations above 5,000 feet and "slopes with a descent from crest to stream of 4000 feet are not uncommon." The Ridge and Valley section, about sixty-five miles wide in northern Tennessee, forms the rest of the region. Numerous creeks feed rivers that follow a northeast-southwest direction in the more open valleys, surrounded by "broad rounded hills, sharp knobs, and narrow ridges, rising from 100 to 300 feet above the streams."[9] Such typically Appalachian physiography allows us to apply conclusions drawn from upper East Tennessee to other locations within the mountain region. When we place upper East Tennessee within a framework for the analysis of isolation (and its converse, integration), we can develop a sense of the region's internal and external connections. This context then helps us understand how external perceptions combined with the residents' self-perceptions to form the enduring images of Appalachia.

## Interdisciplinary Frameworks and Theories

We can understand how images of Appalachia developed by using a theoretical framework to examine the region's internal "connectedness" and its external links to American society more generally. These ties may be relatively concrete (like transportation routes between upper East Tennessee and Virginia) or relatively abstract (such as the sense of loneliness or isolation that people may feel when transportation routes do not exist). A well-established literature in social psychology would call this framework a "multidimensional construct" embracing several distinct "dimensions" and "measures." More simply, "connectedness" implies a variety of parts, each in turn consisting of smaller pieces. We must consider each dimension in relation to the other dimensions rather than separate from them. Otherwise, blanket statements proclaiming a region "isolated" or "integrated" will fail to take into account the different ways in which isolation (or the self-perception of being isolated) can be present in one respect but not in others. By studying the ways in which a region and its people exhibit a range of characteristics, we can develop a more holistic, synthetic, and realistic understanding of a region.

The framework separates connectedness into several component parts, and we must consider each before drawing any conclusions about the region as a whole. For example, upper East Tennessee may be broken down into its political, social, economic, geographical, and perceptual elements. The region may be more isolated in one dimension (such as political structure) and more integrated in others (such as economy or transportation). Therefore, the region may be both isolated and integrated during the same time period. Only after we have weighed all of these dimensions can we determine upper East Tennessee's connectedness. Several cautions must be noted, however. By describing the dimensions separately, we may seem to imply that they were distinct from and unrelated to one another, but they were not separate in upper East Tennessee (or anywhere else); each dimension shared important characteristics with every other dimension. Further-more, different conditions existed *within* the region. When we look at the same dimensions in a variety of locations, we may find different degrees of connectedness. Towns located along the rail-road, for example, may have been more integrated in certain re-spects than those tucked within the folds of mountain ridges and valleys. The sum of these geographical variations shapes our broader understanding of upper East Tennessee.

The process of evaluation continues at a more detailed level, because we must examine each dimension through several "mea-sures." We must weigh these different forms of evidence before we can judge the degree of connectedness for a given dimension. For example, upper East Tennessee's economy may be more isolated regarding subsistence agriculture and more integrated with respect to iron manufacture and livestock trade. We might then conclude that the region's economy should be weighted more toward inte-gration than toward isolation when we rate connectedness. Re-member that many of the measures also address more than one dimension. The early road network, for example, responds to geo-graphical conditions, provides a context for the social develop-ment of a community, and shapes the perceptions of those living within the region.[10]

The proposed framework therefore provides a complex tool for studying a theoretical notion like connectedness. Isolation, often regarded in monolithic terms, can be broken down into its interre-lated parts and analyzed more clearly and critically. To use one metaphor, this framework serves as an interdisciplinary camera lens through which we can take a wide-angle shot of the forest as well as zoom in on the trees. But as experienced photographers know, different lenses clarify certain subjects while obscuring oth-ers. The polarizing filter, which removes the sun's disconcerting glare, also artificially darkens the sky. The lens of community theory—ground and polished over the decades by historians, an-thropologists, and sociologists—helps us understand the outlook and self-perceptions of the Appalachian mountaineers but entails assumptions that inevitably distort our view of the past.

When George A. Hillery, Jr., surveyed the social science litera-ture in 1955, he found *ninety-four* definitions of "community." The majority of them shared only one obvious and simplistic concept: "all of the definitions deal with people."[11] Many current definitions of community identify social structures and activities in a particular locale. For example, Gidean Sjoberg calls a community "a collectivity of actors sharing in a limited territorial area as the base for carrying out the greatest share of their daily activities."[12] Although specific physical location unquestionably plays an important role, some writers argue that it need not serve as a prerequisite for community. As Thomas Bender makes clear, "the concept means more than a place or local activity. There is an expectation of a special quality of human relationship in a community, and it is this experiential dimension that is crucial to its definition." Community, therefore, "is best defined as a network of social relations marked by mutuality and emotional bonds" that "may or may not be coterminous with a specific, contiguous territory."[13] Gunnar Almgren argues in a recent survey of the topic that "the dominant discriminating element and point of debate among definitions remain the role of territorial arrangements."[14] Although my study of Appalachia pays close attention to geographical details, it takes a flexible approach toward the analysis of community in terms of location. "Connectedness" is not limited to a single town, cove, valley, or mountaintop but instead overlaps these different areas.

In addition to freeing the concept of community from its geographical anchor, we must liberate it from its romanticized theoretical tradition. Scholars have often described societies as evolving from a "rural" or "traditional" stage to an "urban" or "modern" one.[15] Such views find their roots in Ferdinand Tönnies's 1887 analysis, *Gemeinschaft und Gesellschaft*, translated as *Community and Society*. At one end of the spectrum, close personal ties bind a community together and produce a society in which "all intimate, private, and exclusive living together. . . is understood as life in Gemeinschaft (community)." At the other extreme, "Gesellschaft (society) is public life—it is the world itself." An atomized society of unconnected individuals characterizes Gesellschaft, the "mere co-existence of people independent of each other."[16] We may consider the colonial New England town, for example, as opposed to modern Manhattan. Alternatively, the familiar world of the mountain hollow can be contrasted with the disconcerting alienness of emigrant destinations like Detroit. In each case, one associates a positive value with the gemeinschaft stage of society. Almgren notes that sociologists have had difficulty with the concept of community for several reasons, "not the least of which has been nostalgic attachment to the idealized notion that the existence of community is embodied in the village or small town where human associations are characterized as *Gemeinschaft*—that is, associations that are intimate, familiar, sympathetic, mutually interdependent, and reflective of a shared social consciousness."[17]

Tönnies's ideas, and the use to which historians subsequently put them, have come under sharp attack. Many historians have designated a particular period during which the shift from a traditional to a modern society took place in America. Unfortunately, they disagree as to when this period occurred. In his perceptive survey of the issue, Thomas Bender examines the works of Bernard Bailyn and Darrett Rutman (who locate the change sometime during the seventeenth century), Gordon Wood and Richard Bushman (who find it in the eighteenth century), and Stephen Thernstrom and Robert Wiebe (who date it to the early and late nineteenth century, respectively).[18] How can the crucial shift in American society have occurred at different points in time, let alone during different centuries? Further complicating the picture, other historians stress the continuation, not the destruction, of earlier social relationships. For the colonial period alone, studies of Massachusetts (Concord, Gloucester, and Marblehead) and Maryland (St. Mary's County) argue for the persistence of societies that resemble Tönnies's gemeinschaft.[19] Other critics take issue with the utility of the concepts of gemeinschaft and gesellschaft. Christopher Lasch, for example, invites readers to "consider some of the many contrasting typologies that Tönnies piled on the basic contrast between community and 'society' or contractual 'association.'" After listing half a dozen of these abstract and ambiguous "contrasting dichotomies" (to use Tönnies's words), Lasch emphasizes "their uselessness either as instruments of sociological analysis or as categories of moral judgment."[20]

Thomas Bender, also a target of Lasch's criticism, nonetheless clears a path through this conceptual jungle. Instead of treating gemeinschaft and gesellschaft as mutually exclusive conditions, Bender reminds us that Tönnies "described these two patterns of social relations that coexisted in everyone's social experience. *Gemein-schaft* and *Gesellschaft* were not places; they were forms of human interaction."[21] Tönnies writes that a society's "whole development tends toward an approach to Gesellschaft in which . . . the force of Gemeinschaft persists, although with diminishing strength, even in the period of Gesellschaft, and remains the reality of social life."[22] An entire society need not shift from "traditional" and "rural" to "modern" and "urban"; instead certain portions of that society may exhibit more of one interaction than the other. Similarly, every segment of society (which may be based in different geographical settings) contains a particular mixture of these relationships at any given time. Even at the individual level, certain persons may view their relationships with society from both perspectives. This insight allows us to use a basic element of Tönnies's ideas without getting mired in shifting definitions of vague terms.

Different individuals saw their world differently. Some held a more locally oriented perspective and focused on their more immediate concerns, while others saw the world more broadly and busied themselves with matters resting beyond the immediate neighborhood. These different perspectives affected the residents' view of their place in American society and their relationship with others both near and far. A local orientation might produce certain forms of isolation, while a broader outlook might lead to different forms of integration; the nature of community and the self-perceptions it generates therefore relate closely to a people's larger sense of connectedness. In upper East Tennessee during the antebellum period, different perspectives on the world shaped the degree to which different groups of residents were isolated from the rest of the United States or were integrated with it. Those with greater connections and a broader worldview described their more inward-looking and less connected neighbors in terms of backwardness. The first group had little idea that the pejorative images they had coined would come to characterize them as well in the eyes of the nation at large.

## ISOLATION, COMMUNITY, AND APPALACHIA

A generation ago, Cratis Williams's 1961 dissertation "The Southern Mountaineer in Fact and Fiction" inaugurated a new period of scholarship on Appalachia. The massive three-volume, 1,600-page work examines the mountaineers' place in both academic research and popular literature over the past three centuries. Williams touches on matters of connectedness, community, and the formation of images essential to the present study. He sees the mountaineer as living in isolation, usually indicated in geographic terms. "The insularity of the mountain region helped to preserve the static quality of its culture and society." Furthermore, as the inhabitants "became isolated as a geographical unit after about 1850, . . . they also became more and more isolated from one another."[23] Despite this emphasis on physical isolation, Williams does identify different forms of isolation, especially regarding access to markets and to state governments. Such awareness of multiple forms of isolation also appears in the works of later scholars with a similar absence of theoretical focus.

Similarly, Williams understands that different groups of mountaineers formed different types of communities within the region. He identifies three social and economic groups: town and city dwellers, valley farmers, and branchwater mountaineers, those who live "up the branches, in the coves, on the ridges, and in the inaccessible parts of the mountain region." Although I agree with Williams that the branchwater mountaineers "became the mountaineer[s] of fiction," I argue for a different process of image formation. Although Williams takes a sometimes fragmented approach to these individuals, he correctly states that the mountaineer "turns out to be a rather complex individual when we examine him closely." Williams set the direction of future research in this area by concluding that "sweeping statements, stereotyped presentations, and generalizations as to his essential character are not to be relied upon as adequate interpretations of mountain life and character."[24]

In the three decades since Cratis Williams's dissertation appeared, many scholars have studied the issues of community and isolation in eighteenth- and nineteenth-century Appalachia. "The search for community," writes Ron D. Eller, "has been central to our work in the region for many years. No theme has been stronger in our literature than the effort to understand the Appalachian character and to explain the nature of the mountain community." Many accounts written earlier in this century describe

the individualistic mountaineer "who cares nothing for coopera-
tion and has no commitment to community beyond what he can
get out of it for himself."[25] Yet a number of more recent, and more
sophisticated, studies implicitly follow the path marked out by
Tönnies and Bender while omitting the terms "gemeinschaft" and
"gesellschaft."

Likewise, earlier works examined the concept of isolation but
never agreed on a definition of it and differed in the extent to
which they viewed the region as isolated.[26] The works usually described physical isolation and failed to articulate how different
forms of isolation can exist at the same time. Lacking a larger
framework such as "connectedness," the earlier works both agree
and disagree with one another and sometimes contradict their
own statements. When recent studies of Appalachian community
and isolation are examined within the framework of connectedness, however, they fit into a more coherent picture. What
emerges is not simply a context in which upper East Tennessee
may be placed for purposes of comparison but also a broader understanding of how the two forces operate throughout the Appalachian region.

Several recent studies have looked carefully at physical isolation but still disagree about its extent and influence. Gene
Wilhelm, Jr., was surely right in 1977 when he rejected "the un-
reasonable assumption that the mountain folk were completely
cut off from the larger, more technologically advanced culture of
the surrounding lowlands. The mountain folk culture has never
existed in a vacuum as many popular writers have described or assumed it to be."[27] Wilhelm, however, chose to study a seventy-
five-mile-long section of Virginia's Blue Ridge Mountains in what
is now Shenandoah National Park. These mountains form a long
narrow ridge (from four to ten miles wide) between the
Shenandoah Valley and Virginia's gently rolling piedmont. The
narrowness of the Blue Ridge and its proximity to the piedmont
make Wilhelm's site more accessible and therefore less likely to be
physically isolated. Ronald D. Eller cites Wilhelm in his 1982
study of the entire Appalachian South and follows Wilhelm's conclusions: "Most mountain families, therefore, were not isolated in
the fullest sense of the word. Traditional patterns of land and water transportation provided opportunities for contact and trade

with other communities and with the rest of the nation, but travel was always difficult and usually time-consuming."[28]

In 1983 Steven Hahn hinted at variations of physical isolation when he argued, "Contradictions [between market and household economies] emerged, however, in a society that had a logic and resiliency rooted, not only in geographic isolation, but in a complex of social relations which served as the foundation of a broad cultural, as well as economic, experience."[29] Hahn's own evidence refutes geographic isolation and strongly supports economic connectedness. He describes how yeoman farmers migrated into the region and out of it; how absentee landlords hired tenants and maintained links with upcountry counties; and, most important, how the residents participated in the wider export market. Diverse elements in upcountry society, from plantation owners and small farmers to merchants and local storekeepers, were tied to such distant markets as "Atlanta, Columbus, Athens, and Augusta by way of railroad, wagon, or pole boat," even though local networks dominated the yeomanry.[30] Clearly, the framework of connectedness can accommodate these different components of the Georgia upcountry better than a monolithic notion of geographic isolation.

We must also reexamine geographic isolation and community in Cades Cove, Tennessee. Durwood Dunn's 1988 study argues that the cove was isolated during early settlement (around 1820) as well as after the Civil War, when "the geographic isolation combined with the regional depression and the developing kinship structure [and] resulted in an intense communal life style which determined internal economic distribution of goods and labor."[31] This situation affected the Baptist church: "It is as though the problems, disputes, decisions, and organization of the church were being conducted in complete isolation from the many social and economic trends which characterized any given decade." For example, the church resisted the establishment of separate congregations, "although the distance and geographic isolation of the Cades Cove group obviously justified such a move." Isolation could affect individuals profoundly as well. John Oliver "could only regard the Confederate cause with abhorrence after the long decades of his isolation in the cove from other Southern political mainstreams."[32]

Yet according to Dunn, the residents of Cades Cove had many connections with the outside world. "Numerous immigrants from various parts of the nation and world had assured the community of frequent exposure to new ideas and attitudes" during the antebellum period. Many trails and five roads had been established by 1860, which "gave the cove people easy access to regional markets for their crops and livestock" and allowed "the technological development of the cove, particularly in farm machinery, [to keep] pace with the rest of Blount County." Dunn wisely emphasizes that "this isolation was always *relative*" and pointed out the "common fallacy of local historians to envision such geographic and social isolation in absolute, either/or terms," but the extent of isolation, geographic or otherwise, in Cades Cove during the antebellum period remains unclear.[33]

Just as Dunn's analysis of the Cove's "isolation" fits within the larger framework of connectedness, so his descriptions of the Cove make plain how community perspectives shape the region. He shows how Cades Cove residents were united by kin networks and the Baptist church but were also directed more individually by the regionally oriented market economy mentioned above. After the Civil War, however, locally oriented relationships came to dominate the cove. A folk culture developed because of "wartime experiences, the expanding kinship structure, economic difficulties which drew families together, and a sense of alienation from the surrounding region." Through a "system of shared values, experiences, and myths of various origins," Cades Cove became a tightly knit and inward-looking community.[34] Such dynamics, when combined with an altered sense of connectedness, help us understand the Cove's place not just in the minds of its residents but also in the region and nation at large.

Altina L. Waller, in her 1988 reconstruction of the Kentucky and West Virginia setting for the Hatfield-McCoy feud, states that "before the building of the railroad in 1889, the Tug Valley home of the Hatfields and McCoys was rural and isolated. . . . No towns existed, and even the county seats . . . were located beyond the mountain ridges which surrounded and defined the valley."[35] Waller disagrees with some of the studies mentioned above in finding that "trade beyond the mountains was almost nonexistent," little in-migration occurred after 1840, and "roads through

and into the Tug Valley fell into disrepair. Apart from an occasional peddler, cattle drover, or circuit preacher, few outsiders visited the mountain hollows." Waller concludes that "although [Tug
Valley residents were] not unaware of events taking place outside
the mountains," they "identified with their local, immediate environment of sheltering mountain ridges and narrow creek beds and
their comfortably familiar set of family, friends, and neighbors."[36]

We might expect such conditions to have given Tug Valley
residents a strong local orientation, but Altina Waller identifies
the ways in which they took a broad perspective. Devil Anse
Hatfield placed one foot within the local Tug Valley society during
the 1870s and 1880s and the other foot beyond it: "he was a bud-
ding entrepreneur, but he was also a man whose outlook and value
system had not transcended traditional values."[37] Industrialization
and modernization, forces that push the inhabitants into the wider
world, win out in the end, and in this respect Waller's study traces
the familiar "decline of community." She breaks new ground, however, by showing that the traditional community did not simply
disappear as it moved into the twentieth century; rather, in myriad
ways both perspectives coexisted and shaped the context within
which outside forces operated.

Several essays collected in *Appalachian Frontiers: Settlement, Society, and Development in the Preindustrial Era*, a volume edited by
Robert D. Mitchell in 1991, display a more complex understanding of different areas within Appalachia as they were connected to
other regions. According to Richard K. MacMaster, cattlemen in
western Virginia from 1760 to 1830 accepted new methods of
feeding and breeding their stock, and drovers led their livestock
directly to eastern markets. As a result, MacMaster strongly refutes
the notion that Appalachian residents were cut off and physically
isolated from the rest of the United States.[38] Similarly, Tyrel G.
Moore shows that subsistence and commercial economies coexisted in antebellum Kentucky. Most residents had established connections with outside regions; even subsistence farmers sold some
goods (such as livestock, coal, iron, and salt) in regional markets.
Moore concludes that "the pioneer subsistence economy and isolation of the Appalachian frontier did not dominate eastern Kentucky throughout the period between 1800 and 1860. Instead,
an evolving regional economy based on agriculture and natural

resources matured, particularly after 1830, in response to both regional and extraregional demands."[39]

The work of H. Tyler Blethen and Curtis W. Wood has particular importance for this study of connectedness. Their essay, "A Trader on the Western Carolina Frontier," describes James Patton's prosperous mercantile business in early nineteenth-century Buncombe County, North Carolina. Patton's story, revealed primarily in a twenty-page autobiographical letter to his grandchildren in 1837, "refutes the stereotype of an economically isolated subsistence economy" and replaces it with a picture of "an economy comparable to that of much of the rural, nonplantation South of that time."[40] Elsewhere, Blethen and Wood describe both the difficulties residents had in moving in the mountains and the existence of transportation networks. They make it clear that although "physical separation was an important political reality" that led to confrontations in the state arena, economic ties placed farmers "in complex webs of interdependence."[41] Citing the work of some recent scholars, Blethen and Wood conclude that "while there were some isolated family farmers, there were also towns and townspeople, as well as rural communities with social gradations and a developed sense of community and interdependence. This more sophisticated understanding of the southern Appalachians explains how the traditional image of isolation could have arisen, while at the same time it reveals how poorly it [isolation] serves as a generalization."[42]

Towns and their role in regional connectedness have also been important for historians studying mid-nineteenth-century western North Carolina. Like Gordon B. McKinney, who concludes that "the acknowledged isolation of the mountain people was relative and did not shield them from the workings of the market economy,"[43] John C. Inscoe asserts that all mountain towns "exerted an influence far in excess of their size" and operated "as links between their own county's residents and the 'outer world.'" Local merchants, serving as the "functional cores" of these towns, supplied goods and services and sold local surplus crops. "Through one means or another, then, most western North Carolinians were involved in this complex trade network. Though the degree of contact varied greatly, from those subsistence farmers who merely bartered occasionally . . . to those larger farmers and businessmen who maintained close regular ties with their counterparts in South Carolina and Georgia, that dependence on southern markets was pervasive throughout the mountain counties."[44]

Yet the picture of such connections, according to Inscoe, must be balanced by the realization that "though greatly exaggerated and less true of the antebellum period than of later years, images of the isolation and seclusion of mountain families were not entirely false." As the better, more accessible land was claimed, later set-tlers had to seek more remote sites. "By their distance and terrain, these locales tended to separate those who settled there from much of what went on beyond them. In other instances, areas that had been fairly accessible and well traveled at the time of settle-ment became more isolated as trade routes changed and migration dwindled. Some communities were bypassed by traffic that earlier had provided their primary contacts with the outside world."[45] These residents "were willing to settle for just enough land to sup-port a family, and an adequate supply of water, wild game, and tim-ber or stone for building. . . . Such families often maintained a pioneering lifestyle of subsistence farming with only minimal con-tact with anyone other than neighbors, the closest of whom were sometimes several miles away."[46] Such circumstances shape our understanding not only of a region's connectedness but also of the inhabitants' self-perceptions of community.

Ralph Mann has recently shown how social networks gener-ated a sense of community and produced "an egalitarian identity" among the inhabitants of antebellum Burkes Garden, Virginia. The community protected even the most economically marginal residents—tenants and farm laborers—"from coercion by their own kin networks, by the mutual dependencies that grew up where various kin networks interacted, and by the neighborhood ties that facilitated agricultural exchange in Burkes Garden." Al-though the tenuous economic position of the landless placed them "outside much of the community exchange," they were able to use their labor to enter into the local economy. Therefore, "being landless did not isolate them from the networks that held the Gar-den together as a farm community." This snapshot of one Appala-chian community shows that the residents "lived partly in a traditional world imposed and protected by the mountains and partly in a modern world of courts and capitalism."[47] In short, economic, family, and neighborhood networks united the local community and the broader society in Burkes Garden.

Other historians have recently examined Appalachian locales at an even earlier time period, the eighteenth century. Building on Robert D. Mitchell's earlier work describing the Shenandoah Valley's economic connections, Warren Hofstra focuses on early settlement in Frederick County, in the northern end of the Valley. The Scotch-Irish first settled the area in the 1730s and "established social patterns that fostered community cohesion for three generations and at least sixty years." They were held together by family property and values passed on from generation to generation, kinship networks that arose from marriages, ethnicity, and the Presbyterian religion. These settlers were also united by forces that I have already discussed: the emergence of towns as county seats and centers for defense, and a local economy that linked residents in webs of debt from local trade.[48]

Yet Frederick County residents were not simply locally oriented; other forces separated people, especially during the last third of the eighteenth century. The third generation of settlers migrated to western lands. Commercial production, especially of wheat, fed a regional and national economy and created a demand for more imported goods, encouraged more stores to open, and promoted the use of cash and credit. Furthermore, as we may recall from Thomas Bender's definition of "community," bonds entail mutuality rather than just physical proximity. The Millwood settlement, seven miles east of the county seat of Winchester, contained emigrants from relatively affluent Tidewater families, in contrast to the majority of settlers, who had migrated south from Pennsylvania. With few economic or kin connections between them, the two neighboring populations remained largely separate.[49]

Most recently, several essays in the 1995 volume *Appalachia in the Making: The Mountain South in the Nineteenth Century* directly address the issues of isolation and community. The editors Mary Beth Pudup, Dwight Billings, and Altina Waller argue in their cogent introduction that by "refusing the 'world we have lost' romanticism about a traditional mountain subculture as well as assumptions about a unified historical experience, the essays are distinguished by their careful attention to the often subtle nuances of geography and often stark realities of social structure."[50] In particular, Ralph Mann discusses how the Virginia and Tennessee Railroad enhanced connections between portions of Tazewell County, in southwestern Virginia, and surrounding locales. Such improved transportation not only brought outsiders to live in the area but also encouraged greater commercial farming among some communities. While the railroad broadened the outlook of some inhabitants, others (like those in Abb's Valley) maintained their local orientation.[51] Similarly, Gordon B. McKinney notes for the 1860s that "while most western North Carolina farm families were subsistence farmers—that is, they sought to provide for their own needs as their primary objective—they were constantly involved in an exchange of goods and services. . . . Even the most isolated family was dependent at some point on outside labor for survival."[52] Clearly, this combination of perspectives existed in many Appalachian locales.

All of the current scholarship reminds us that when we analyze self-perceptions within the larger framework of connectedness, we must consider how the different dimensions and measures interrelate. For example, migration may separate people, but kin and family ties may unite those individuals over great distances. To what degree do community and integration exist if one marries within the kin network but spends every waking hour looking toward the Philadelphia or Baltimore markets? Are inhabitants of Cades Cove more concerned about their Baptist neighbors or about their distant suppliers of farm machinery? Until recently, such questions often produced a confused and contradictory picture of life in the Appalachian region. The framework for connectedness, when combined with an awareness of local and broad perspectives, brings a sense of order to these earlier studies. Isolation and integration can exist at the same time in the same place but in different parts of individual lives. A region's particular mixture of isolation and integration, when combined with the residents' perceptions of connectedness, plays a crucial role in our understanding of the larger images of the Appalachian region.

## Connectedness, Community, and Stereotypes

The settlement, development, and characterization of upper East Tennessee can be described in terms of running water, an image

popular at the turn of the twentieth century. According to John
Fox, Jr.: "mountains have dammed the streams of humanity, have
let them settle in the valleys and spread out over the plains; or
have sent them on long detours around. When some unusual pressure has forced a current through some mountain-pass, the hills
have cut it off from the main stream and have held it so stagnant,
that, to change the figure, mountains may be said to have kept the
records of human history somewhat as fossils hold the history of
the earth."[53] As historians looking at America generally, we must
agree with Fox that the "streams of humanity" came late to the
mountains, in a trickle as the torrent rushed into the Old Northwest and the Old Southwest. A closer look at the Appalachian region, however, reveals that the banks of the larger and more
accessible mountain rivers were settled and developed before
other locations. Finally, when we examine one particular mountain region, we notice that upper East Tennessee has its own
"main stream" of development in the more open Holston and
Watauga river valleys to the west and smaller rivulets branching
off into the Unaka Range. On the one hand, residents in this
mainstream established important ties to other parts of the United
States. These waters were fed by, and in turn flowed into, larger
rivers leading to Philadelphia, Charleston, and other destinations.
On the other hand, the small rivulets penetrated into the most
mountainous regions only by the 1830s, and residents in these areas were much more physically isolated by the terrain. Although
the rivulets never became stagnant pools, their waters did not flow
swiftly into the mainstream of either upper East Tennessee or
places more distant.

  I argue that the rivulets became the subject matter for later
characterizations of Appalachia. This book analyzes the development of upper East Tennessee from the first settlement in the eighteenth century to the Civil War and traces the evolution of
external images and local self-perceptions over eight decades.
Voices from outside the region first articulated images of Appalachian distinctiveness only to be drowned out by a rising chorus of
internal opinions. During the 1780s and 1790s, a period of social
and political upheaval within the region, outsiders believed that
the mountaineers differed from themselves. At the same time,
residents within upper East Tennessee saw little difference among

themselves or from those living in coastal and piedmont regions. During the antebellum period, however, such self-perceptions changed.

By applying a variety of methodological approaches to different dimensions (such as growing transportation networks, the changing economy, population movement, and the local topography) within the framework of connectedness, I show how these growing perceptions of difference *within* the mountain region led to more general characterizations of Appalachia as a whole. Town residents living in upper East Tennessee's more accessible valleys held broader worldviews. Such perspectives led them to promote the construction of a railroad and to describe nonsupporters, living in the more remote coves with a more locally oriented perspective, in terms that imply backwardness. Popular magazine writers who would eventually contribute to the local color movement did not actually visit the most remote mountain areas but instead talked with the more accessible town residents, tapped into these local perceptions, and publicized an image of Appalachia that has persisted ever since. Americans in the late twentieth century have become familiar with notions of Appalachian exceptionalism. Images of backwardness and violence come easily to the imagination, but few individuals realize that the underlying notions have existed for centuries. For upper East Tennessee, the images first emerged from the battles of the Revolutionary War.

# CHAPTER ONE

# Perceptions and Self-Perceptions in the Revolutionary Era

THE INHABITANTS in what would become upper East Tennessee were perhaps first described in Appalachian images during the American Revolution. At the battle of King's Mountain in October 1780, revolutionaries from the mountainous regions of western Virginia and North Carolina (including what is now upper East Tennessee), and northern Georgia destroyed a Tory army from South Carolina commanded by British Major Patrick Ferguson. In order to drive wavering Americans into his Loyalist camp, Ferguson issued the following proclamation on 1 October 1780:

> Gentlemen: Unless you wish to be eat up by an innundation of barbarians, who have begun by murdering an unarmed son before his aged father, and afterwards lopped off his arms, and who by their shocking cruelties and irregularities, give the best proof of their cowardice and want of discipline; I say, if you want to be pinioned, robbed, and murdered, and see your wives and daughters, in four days, abused by the dregs of mankind—in short, if you wish to deserve to live, and bear the name of men, grasp your arms in a moment and run to camp.
>
> The Back Water men have crossed the mountains; McDowell, Hampton, Shelby, and Cleveland are at their head, so that you know what you have to depend upon. If you choose to be degraded forever and ever by a set of mongrels, say so at once, and let your women turn their backs upon you, and look out for real men to protect them.[1]

Ferguson certainly exaggerated here for effect, but a close examination of his public and private correspondence reveals that he indeed attributed special characteristics to the "Back Water men." The events relating to the battle of King's Mountain therefore provide a starting point for our interpretation of early descriptions and perceptions of Appalachia.

The residents of the western waters, united by the constant threat of Indian, British, and Loyalist attacks during the southern campaigns, forged a number of physical and psychological bonds among themselves. Yet from the perspective of the enemy, illustrated by Patrick Ferguson, the realities of war in the South served to break some of the external connections linking the mountaineers with those same Indian, British, and Loyalist groups. The chaos of war fostered a situation in which outsiders, ever more physically and psychologically separated from the mountaineers, could characterize their enemies as barbarians.

The bonds formed among the mountaineers during the war shaped the development of internal perceptions immediately following the war's conclusion. Ferguson's backwater men in what is now upper East Tennessee fought among themselves over whether or not to separate from North Carolina and form the independent state of Franklin. Local disputes, often quite violent, divided these mountain residents. Yet the bonds formed during the war combined with larger economic and political forces to mute the differences and discourage the development of perceived difference within the region. This broad array of forces can be understood within the framework of connectedness. The battle of King's Mountain shows how war could lead outsiders to develop distinct images of the mountaineers, while the events surrounding the state of Franklin show how the residents' shared concerns led to self-perceptions of commonality, rather than difference, within the population of upper East Tennessee.

## INTERNAL CONNECTEDNESS

Participants on both sides of the war spoke of the battle of King's Mountain as a turning point in the American Revolution. Sir Henry Clinton, the British commander-in-chief for North America, noted the debacle at King's Mountain as the "event which was immediately productive of the worst consequences to the King's affairs in South Carolina, and unhappily proved the first link of a chain of evils that followed each other in regular succession until they at last ended in the total loss of America."[2] David Vance, a Whig militiaman from North Carolina, placed the battle in "the most disasterous period for Liberty and Independence from the time of its Declaration to the end of the war. . . . Furgurson's [sic] defeat was the turning point in American affairs. . . . The loss of this battle would, in all probability, have been the loss of American Independence and the Liberty we now enjoy."[3]

The war in the southern colonies had taken a disastrous turn for the revolutionaries during the spring and summer of 1780. Major General Benjamin Lincoln surrendered 5,500 men and the city of Charleston in May, and General Horatio Gates lost another army at Camden in August. During the intervening months, support for the revolution diminished as the British swept through South Carolina. King's Mountain halted the string of British victories. Major Patrick Ferguson, leading a force composed almost entirely of American Loyalists from the coastal and piedmont regions, traveled along the eastern edge of the Blue Ridge Mountains, tracking down rebels and silencing outspoken civilians. William Campbell, John Sevier, Isaac Shelby, Benjamin Cleveland, and other militia leaders from the mountain areas, upon learning of Ferguson's movements, gathered about 900 men at Sycamore Shoals and Quaker Meadows, marched over the mountains, and pursued Ferguson and his army to the border between North and South Carolina (see Map 1 and Figure 1). On the afternoon of 7 October 1780, the revolutionaries killed 150 men, including Ferguson, and captured 800 others. During the battle, 28 mountaineers were killed and 62 were wounded. Afterward, most of the revolutionaries quickly dispersed to defend their homesteads from Indian attacks. Those who remained led the captured soldiers toward a prison camp in western North Carolina. During this march, resentment against the Loyalists ignited into a desire for summary executions. At Gilbertown, some mountaineers accused thirty-six prisoners of raiding and ravaging innocent citizens; all were found guilty, and nine were hanged before the commanders interceded. Many of these backwater men participated in the subsequent battles that culminated in Cornwallis's final defeat at Yorktown the following year.[4]

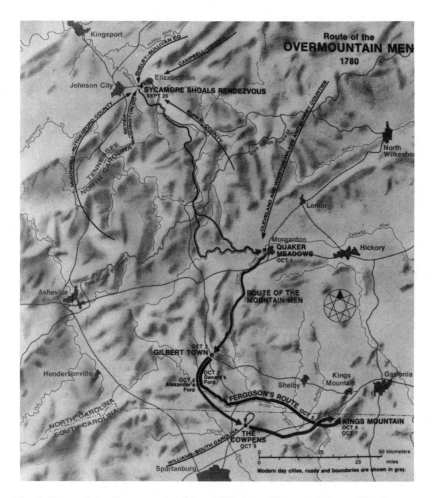

Map 1. Route of the Overmountain Men, 1780. From Wilma Dykeman, *With Fire and Sword: The Battle of King's Mountain, 1780* (Washington, D.C.: National Park Service, 1978).

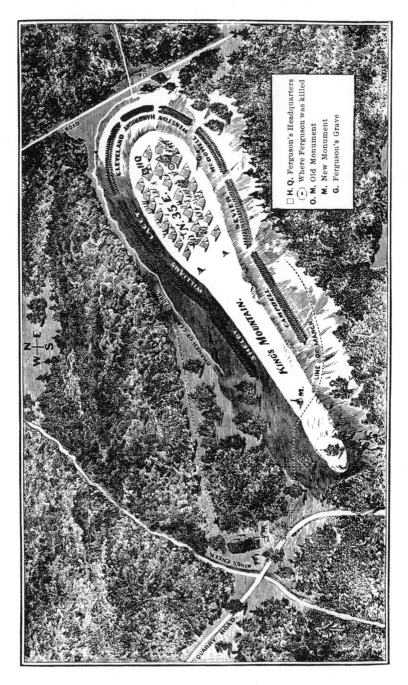

Fig. 1. "Diagram of the Battle of King's Mountain." From Lyman C. Draper, *King's Mountain and Its Heroes* (1881).

This brief sketch of the circumstances surrounding the battle reveals the many elements that linked the mountaineers with one another. The British, with their Indian and Loyalist allies, provided an external threat that forced the revolutionaries together, especially those in the mountains. Lord Cornwallis reveals the extent of the threat in a letter to Sir Henry Clinton written soon after King's Mountain: "When the numerous and formidible bodies of back-mountain men came down to attack Major Ferguson and showed themselves to be our most inveterate enemies, I directed Lt.-Col. Brown to encourage the Indians to attack the settlements of Watoga, Holsten, Caentuck, and Nolachuckie, all of which are new encroachments on Indian territories. The good efforts of this measure has already appeared. A large body of mountaineers marched lately to join the rebels near King's Mountain, but were soon to return to oppose the incursions of the Indians."[5] Nathanael Greene, commander of the revolutionary forces in the South, testifies to the success of the strategy Cornwallis describes. "The inhabitants of this country live too remote from one another to be animated into great exertions," he wrote to George Washington, "and the people appear, notwithstanding their danger, very intent upon their private affairs."[6] The private affairs without question included the dangers brought on by the war. The ways in which the mountain residents organized themselves to meet the different threats reveal the depth of the ties that bound the inhabitants together in a community that withstood the internal pressures of the revolutionary period.

The backwater men organized themselves against Ferguson by a militia company within each of the affected counties. The political structure connected the residents with one another and helped create a shared identity and interest. Americans had established permanent settlements in what is now upper East Tennessee by 1770. While many followed the Shenandoah Valley south from Virginia, others moved west from North Carolina across the peaks of the Appalachian Mountains. They gravitated toward the Holston, Nolichucky, and Watauga Rivers and formed in 1772 a local government called the Watauga Association. After the association had submitted a petition to place itself under North Carolina government, the state legislature created the Washington District in late 1776 and appointed twenty-one justices of the peace. At the end of 1777, North Carolina converted the district into Washington County and created the Court of Pleas and Quarter Sessions. Beginning in 1778, the court met on the fourth Monday of February, May, August, and November.[7]

From its inception, the court served the approximately 2,500 residents of Washington County by performing a bewildering array of administrative and judicial functions. In 1778 alone, the court appointed county officers, named jurors to the state supreme court, selected tax assessors, licensed attorneys, registered livestock marks and brands, recorded land sales and property exchanges, accepted oaths of allegiance, bound orphans to adults, chose surveyors for roads, summoned men to serve on the grand jury, administered wills and estates, decided the county boundaries, sent men to record depositions, authorized the construction of gristmills, and decided a number of criminal cases. During the war, the court also determined the value of different currencies, set tavern and ferry rates, collected taxes, and provided charity for the poor.[8] The scope of the court's activity indicates its importance in connecting the inhabitants with one another.

Loyalists (or Tories) form a second force that united Washington County residents. At first glance we might expect loyalism to fracture local society and thereby to promote images of distinctiveness within the mountain region. Loyalism within Washington County, however, never reached a level that could produce such divisiveness, for the court heard only fourteen cases of "high treason" from 1778 to 1783. The first case, *State* vs. *Moses Crawford* on 25 August 1778, illustrates how the court controlled the situation. It decided that "the def[endan]t be imprisoned . . . and the Sheriff taking the whole of his Estate into Custody which must be valued by a jury at the Next Court, and that the one half of the s[ai]d Estate be kept by the sd. Sheriff for the use of the state, and the other half remitted to the family of the Deft."[9] The next day, Crawford failed to appear before the court to take the oath of allegiance to the state. The court ruled that he could remain in the state but declared that he "hath Incured the penalties [and] shall be subject to all the [?] in such case . . . of Treason & providing punishment adequate to crimes of both classes and for preventing the dangers that may arise from persons Disafected to the State."[10] After hearing further testimony the court decided to

send Crawford "to the district Gaol for further Tryal" but eventually took a more lenient stance, and allowed Crawford to stay
upon "his Taking the State Oath & giving bond and sufficient
sec[ur]ity in the sum of 10,000 [pounds]." Crawford raised the
bond, with seven men signing as securities.[11] The court bound
these seven men, Crawford, and Washington County together in a
web of social, legal, and economic connections.

The divisive effects of loyalism are tempered further when we
see that the court found almost half of those charged with treason
during the war years to be not guilty. On the same day that the
court sent George Lewis to the district jail for being "a spie or an
officer from Floridia out of the English Army," it decided that John
Holly, Jr., "is not guilty and is ord. to be discharged."[12] The court
used similar language and reached the same verdict in the cases
against Thomas Barrker, Jonathan Holly, Alexander Chatawood,
Francis Holly, and William Bryant.[13] The court even allowed a
small number of professed Loyalists to return to Washington
County under certain conditions. They permitted Joshua
Boulding to do so, "on proviso that he comply with the laws provided for persons being inimical to the state and have Rendered
service that will expiate any crime that he has been Guilty of inimical to this state or the United States."[14] Others may have been
driven to abandon their loyalism, pressured by forces extending
beyond the county court. Vigilantism might explain the case of
Samuel Weaver, who "came into Court and volentarily confest
that he . . . had been with the English Army some time and had
been in several engagements against the American people During
his stay with the Enemy & c." Similarly, Isam Yearly "volentary
confest that he had been Incrimical to the common Cause of Liberty also having theretofore the . . . testimony of sundry witnesses
against the said Isam Yearly."[15] These cases, describing the protection available under the county court, speak to the different forms
of social control that drew the inhabitants together. Clearly, the
internal connections among Washington County residents withstood this degree of loyalism.[16]

Indian activities compose the third force that encouraged internal connections among the mountain residents. Throughout the
war, the British enlisted the Cherokees (and later the Chickamaugas, a group that broke away from the Cherokees) to help in

the southern campaigns.[17] John Stuart, the superintendent of Indian affairs in the region, notified Sir Henry Clinton in the spring of 1776 that the Indians would participate "in the execution of some connected plan jointly with the friends of Government, or to favor the operations of His Majesty's forces by drawing the attention of the Rebells."[18] Spurred by British deliveries of supplies and promises of territory to be emptied of western encroachers, the Cherokees launched a number of attacks against the inhabitants of upper East Tennessee.

In July 1776, the Cherokees conducted a three-pronged attack into upper East Tennessee. Dragging Canoe led about 200 Cherokees against the settlements near the Long Island of the Holston River on 20 July 1776. At about the same time, Chief Raven and about 100 Cherokees attacked the scattered settlements in Carter's Valley further to the west. Finally, Chief Old Abram of Chilhowee guided 300 to 400 Cherokees first against Fort Lee on the Nolichucky River and then Fort Caswell on the Watauga River on 21 July 1776. Chief Raven's foray succeeded in destroying property throughout Carter's Valley, but the settlers repelled Dragging Canoe's attack at Long Island, and the Fort Caswell inhabitants endured a two-week siege before Chief Old Abram finally withdrew. In response to these attacks, William Christian led a retaliatory campaign manned by soldiers from what is now southwestern Virginia, northwestern North Carolina, and upper East Tennessee. In the face of this force of 1,800 men, the Cherokees pulled back southward and began to negotiate with Christian. The counterattack and the discussions that followed produced two changes in the revolutionaries' relations with the Cherokees: first, the discussions led to a treaty with the Cherokees the following June that established a boundary line between the two peoples and opened more land to white settlement; and second, Dragging Canoe and other Cherokees became disgusted by the negotiations and departed for new lands on Chickamauga Creek in order to continue their battles against the western settlers.[19]

The Cherokee threat connected the mountain inhabitants on several different levels. The siege of Fort Caswell forced the occupants into a well-defined space and united them in the effort to survive the attack.[20] This sharply circumscribed sense of attachment among residents of a small part of upper East Tennessee fits

Fig. 2. John Sevier. Painting by Charles Willson Peale, 1792. Courtesy of the
Tennessee State Museum, Tennessee Historical Society Collection, Nashville.

into a larger sense of connectedness with mountain residents in
Virginia, North Carolina, and Georgia. Men from the different states
rode together under Christian, defended their home settlements,

and came to the aid of their neighbors, thereby forming bonds of mutuality among themselves. Finally, as one incident in Greasy Cove demonstrates, the ties connecting the militia with their homes were never stretched too thin by forays into Cherokee territory. Although physically separated from their homes and mentally focused on an attack, upper East Tennessee soldiers constantly had their communities in mind.

In August 1780, residents of Greasy Cove in southern Washington County discovered signs of an impending Cherokee attack. Once their suspicions were confirmed, John Sevier "concluded to carry on a campaign against their [the Cherokee] towns, and men to the number of a hundred had collected at the Greasy Cove, and others expected to join them," according to the later testimony of Major James Sevier. One of these men stumbled upon an Indian, exchanged fire, and ran back to camp. A party returned to find the dead Indian as well as signs that others had recently camped in the area. "This circumstance, it was thought," related James Sevier, "was the means of breaking up the campaign. William Fain, an officer, said he would not go—that it was clear that Indians were lurking on the frontier, and if they went out to the nation, then the Indians would fall upon their defenceless families and massacre them." The bonds between the soldiers and their homes remained strong. John Sevier "had Fain arrested and broken, but by this time the people who had collected were so filled with apprehension that it was deemed best to abandon the expedition."[21]

External threats from the British, Loyalists, and Indians served to unite the inhabitants of upper East Tennessee with one another and with those living in the neighboring mountain regions. The physical nature of the connections can be seen most clearly during the days leading up to King's Mountain. The road network played an important role in helping the "over-mountain men" to gather their forces. Isaac Shelby rode, via several local roads, from his home in Sullivan County to Washington County forty miles away, where he consulted John Sevier. The two militia colonels persuaded militia companies from neighboring counties to rendezvous on 25 September 1780 at Sycamore Shoals, on the bend of the Watauga River. Shelby and Sevier arrived with 240 militiamen apiece. They joined the 160 Burke and Rutherford County men, commanded by Charles McDowell and Andrew Hampton, who had already engaged Ferguson's army in their home territory east of the mountains and had retreated to Sycamore Shoals. In addition, William and Arthur Campbell brought 400 militiamen from the Holston River valley of Washington County, Virginia.

On the clear and sunny morning of 26 September 1780, the force of more than 1,000 men began their pursuit of Patrick Ferguson. They rode twenty miles southeast through the mountains, following the twisting course of Gap Creek and the Doe River. The next day they passed through the gap north of Roan Mountain on Bright's Trace, a common footpath, and camped along Roaring Creek that night. The men reached the North Toe River the next day and followed its rough and stony ravines for about a dozen miles. On Friday, 29 September, the men finally passed through the Blue Ridge at Gillespie Gap and on the following day gathered at Quaker Meadows. Here the remainder of the King's Mountain force had converged: Elijah Clarke's militia from Savannah, Georgia, and North Carolina militia from the eastern side of the mountains under Charles and Joseph McDowell and Benjamin Cleveland. On October 1, the nearly 1,500 revolutionaries set off southward toward the Carolina piedmont and caught Ferguson's Loyalist army a week later.[22]

These militia forces were able to gather at Sycamore Shoals and cross the steep mountains because roads, trails, and paths had formed a network of physical connections within upper East Tennessee and among its neighboring counties. The men under William Campbell and Isaac Shelby reached the Watauga River on roads that ran parallel to the northeast-southwest orientation of the ridges and valleys. John Sevier's militia converged on Sycamore Shoals from neighboring areas by using local roads that had been surveyed and cut ever since the earliest years of settlement. These men then wound their way past Roan Mountain to Quaker Meadows on one of the few routes that crossed the Appalachian Mountains from northwest to southeast.[23] Such physical connections allowed the men to act upon the concerns that united them in less obvious ways. The threats posed by the British, Loyalists, and Indians throughout the Revolutionary War physically and psychologically connected the mountaineers in ways that fostered the development of a common identity. The men

were "so often called together that they were like a band of brothers raised in the same family."[24]

## PATRICK FERGUSON AND EXTERNAL PERCEPTIONS

Patrick Ferguson's description of the backwater men as "barbarians" and "the dregs of mankind" illustrates some outsiders' perceptions of the mountain inhabitants. A close examination of his
language and correspondence reveals that Ferguson described the
backwater men with terms and images more distinctive than those
used in his descriptions of earlier opponents in New York. Such
views have some basis in the realities of war, which turned particularly savage in the South. The images may have become even
more extreme when war's social and political disruptions severed
many of the ties that had connected the British with the Loyalists
and other inhabitants of the backcountry. Generally speaking, a
particular set of images becomes firmly established as individuals
have fewer opportunities to balance their perceptions with direct
observation. The turmoil and disruptions caused by the war separated the British from their opponents, and the separation helped
give rise to distinctive images of the backwater men.

Patrick Ferguson's correspondence reveals an increasing tendency to describe his mountain opponents in distinctive terms.
The references remain fairly general during the summer of 1780.
In August, he wrote to Cornwallis about "the very great use the
rebels derive from a militia (which altho at present more warlike
than ours, is certainly not equal in numbers to the real loyalists of
the Carolina, nor established on so good & promising a foundation), may afford some hope that advantage may be made of the
many thousand loyalists that are sincerely with us." Ferguson then
hinted at the abilities of the enemy's militia. "Gen'l Sumpter with
a few militia kept Hanging Rock & Rocky Mount in constant
alarm, brought the troops there into danger, & commanded the
country round." In particular, the militia "have more than once
shown that regular troops have not the same advantage over them
in small detach'ts, that they have collectively in an army, being
able in one case to elude the charge of a small front & to wear
down the regular troops by distant scattered shots from superior
marksmen."[25] While elucidating the militia's advantages in order

to win Cornwallis's permission to use such forces, Ferguson displays an appreciation for the revolutionary militia.[26]

After a battle against Elijah Clarke's forces from the mountains of northern Georgia in early September 1780, Ferguson's men retreated, hoping to entice Charles McDowell's North Carolina militia "to advance if in any force to a gap in the mountains which they boasted of as impassible, & on the 11th . . . , understanding that the rebels had actually occupied that pass, I marched by an unexpected detour with 40 soldiers & 100 militia." Although the rebels may have shown surprising ability in marching through difficult terrain to control the gap, Ferguson made it clear that the Americans were not equally skilled in fighting. "At the instant that my advanced guard was scattered on our left in pursuit of a small party, Colonels Macdougals & Hampton appeared suddenly from a commanding ridge, up to which they immediately retreated." Once Ferguson turned to attack, "their center . . . gave way & their whole party fled with little loss." One man was badly wounded from "skulking shots on the flank." Ferguson estimated that the enemy numbered more than 200, "part of whom are skulking in scattered parties in the mountains & part at home to avail themselves of the inclosed declaration," which promised amnesty to those who surrendered to the British. Ferguson attacked the following evening, and "by a march of our horse round the rear of the rebels, they were reduced to the necessity of retreating through the gap of the mountains to the western waters to avoid being intercepted."[27] Ferguson depicted the enemy as skilled in some respects but ultimately weak, fleeing when attacked, hiding in the woods, shooting from cover, and afraid to face the British in open battle. The enemy was not a determined and unified force but a group of civilians ready to sign their allegiance to the King. Although Ferguson's emotions are more tempered here than in the proclamation of 1 October, he clearly disdains the abilities and character of the overmountain rebels.

These letters to Cornwallis emphasize the distinctions Ferguson made between the mountaineers and other revolutionaries. Whenever appropriate, he used a geographically descriptive phrase: "The account I sent . . . respecting the back mountain men, MacDowal, Cleveland, & Berard, have been confirmed from various quarters."[28] In one letter, Ferguson even went so far as to spell out "Back Water men" in code. "There are different arrivals from Nolachuki & Holstein maintaining D.D.H. 5.6.4.9. 21.6.24.2.14. 7.2.18. [800 back water men] being on their way but, I believe Hampton & Shelby together will not 5.14.10.18.12. [?].H.H. [bring 300]."[29] By making the effort to spell out "Back Water men" explicitly rather than use some shorter term like "enemy" or "rebels," Ferguson showed that he viewed this mountain militia as different.

Although Ferguson became increasingly concerned during the first week of October about an impending battle, he remained confident about the outcome. He predicted that "3 or 400 good soldiers, part dragoons would finish the business" but warned that "something must be done soon. This is their last push in this quarter, and they are extremely desolate and awed."[30] With such reinforcements, "the happiest opportunity offers of crushing the back mountain men who cannot at other times be reached and be a serious thorn in the rear of your [Cornwallis's] army, & have it at all times in their power to be formidable support to the malcontents & bring this district into danger."[31] The mountain militia appear elusive here. They have the ability to harass the British while avoiding confrontations. Ferguson sees them as both weak and strong—too weak to defeat his forces but also quite able to foment a general resistance that would be difficult to quell.

All of these views find expression in two letters Ferguson wrote on 6 October 1780, the day before the battle. He notified his commander: "I arrived today at King's Mountain & have taken a post where I do not think I can be forced by a stronger enemy than that against us. . . . I understand that we have little or no reinforcement to expect. . . . We do not think ourselves inferior to the enemy if you are pleased to order us forward, but [with] help so near at hand it appeared to me improper of myself to commit anything to hazard."[32] His opinion derives from a combination of caution, confidence in his troops, and disdain for the enemy. That same day Ferguson wrote a more private letter to Robert Timpany, an officer of the same rank and, we may suspect, a friend as well. Ferguson writes:

Between you and I, there has been an inundation of Barbarians, rather larger than expected. . . . They give themselves out for 3800 men, I expect they are not above half that

number. . . . We are inferior in number but as to quality—
but we must not praise ourselves. I did not think it necessary
to stake our young militia to an overmatch without orders—
but with the advantages of arms, our people and the four officers from Cruger, I should have thought myself justifiable
in committing myself, had I not expected reinforcements.
The word said—presto you will hear of a scramble, till when
you need not bring forward our commoditys.[33]

Although Ferguson's ringing self-confidence would prove to be un-
founded, how could we describe his opinion of the mountaineers?
By using the term "barbarians" in both his official and private correspondence, Ferguson clearly expressed his view that the overmountain men were a different, uncivilized people. He attributed
distinct characteristics, in this case mostly negative ones, to the
residents of a specific geographical region, the western mountains.

Ferguson did not describe all of his opponents in such stark
terms.[34] He regarded as uncivilized not all revolutionaries but only
those he encountered in western North Carolina. Through most
of 1779, Ferguson was stationed at the fort at Stony Point, just
north of New York City on the Hudson River. He submitted rec-
ommendations to Clinton for reinforcing the fort with cannon
and troops and then tried to persuade Clinton not to abandon the
fort to the rebels. In this correspondence, Ferguson often dispar-
aged the enemy's abilities but never in the language he came to
use at King's Mountain.[35] After describing the proper design for a
fort, Ferguson concluded that "such works, elevated as their situations are, with British troops, would stand a tough and serious siege, and require a numerous, gallant, disciplined, and well-
provided army (such as the rebels have not)."[36] He scoffed at the
American army: "If the rebels had any design of investing this
post, it must have been upon the supposition that the expeditions
had failed; and as to assault, they would only break their shins."[37]
Even when Ferguson criticized the actions and intentions of the
revolutionaries on the grounds that he would use in 1780, he
never used terms such as "inhuman" or "barbarian." For example,
he remarked that "the rebel troops live as much as they may be on
the country here without regards to friend or foe, collecting indiscriminately the cattle, grain, & forrage."[38] Ferguson always spoke

of "the rebel troops" or the "rebels," whereas in the Carolinas, he usually identified his enemy by their geographic origin, as "Back Water men" or "over-mountain men."

Patrick Ferguson sometimes saw his overmountain opponents as clever and capable but not savage. "The rebels are putting themselves in a situation either to throw their whole force towards New York and cooperate with the French fleet should it arrive, or . . . to push for the posts here." The forts would be in a difficult position because "as the first gun or howitz opened by the rebels will drive the shipping from their station and then [British ships] may only be able to communicate with us by boats in the night, if the rebels knowing our wants are delinquent."[39] Ferguson apparently regarded this foe as capable and organized, a view he did not hold before King's Mountain. Most important, his letters in 1779 show that he was not prone to call all Americans "savage barbarians."

Clearly Patrick Ferguson perceived the backwater men as a distinctive group, but it remains for us to determine why he characterized the inhabitants as savage and barbarous. The answer has in part to do with the accuracy with which Patrick Ferguson described the revolutionaries' actions in the South. "Two old men," he wrote on 1 October 1780, "have been brought in here today most barbarously maimed by a party of [Benjamin] Cleveland's men, who after drinking with them in disguise for some time fell upon them altho unarmed, & after butchering two young men, one of whom a son to one of the old, left them for dead & I fear past recovery. It appears from various accounts that Cleveland gives orders for such cowardly acts of cruelty."[40] Had Ferguson lived through the battle of King's Mountain, he would certainly have pointed to the forced march and summary executions of Loyalist prisoners after the battle as an example of what his opening proclamation called "shocking cruelties" committed by the "dregs of mankind."

The British captain Alexander Chesney remembered that "officers [were] in the rear and obliged to carry 2 muskets each, which was my fate although wounded and stripped of my shoes and silver buckles in an inclement season without a cover or provisions untill Monday night [two days] when an ear of Indian corn was served to each."[41] A British magazine reported that "orders were given by [Colonel William] Campbell, should they be attacked, to fire on and destroy every prisoner. The party kept marching for two days without any kind of provisions. On the third day's march all the baggage of the officers was seized and shared among the rebel officers."[42] Campbell, leader of the overmountain forces, issued general orders that attest to his difficulty controlling his own troops. Four days into the march, he ordered "the officers of all ranks in the army to endeavour to restrain the disorderly manner of the slaughtering and disturbing [of] the prisoners. If it cannot be prevented by moderate measures, such effectual punishment shall be executed upon delinquents as will put a stop to it."[43] Prisoners were not the only victims. Campbell had heard "the complaints of the inhabitants on account of the plundering parties who issue out from the camp, and indiscriminately rob both Whig and Tory, leaving our friends, I believe, in a worse situation than the enemy would have done. I hope the officers will exert themselves in suppressing this abominable practise, degrading to the name of soldier."[44] The situation deteriorated further, however, in the days to come.

At Gilbertown one week after the battle, stories began to circulate about various Tory atrocities, including the hanging of revolutionaries. These tales stirred old resentments and frustrations that led quickly to a summary trial. "A copy of the law of North Carolina was obtained," recounted Isaac Shelby, one of the militia leaders, "which authorized two magistrates to summon a jury, and forthwith to try, and, if found guilty, to execute persons who had violated its precepts." The magistrates found thirty-six prisoners guilty of "breaking open houses, killing the men, turning the women and children out of doors, and burning the houses."[45] The mountaineers hanged nine before several commanders stopped the proceedings. Colonel Benjamin Cleveland, one of the presiding justices, apparently condemned John McFall to death by saying, "That man, McFall, went to the house of Martin Davenport, one of my best soldiers, when he was away from home, fighting for his country, insulted his wife, and whipped his child; and no such man ought to be allowed to live."[46] Cleveland, the most active of the officers in these trials and executions, relentlessly pursued Tories; his actions serve as another test for Patrick Ferguson's conclusion that the mountaineers were "barbaric."

Benjamin Cleveland, forty-two years old at the time of the battle, led militiamen from Wilkes County in northwestern North Carolina. Although he fought Tories throughout the revolution-

ary period, Cleveland was especially active during the year following King's Mountain. He continued to carry out summary executions even when the British threat had eased in the region. In
November, Cleveland's men caught two Tories who had been raiding
the countryside. The men brought the prisoners to Cleveland,
who ordered them to hang from the ropes they had stolen. In April
1781, a Tory party captured Cleveland, but he was subsequently
rescued by his soldiers; the three captured Tories were quickly
court-martialed and hanged. Cleveland was also responsible for
executing Bill Nichols, Bill Harrison, and a third Tory named
Tate. When presented with two horse thieves, Cleveland had one
hanged and said to the other, "You have your choice, either to take
your place beside them, or cut your own ears off, and leave the
country forever." The prisoner cut off his ears and was never seen
again.[47] Cleveland sometimes showed leniency, but in all cases he
acted as a speedy judge and a decisive jury. Ferguson had written,
in the proclamation quoted at the start of this chapter, that two
elderly men were "most barbarously maimed by a party of Cleveland's men"; Cleveland's subsequent record provides little reason
to doubt Ferguson's accusation.

Yet far from acting alone in the backcountry, Benjamin Cleveland joined both Whigs and Tories in a cyclone of terrorism and
savagery that swept up civilians and soldiers alike.[48] Taking stock
of the situation at the close of 1780, General Nathanael Greene
summarized the situation in which he had to command: "The
Spirit of Plundering which prevails among the Inhabitants add not
a little to our Difficulties. The whole Country is in Danger of being laid Waste by the Whigs and Tories who pursue each other
with as much relentless Fury as Beasts of Prey." In a second letter,
he remarked, "A great part of this country is already laid waste and
in the utmost danger of becoming a desert. The great bodies of militia that have been in service this year employed against the enemy and in quelling the Tories have almost laid waste the country
and so corrupted the principles of the people that they think of
nothing but plundering one another."[49] Little wonder, then, that
external observers like the British would characterize the mountaineers as savage or barbarous. They could reasonably have said
the same of their opponents throughout the South.

The British and Loyalist depredations, however, suggest another way of explaining the characterizations of the mountaineers. Tory atrocities, when combined with similar Whig actions, drove soldiers and militiamen out of the military and encouraged civilians to dissociate themselves from the horrors of the war. The inhabitants sought to distance themselves from the perpetrators of such killing and destruction. As British soldiers like Patrick Ferguson became increasingly removed from the enemy and the civilian population, they saw little apart from the brutal fighting upon which they might base their generalizations. While many charges of savagery were justified, the British had ever fewer opportunities to see the opponent engaged in peaceful pursuits. As a result, direct contact paradoxically combined with the growing scarcity of nonhostile contacts to promote savage images of the backcountry inhabitants.

The conditions in the backcountry during the war placed residents in a very delicate position. As the historian Ronald Hoffman has written, "Authoritative personages on both sides demanded that common people supply material, reduce consumption, leave their families, and even risk their lives. Forced to make hard decisions, many flailed out in frustration or evaded and defied first one side, then the other, each contender's popularity fluctuating in rough accord with the seeming balance of power, or the balance of demand upon them."[50] Such dangers and demands helped put distance between the residents and the Whig government and military. Paul D. Escott and Jeffrey J. Crow have shown that in the face of demands for oaths of allegiance and for property, "the neutral and disaffected who from the beginning had questioned the legitimacy of the new regime began to turn to noncooperation and resistance."[51] Similarly, A. Roger Ekirch stated that North Carolina's "whig authorities frequently found themselves on the run. From 1780 to 1782, the assembly often could not convene because of the threat of Tory raiders."[52]

The inhabitants were not necessarily driven to form connections with the opposing side, however. Tory atrocities in the South, of which examples are abundant, surely discouraged the inhabitants from attaching themselves to the British. Patrick Ferguson himself, as inspector general of militia for South Carolina, had orders to prevent the Loyalist militia "from offering violence to innocent and inoffensive people, and by all means in your power [to] protect the aged, infirm, the women, and the children of every denomination from insult and outrage." Yet civilians suffered abuse from the likes of Samuel Brown, who earned the nickname "Plundering Sam," and William Cunningham, who came to be called "Bloody Bill." Cunningham once led a band of 300 Loyalists against Whig activists Joseph Hayes and Sterling Turner in western South Carolina. First they killed Turner and his men, and then they set fire to Hayes's fort. "Upon being reassured that their lives would be spared," recounts historian John S. Pancake, "the defenders surrendered. Hayes and his entire command, about thirty-five men, were promptly sabered to death. Bloody Bill was reported to have wielded his sword until he collapsed from exhaustion."[53]

As a result of these British actions, the inhabitants of the backcountry disconnected themselves (as much as they were able) from the British. As one Whig officer wrote, "If some means is not fallen upon to support the Civil Law . . . , the peaceable Inhabitants must be under the necessity of removing themselves very speedily." In response to the fighting and chaos in the backcountry, another Whig officer observed in August 1781, "It seems . . . to be the general opinion of those yet at liberty to withdraw themselves to places of safety."[54] Nathanael Greene reported that many Tories gave themselves up to the Whigs, "being tired of such a wretched life and not finding the Support, Respect, or attention which they expected from the British army."[55] When Whig governments finally initiated lenient parole and pardon laws that allowed Tories to return in relative safety, the separation from the British increased even more. Colonel Thomas Wade's promise to grant parole to those who would serve three months with his troops brought "upwards of one hundred of those deluded peoples . . . under arms. . . . [though first] we had to Kill . . . a few Outliers, which Ansured [ensured] a good End."[56] Cornwallis also provides evidence of the growing distance between the British and their former American allies. In April 1781, Cornwallis wrote that he hoped to have the aid of "our friends in North Carolina," but "Our experience has shown that their numbers were not so great as had been represented and that their friendship was only passive. For we received little assistance from them since our arrival in this province, and . . . not above two hundred have been prevailed upon to follow us either as Provincials or Militia."[57]

British soldiers like Patrick Ferguson, who characterized the mountaineers as "barbarians" and "the dregs of mankind," developed their images from the nature of warfare in the South. The brutal partisan fighting that engulfed both backcountry Whigs and Tories led each side to commit numerous atrocities and to act in ways that Patrick Ferguson accurately described. Ferguson did not describe New York revolutionaries in comparable terms because this type of warfare was largely confined to the southern theater. The savagery of southern warfare also ruptured ties between the British and the Whig, Tory, and neutral Americans. The framework of connectedness helps us see how Tory atrocities severed many physical and psychological bonds. As previously noted, British images of backcountry and mountain Whigs, formed under battle conditions, were not balanced by observations of ordinary civilian life. The nature of the fight, combined with its effect on connections within the mountain community, illuminates this early example of Appalachian imagery. In order to understand why the broad range of Appalachian stereotypes does not appear at this time, we must examine events in upper East Tennessee immediately following the war.

## THE STATE OF FRANKLIN

Many of the overmountain men who defeated Ferguson at King's Mountain also took part in the struggle with North Carolina over the state of Franklin from 1784 to 1789. The issues raised and the rhetoric used during this episode cast additional light on the relationship between imagery and connectedness. In the struggle to assert their political independence, the Franklinites portrayed themselves as different from their North Carolinian neighbors to the east. Their efforts then helped shape distinctive images of the mountain residents in the minds of others.

The state of Franklin arose in what is now upper East Tennessee on land originally claimed by North Carolina.[58] The state, pressured by Congress to cede its western lands to the federal government, relented on 2 June 1784 by transferring its land from the Blue Ridge Mountains in the east to the Mississippi River in the west. The act guaranteed the validity of all land entries made under North Carolina law and maintained the state's control over the region until Congress accepted the cession. The settlements on the Watauga, Holston, and Nolichucky Rivers received the news, called a convention at Jonesborough in late August 1784, elected John Sevier president of the convention, and declared themselves independent. In the meantime, opponents of the cession act in North Carolina pushed for its repeal and succeeded in the assembly's November session. At the same time, the assembly created the Washington judicial district for the mountain region, which provided a superior court and militia brigade for the region. It appointed David Campbell assistant judge and John Sevier the brigadier general. The news of the repeal, however, did not reach the mountains until after the residents had already convened a constitutional convention on 14 December 1784, formed a separate state, and adopted a constitution almost identical to that of North Carolina. When Sevier learned of North Carolina's repeal, he initially balked at continuing the move for independence but soon decided to follow the people's wishes and to lead the separate state. The first Franklin Assembly in March 1785, held in Jonesborough, elected Sevier governor.

Throughout 1785 and 1786, the Franklin government functioned in many respects as an independent state, signing treaties with neighboring Indians, opening land offices, and collecting taxes. During this period, the North Carolina government continued to oppose the Franklin government and cited the repeal of the cession act as the basis for nullifying any western claims of independence. Support for the movement, however, had never been unanimous within Franklin. The factions became increasingly hostile beginning in the summer of 1786. In July, North Carolina ignored any Franklin claims to authority by holding elections to the General Assembly in the mountain region. The Franklinites, represented by John Sevier, received 254 votes, while the North Carolina faction, led by John Tipton, had 179 votes.[59] From this point onward, both groups tried to exercise local political and legal authority, though with increasingly bitter and violent results. Anthony Bledsoe observed during the spring of 1787: "Politics in this part of the Country [Holston River area] run high. You hear in almost every collection of people frequent declarations, whorah for North Carolina! And others in the manner for the State of Franklin. I have seen it in much warmth. The Franklin Assembly has Passed an Act to punish by imprisonment any Person that shall Act in the commission of the Peace or other civil office under the Assumed Authority of North Carolina. God only knows where this confusion will end. I fear it ends in Blood."[60] Bledsoe predicted all too well. Despite both sides' efforts to compromise, violence broke out in 1788.

The confrontation started when John Tipton's men seized Franklin court dockets and personal property, including some of Sevier's slaves. Sevier responded at the end of February by marching more than 150 men to Tipton's home (which was guarded by 45 men, who were soon reinforced) and placing it under siege. Each side demanded the other's surrender. On 29 February 1788, the shooting began. The Tipton forces lost two men, and six more were wounded, while the Franklinites suffered two casualties, one of whom later died. The Tiptonites also captured nineteen prisoners, including two of Sevier's sons and one cousin. At first Tipton wanted to hang the two sons, but he was soon persuaded to release them on bond. After the fight the Sevier forces retreated, and the uneasy truce continued until October, when Tipton, under orders from the North Carolina governor, arrested Sevier. A group of friends and relatives quickly rescued Sevier, but the Franklinites' determination to continue the fight had weakened. The new federal constitution proclaimed in Article IV, section 3, that any new state formed from the territory of an existing state could be admitted to the Union only with the consent of the parent state. Nearly every mountain resident sought citizenship in the United States, and consequently support for Franklin waned. In February 1789, Sevier took the oath of allegiance to North Carolina, and in November, he represented Greene County in the North Carolina Senate and received an official pardon from the assembly. The next month, North Carolina again ceded its western lands to the federal government. Congress accepted this cession in February 1790 and three months later created the Territory South of the River Ohio to administer the region. The creation of Tennessee in 1796 completed the movement for a western state that had begun a dozen years earlier.

Many North Carolinians came to see the Franklinites as a distinctive group of people. The North Carolinians' images arise from both respect for the mountaineers' physical abilities and criticism of their separatist behavior. When Governor Alexander Martin was considering arguments for invading Franklin in 1785, he cautioned that "we shall have to do a great deal more than make a few token arrests. Do you think that men who fought at King's Mountain and have engaged in so many Indian campaigns will allow themselves to be made prisoner? If we want to subdue [them] by force, we shall need far more troops than are enlisted in our entire militia." When he asked other states to send help, South Carolina replied, "Sevier may be a fool. But he and his riflemen don't shoot like fools. It might be necessary to muster all the veterans of the recent war in order to force their surrender."[61] The Franklinites understood that others regarded them as inferior and as different from the more established regions of North Carolina. "Reflect upon the language of some of the most eminent members of the General Assembly of North Carolina at the last Spring session [1784], when the Members from the Western Country were supplicating to be continued a part of your State," the Franklin legislature asked. "Were not these their epithets: The inhabitants of the Western Country are the off scourings of the Earth, fugitives from Justice, & we will be rid of them at any rate."[62] These sentiments helped persuade the Franklinites to separate from North Carolina. "Some of your politicians," continued David Campbell to Governor Caswell, "think we have not men of abilities to conduct the Reigns of Government."[63] John Sevier leveled further criticisms against the members of the North Carolina Assembly in 1787: "[You have] done everything to disorder, and not to reconcile, the people of this country; and have calculated matters as they expect on purpose to set friends to cutting each other's throats. However I trust in this they will be disappointed and convinced although we live on the west of the Appalachian Mountain that we are not such dupes nor fools that will render us void and destitute of rational understanding."[64]

Such perceptions of difference stem from a growing political and geographical separation acknowledged by both sides. For example, the first Franklin Assembly sent a letter to North Carolina governor Alexander Martin in March 1785 explaining the reasons for its actions. The assembly insisted that "the inadequate allowance made the Judges who were appointed to attend the Courts of Criminal Justice, and who had to travel over the Mountains, amounted to prohibition as to the administration of Justice in this quarter." As a result, "the Western Country found themselves taxed to support Government, while they were deprived of all the blessings of it. Not to Mention the injustice done them in taxing their lands which lie five hundred miles from trade equal to land of the same quality on the sea shore."[65] The Franklin legislature exaggerated when it stated that "the Influence of the Law in Common Cases became almost a Nullity, & in criminal Jurisdiction had intirely ceased, which reduced us to the verge of Anarchy"; after all, the Washington County court records clearly reveal that a local legal system existed in the mountains.[66] Franklin's location, however, made access to higher level courts difficult, expensive, and time-consuming.

Franklinites also claimed that "almost every sensible disinterested traveler has declared it incompatible with our Interest to belong in Union with the Eastern part of the State." The mountains disconnected the inhabitants, in a deterministic fashion, not just from the legal system but also from every aspect of society. "For we are not only far removed from the Eastern parts of North Carolina, But Separated from them by high & almost impasable Mountains, which Naturally divide us from them; have proved to us that our Interest is also in many respects distinct from the inhabitants on the other Side & much injured by a Union with them."[67] Governor Martin agreed in part with these geographically based arguments when he reminded them that the assembly had removed "the only general inconvenience and grievance they might labour under, [the] want of a regular administration of criminal Justice and a proper and immediate command of the Militia, [and] a new District was erected, an assistant Judge and a Brigadier General were appointed."[68]

The Franklinites considered physical separation, distance, and the mountain environment critical in deciding whether or not an independent state should exist. Throughout 1786 and 1787, discussions between Franklin and North Carolina included these topics. "Our local and remote situation," wrote John Sevier, "are the only motives that induce us to wish for a separation. Your Constitution and Laws we Revere, and consider ourselves Happy that we have had it in our power to get the same established in the State of Franklin, although it had occasioned some confusion among ourselves." What advantages of political connectedness could outweigh the problems of location and distance?

> Our trade and commerce is altogether carried on with other states. Therefore neither party is benefited on that head. And whether it can be suggested that the benefit of the government can be extended from five to eight hundred miles distant, is a matter I leave to your own good sense to judge of. And further, it cannot be supposed that the inhabitants who reside at that distance are not equally entitled to the blessings of civil government as their neighbors who live east, south, or any other point, and not one-fourth of the distance from the seat of government; besides the incomparable advantages of the roads and other easy communications that you have on the east of the Appalachian.[69]

David Campbell implored Governor Richard Caswell similarly. "Nature has separated us—do not oppose her in her works; by acquiesing you will bless us . . . by uniting the disaffected, and do yourselves no injury, because you lose nothing but people who are a clog on your Government & to whom you cannot do equal justice by reason of their detached situation."[70]

The Franklinites summarized the effects of distance and location in a petition to the North Carolina Assembly in December 1787, predicting a dark future if political connections with the state were continued. Echoing Sevier, they mentioned the assembly's "great difficulty in ruling well & giving protection to so remote a people." This petition, however, went into greater detail about how the "almost impassable mountains Nature has placed between us" made it "impracticable for us to furnish ourselves with a bare load of the necessaries of life, except we in the first instance travel from one to two hundred & more miles through some other State 'ere we can reach your government." They would never see the benefit of taxes paid to North Carolina because they had no products "that could bear the carriage or encourage purchasers to come so great a distance" to the west. Eventually, "the people here must pay a greater sum than the whole of the medium now in circulation for the Exigencies and support of your Government, which would be a sum impossible for us to procure," and as a result "our property would gradually diminish and we at last [would be] reduced to mere poverty and want by not being able equally to participate with the benefits and advantages of your government." They did not see the mountain region as devoid of natural advantages and asserted hopefully "that having settled west of the Appalachian Mountains ought not to deprive us of the natural advantages designed by the bountiful hand of Providence for the conveniency & comfort of all those who have Spirit and sagacity enough to seek after them."[71]

Governor Caswell shared many of the Franklinites' sentiments about the mountain environment and the destiny of its inhabitants. "My Ideas are that nature in the formation of the Hills between us & directing the courses of water so differently had not in view the Inhabitants on either side being longer subject to the same Laws and Government."[72] Yet he could not encourage political independence when the mountain region was so torn by factionalism. "I have not a doubt but a new Government may be shortly established if the people would unite, submit to the form of Government & Petition for a Separation. This, I think, the only Constitutional mode; and I firmly believe, if pursued, will be a means of effecting the Separation on Friendly Terms, which I much wish."[73] Both parties agreed that geographical circumstances had separated the two sides; the debate centered on the way in which political separation would be achieved. That the Franklinites seized their independence when the North Carolina government wished to grant it helps explain some of the images of the mountaineers that emerged from this context of political and geographical disconnectedness.

## INDIANS, SPANIARDS, AND INTERNAL CONNECTEDNESS

Like the early external perceptions of difference, internal perceptions began to develop during the period when the state of Franklin existed. The internal perceptions did not develop sufficiently, however, to produce characterizations and images common to modern Appalachia. The disagreements between the Tiptonites and the Franklinites eventually led to violence, but all of the inhabitants remained united by connections to and concerns with issues beyond their immediate region. Continued threats from the Cherokee and Chickamauga Indians, combined with negotiations with Spain for commercial access to New Orleans, linked the residents as they pursued common goals. The divisions within upper East Tennessee created an acute but limited crisis that did not destroy the internal connectedness of the region. As a result, internal perceptions of difference among the inhabitants did not match those held by outsiders.

Most accounts of the state of Franklin focus their attention on the blood shed by the Tipton and Sevier factions in 1788. While the shootout at John Tipton's home and the subsequent arrest of John Sevier serve as the most familiar examples of internal division, the actions of more anonymous individuals afford a complementary view of internal disconnections and perceptions. The historian must use the sources with care; people sometimes exaggerate when describing their enemy to an ally. For example, Evan Shelby wrote North Carolina governor Richard Caswell criticizing the actions of the Franklin government: their "methods, with many others, such as appointing officers to carry into execution their treasonable acts and designs, [creates] a total subversion of all laws and good government[;] even every sense of civilization is lost amongst them."[74] Court depositions of very specific events can provide similar distortions—first because depositions by their nature record unusual events and second because the surviving court records tend to favor the North Carolina supporters—but such sources have the advantage of capturing a level of detail absent from the typical correspondence between the leaders of the two factions.

The differences between the two governments appear at the level of the individual in the deposition of Jonathan Pugh, sheriff for Washington County under North Carolina and a devoted supporter of the Tipton faction (Pugh was one of the two Tiptonites killed in the fighting against the Franklinites in 1788).[75] On 31 July 1787, Pugh and one of his deputies traveled to Jonesborough to remind certain citizens to report their taxable property. While in town, Pugh reported: "A certain James Sevier came up to the deponent and shook hands with the deponent and asked the deponent how he was. Whereupon the deponent arrested the said James Sevier by virtue of the precept upon a bill of indictment against him found; upon which the deponent demanded security for his appearance at next court, which he refused to do, and said that he despised the deponent's authority, and that he would not pay obedience to the laws of North Carolina." An apparently civil greeting by John Sevier's son had turned into a legal and political confrontation that soon escalated into violence. As soon as Pugh had arrested James Sevier, "a certain Andrew Caldwell came to the deponent and asked him if he was the person that had been serving a writ." When Pugh answered that he had, "the said Caldwell violently struck and abused the deponent, and after having so done, he, the said Caldwell, under the character of Sheriff of the State of Franklin, threatened to put him, the deponent in the common jail; upon which the said Caldwell departed."

What began as an exercise of North Carolina authority turned into a display of Franklin power when Caldwell returned after a few minutes and "affirmed that he would put the deponent in jail; upon which some of the bystanders said he had better not. To which the said Caldwell replied that he had his orders from a higher power than any of them, and immediately secured the deponent and put him in prison and shut the door and departed." After Pugh had "continued some time in prison, the said Caldwell came and opened the prison door, upon which the deponent came out of prison and met John Sevier, the pretended Governor of Franklin, who asked the deponent what business the deponent had there, serving a writ." When Pugh explained his original business and that he had no choice but to serve the outstanding writ when his son appeared, "the said John Sevier replied that they paid no obedience to the laws of North Carolina, and that they despised her authority." Sevier's defiant words apparently ended this specific incident, for the deposition concludes with Pugh asking Sevier on the following Saturday "if he was not the man that had ordered him to jail some days ago" and Sevier replying that he had.

This incident illustrates several different tensions between internal connectedness and division in the mountain region. We see local government, operating in the face of difficulties, reminding people to report their taxable property, while the larger political dispute hinders its efforts. Commonplace social relations, such as James Sevier's initial friendly greeting to Pugh, were also transformed. In the future, we may suspect, James Sevier might be more wary than warm when greeting an acquaintance. Violence, threats, strong feelings, angry words, and proud defiance arose on each side. Both men were strongly committed to upholding the law (in their positions as sheriffs) and freely engaged from time to time in breaking what the other side considered to be that law. In this context, we may readily guess what types of perceptions would be fostered by the situation. Pugh, angry at having been jailed for following what he believed to be the law, probably saw the Seviers not just as leaders of an illegitimate government but also as haughty and self-important men. James and John Sevier, on the other hand, may have seen Pugh as a misguided official of a government out of power who was policing an area no longer under the jurisdiction of North Carolina. The dispute over the state of Franklin could therefore affect the ways the mountain residents viewed each other.

David Deaderick's deposition depicts John Sevier as even more angry, demanding, and abusive.[76] At seven o'clock in the evening of 9 November 1788, Deaderick "was peaceably sitting in his shed adjoining his store house, with Andw. Caldwell." Deaderick's son told him Sevier had appeared at the store door. Deaderick "happened to be whistling as he opened the door, and was surprised to see a number of men on horseback; . . . John Sevier, Senr., at their head, who immediately on the deponent's opening the door, said we want no whistling, we want Whiskey or Rum. The deponent replied, as to whistling he hoped he might do as he pleased, but whiskey or Rum he had none." Sevier insisted that the liquor was available and offered to pay for it, but Deaderick repeated that he had neither whiskey nor rum. Sevier then asked Caldwell the same question and received the same reply.

> After hesitating a very little time he (Sevier) began to abuse this place; then its inhabitants without distinction, until the deponent thought the abuse so pointedly leveled at him, that he asked Sevier if he aimed that discourse or abuse at him. His answer was Yes, at you or anybody else. After exchanging several high words, Sevier called the deponent a son of B———ch. The deponent replied he was a d———d son of a B———ch, and stepped close to Sevier, who immediately drew out his pistol, or pistols. O, says the deponent, if you are for that I have pistols too, and turned, run into his store, & . . . returned with his pistols.

Caldwell blocked the door to prevent Deaderick from going out, "lest as Caldwell said, they should abuse him." After some delay Caldwell finally relented, and when "the deponent run out Sevier immediately presented a pistol at the deponent, who moved towards him & desired an equal chance, . . . & the deponent is of opinion, if Sevier had seen him raise his pistol he would have shot him; being then to the best of his Recollection not above fifteen feet separate." In the heat of this confrontation, Caldwell began to argue with Sevier, demanding payment for outstanding debts. Sevier claimed to owe nothing. "Caldwell said he was d——d eternal liar. Sevier swore by G——d he would shoot him, & rais'd his pistol. It went off, and wounded a certain Richard Collier. Sevier & his party left the town shortly after firing his pistol." At about two o'clock the next morning, Tipton, Caldwell, and several other men picked up Deaderick at the store and "pursued Sevier whom they overtook & Apprehended about day light next morning, and further this deponent saith not."[77]

The violent image of John Sevier that emerges from David Deaderick's deposition is akin to Patrick Ferguson's barbarous "Back Water men" and prefigures modern descriptions of the mountain residents. Yet such images may not be reserved exclusively for the mountain residents. According to Bertram Wyatt-Brown, the ethic of honor suffused the Old South, and one form manifested itself in dueling. Its essential function, the "public recognition of a man's claim to power, whatever social level he or his immediate circle of friends might belong to," was not necessarily played out in the specific rituals of the duel. "A street fight could and often did accomplish the same thing for the victor." Violence associated with honor, Wyatt-Brown argues, "pervaded all the white social classes. Whether the combat took a prescribed form or consisted of sheer unchecked fury did not make too much difference, if one or both of the contestants died."[78] Similarly, according to John Hope Franklin, "violence was inextricably woven into the most fundamental aspects of life in the South and constituted an important phase of the total experience of its people."[79] Furthermore, Sevier's capacity for violence, elicited by Tories and Cherokees during the preceding decade, had helped him reach the political and social position he now enjoyed. In fact, Sevier's continued military efforts against the Indians and his diplomatic efforts toward the Spanish helped establish internal connections that survived the wounds created by local political battles.

The continuous threat posed by the Indians muted perceptions of difference within the state of Franklin. The followers of both Tipton and Sevier met every year of Franklin's existence to negotiate with the Cherokees, Creeks, and Chickamaugas or to fight them. For example, the Treaty of Dumplin Creek in May 1785 enabled Franklinites to settle on Cherokee lands south of the French Broad River. Six months later, however, the Treaty of Hopewell prohibited settlement in large sections of Franklin's territory. As a result, the Franklinites marched on the Cherokees in 1786 and with the Treaty of Coyatee forced the Cherokees to sell the disputed land. Hostilities escalated to the point where John Sevier, Jr., called the campaigns against the Cherokee and Chickamauga in 1788 "the hottest Indian war that I ever witnessed."[80]

Indian activity outside what is now upper East Tennessee also brought calls for action during 1787. From the Cumberland region to the west, James Robertson sent a desperate letter to John Sevier in August, predicting that "without some timely assistance, we shall chiefly fall a sacrifice. Ammunition is very scarce; and a Chickasaw now here tells us they imagine they will reduce our station by *killing all our cattle, etc., and starving us out.* . . . Relieve us in any manner you may judge beneficial. We hope our brethren in that country will not suffer us to be massacred by the savages without giving us any assistance; and I candidly assure you that never was there a time in which I imagined ourselves in more danger."[81] Georgia felt similar threats from the Creeks and sought to raise 3,000 men to join with 1,500 Franklinites in a November campaign. For the Cumberland, Sevier promised to "[surmount] every difficulty to raise a formidable force," and for Georgia he lured volunteers with a generous land bounty. "This great and liberal encouragement," he concluded, "will, certainly, induce numbers to turn out on the expedition, which will not only be doing something handsome for themselves, but they will have the honour of assisting a very generous and friendly sister state to conquer and chastise an insolent and barbarous savage nation of Indians."[82] Although in the end no Franklinites fought in either campaign—the dissipation of the Indian threat in the Cumberland and the start of negotiations with the Creeks rendered their involvement unnecessary—the Creeks, Cherokees, and Chickamaugas throughout the southeast served to unite the inhabitants during this period.

In September 1788, fearing an alliance between the recently defeated Cherokees and the Creeks, Choctaws, and Chickasaws, John Sevier asked the Spanish minister Don Diego de Gardoqui for his "imposition with those Tribes in our behalf, and to inform them that the Cherokees have wantonly brought on the War themselves by frequently murdering and committing other acts of hostility against the Citizens of this Country." All inhabitants of upper East Tennessee felt concern about Spain's influence in this matter, but Spain's control of the Mississippi River played a far more important role in fostering a shared concern and an internal connectedness among the residents.[83] The closure of the Mississippi River to American commerce, one component of the Jay Treaty, caused western residents to howl in protest. Some inhabitants urged separation from the United States and allegiance to Spain for the sake of commercial advantage. James Madison quite reasonably asked, "Will it be an unnatural consequence if they [Westerners] consider themselves as absolved from every Federal tie and court some protection for their betrayed rights? . . . I should rather suppose that he [Gardoqui] means to work a total separation of interest and affection between the western and eastern settlements and to foment the jealousy between the eastern and southern States."[84] Thomas Jefferson replied, "I will venture to say that the act which abandons the navigation of the Mississippi is an act of separation between the Eastern and Western Country. . . . If they declare themselves a separate people, we are incapable of a single effort to retain them. Our citizens can never be induced, either as militia or as souldiers, to go there to cut the throats of their own brothers and sons, or rather to be themselves the subjects instead of the perpetrators of parricide."[85] The Jay Treaty galvanized local opinion in a way that united the Tipton and Franklinite factions.

For its own part Spain tried to lure the western settlements of Franklin, Cumberland, and Kentucky into declaring independence, if not an alliance or outright incorporation under Spanish rule. To protect their own holdings from the growing population of western settlers, the Spanish offered relief from Indian attacks and access to New Orleans. As Gardoqui wrote John Sevier, "His Majesty is very favorably inclined to give the inhabitants of that region all the protection that they ask for and, on my part, I shall take very great pleasure in contributing to it on this occasion and other occasions."[86] Sevier informed Gardoqui that "upon consulting with the principal men of this country, I have been particularly happy to find that they are as well disposed and willing as I am in respect to your proposals and guarantees." He assured Gardoqui that "you may be sure that the favorable hopes and ideas that the people of this country maintain with respect to the future probability of an alliance and concession of commerce with you in the future are very ardent and that we are unanimously determined to that effect."[87] While Sevier sought military and economic benefits for the people he served as governor of Franklin, he probably did not intend to make the region subservient to Spain.[88] His statement provides valuable insight, however, into the important role that Spain played in forging a sense of common identity and purpose within what is now upper East Tennessee.

Divisions clearly existed within this region during the 1780s, the product of tensions that strained relationships between inhabitants and led to physical violence and bloodshed. Considered more broadly, however, these divisions appear more transient than permanent, more the product of a passionate moment than of any deep, lingering resentment. The evidence supporting this perspective ranges widely: the entire Franklin period lasted less than five years; the animosity manifested itself largely in name-calling; and the two factions' bloodshed involved relatively few bodies. Perhaps most telling, John Sevier, the governor of Franklin, readily accepted North Carolina's offer of a pardon and quickly took his seat in the state senate. Bearing in mind also the external threats posed by the Indians and by the Spanish closure of the Mississippi, we can understand why internal self-perceptions of difference might have been relatively absent, in contrast to the outsiders' perceptions during the Revolutionary War period and the tenure of the state of Franklin. Yet self-perceptions of distinctiveness do begin to emerge within the region after the 1770s and 1780s, as political and social turmoil gave way to stability. The growth and dispersion of the population in upper East Tennessee by 1800 shows how inhabitants would become, in different ways, more connected with some of their neighbors and more disconnected from others.

# CHAPTER TWO

# The Early Roads

IN THE AFTERMATH of the War for Independence and the movement to create a state of Franklin, the inhabitants of upper East Tennessee returned to the more routine concerns of everyday life. The stability of the 1790s fostered regional growth and development. Cabins and farms no longer simply hugged the banks of the Watauga, Holston, and Nolichucky Rivers, for settlers pushed deep into Washington County's wooded rolling valleys. A rudimentary but vigorously developing road system connected the scattered settlements with one another and to places beyond the county boundaries. The web of roads that developed from 1780 to 1800 describes the geographical dimension of transportation and communications and thereby reveals the physical nature of isolation and integration. The roads not only mapped the community's shifting territorial boundaries but also indicated where the network of social relations varied from the political and physical units of town, county, and valley.

The road system in upper East Tennessee helped shape the character and boundaries of the region by connecting the residents both internally and externally. Settlements on different creeks and rivers were tied to each other by many small roads, while larger routes linked upper East Tennessee with different states. These roads, however, served some areas better than others, for certain portions of the region remained fairly inaccessible. Furthermore, overland travel during the period, no matter how well constructed the road, involved considerable effort and expense. An examination of the transportation routes—not only where and when roads were built but also the relative difficulty with which people traversed them—shows how the residents of upper East Tennessee were geographically isolated from or integrated with others. The network also describes the area within which the social and psychological ties of community were most likely to form. The various steps that settlers took to link themselves with neighbors both near and far demonstrate that by 1800 they were connected geographically and emotionally, albeit tenuously in places, to points scattered across the map. These ties suggest that no basis exists in the area's early history for modern depictions of Appalachian residents as a people isolated from the time of first settlement.

## Mapping the Early Road Network

People moved into upper East Tennessee from regions both to the north and to the east. The majority of the first settlers followed the Shenandoah Valley south from Virginia. Jacob Brown, leader of a company at King's Mountain, arrived from western Virginia in 1771 and arranged a long-term lease from the Indians for large tracts of land in the river valleys. By trading and subletting portions of the land to settlers who came after him, Brown acquired the financial resources to buy the property when the opportunity arose.[1] John Sevier, who eventually settled near Jacob Brown, also migrated south from Virginia. After visiting the region in 1771 or 1772 with the intent to trade, he settled first in Sullivan County and then in Washington. In the spring before King's Mountain, Sevier established a mill on Big Limestone Creek, six miles west of Jonesborough. By 1783, he lived directly south of town on the Nolichucky River.[2] David Deaderick, like the others, came to upper East Tennessee as a trader. Before the end of the Revolutionary War, he arrived in Jonesborough and established his mercantile business. Born in 1754 in Winchester, Virginia, at the northern end of the Shenandoah Valley, Deaderick probably took the Great Wagon Road and followed the valley south to the broad Holston River valley of East Tennessee.[3] This ancient trade route, established by the Cherokees and others, passes within twenty-five miles of Jonesborough. Christian's War Road, however, loops south of Bay's Mountain and comes ten miles closer to the town.[4] The connections between upper East Tennessee and Virginia, therefore, were well established in the late colonial period and provided a popular route for settlement from the north.

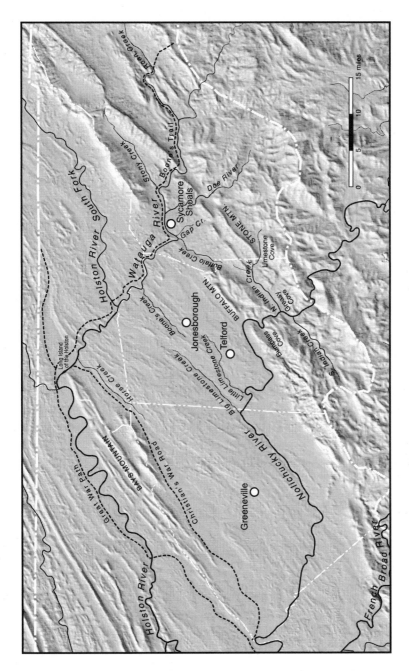

Map 2: Early Transportation Routes

Fig. 3. "Travelling." From "A Winter in the South," *Harper's*, May 1858.

Settlers also arrived by moving west from North Carolina across the crest of the Appalachian Mountains. Daniel Boone blazed a trail through the region in 1769 and entered the eastern tip of what is now Tennessee via Roan Creek and followed the Watauga River westward to the south fork of the Holston River. Boone's Trail crosses Christian's War Road at the Long Island of the Holston before continuing northwest into Kentucky.[5] Early settlers like Andrew Greer and Julius Dugger may have followed this route to the Watauga River, where they settled during the early 1770s. Charles Robertson, dissatisfied with the poor soil in central North Carolina and harried by the political persecution of the British colonial government, likewise moved to the Watauga River area before the Revolutionary War began.[6] Fewer settlers migrated over the mountains from North Carolina than came along the Shenandoah Valley, but transmontane routes existed early in the period of permanent settlement. In its connections to outside regions, therefore, the Great War Path crossed upper East Tennessee from northeast to southwest and Boone's Trail and other routes crossed the region from southeast to northwest.

Such external connections played an important role in the early legal jurisdiction of the mountain region. The dispute over the state of Franklin in the 1780s, as shown in chapter 1, arose in part because of the inadequate communication links over such distances. Individuals could penetrate the region, but the movement of larger numbers of people proved more difficult. For example, the North Carolina General Assembly decided to send a superior court judge to Jonesborough twice a year "for the trial of all criminal causes whatsoever within the limits of the counties of Washington and Sullivan." It felt that "the extensive mountains that lie desolate between the inhabited parts of Washington and the inhabited parts of Burke counties make the transportation of criminals from the former to the latter difficult and on the way may frequently find means to break custody and escape."[7] Similarly, Washington County's own court could send individuals to distant spots in order to take depositions for a particular case. On 7 August 1784 alone, the court sought depositions from the Charleston district in South Carolina; Ettingham County, Kentucky; Rutherford and Burke Counties, North Carolina; Rockingham County, Virginia; and neighboring Greene County.[8] Individuals in Washington County could reach a variety of locations and were not, as the historian Harold Browning contends, "completely isolated from the eastern settlements."[9]

Residents depended upon internal road connections not only to reach roads leading to other regions but also to link them with their neighbors. Such ties did not unify local government, because distance, terrain, and inaccessibility helped create separate counties within upper East Tennessee.[10] Still, the residents maintained a degree of communication and transportation with each other. The road network fell under the control of the Washington County Court of Pleas and Quarter Sessions, which served about 2,500 people in 1778 (the number grew to 5,862 in 1791 and to 11,192 by 1800) within an area of approximately 1,150 square miles.[11] A typical resident such as David Deaderick, from his residence in Jonesborough, would have had ample opportunity to see the Washington County Court of Pleas and Quarter Sessions at work ordering residents to survey, clear, and oversee 161 different roads from 1778 to 1800. By looking at when these roads were cleared, where they went, and how they were administered, we may map the community's proliferating physical connections.

Deaderick undoubtedly knew where the roads went, but the modern historian must wrestle with several methodological problems that complicate the process of pinpointing the roads' exact locations. When a typical entry in the court's minute book reads, "Ord that Adam Willson, Robert Willson, James Stinson, Jos Gest, & James Rodgers be appointed to make and Lay out a road

Fig. 4. "A Full View of Deaderick's Hill." Painting by Rebecca Chester, 1810 or 1811. Located in Jonesborough, the hill was named for David Deaderick. His general store on Main Street appears in the left foreground with his name over the door, and his residence appears above it. Courtesy of the Tennessee State Museum Collection, Nashville.

the most convenient & best way from the Court House of Washington down to Benja Gest Esqrs & Make return to our next Court," one end point can be easily located (Jonesborough, the county courthouse), but the other is far more difficult to place accurately. Although I have been unable to locate Benjamin Gest using primary and secondary sources, I can place him approximately by knowing that surveyors and workers on roads usually live near the proposed road and by using primary and secondary sources to locate Adam Wilson and James Stinson in the Telford region, six miles southwest of Jonesborough on Little Limestone Creek.[12] Even if the road cannot be placed exactly, we can be fairly confident of its general location.

Several problems arise from using such methods to locate people and roads. The primary documents, including other road requests and the occasional tax list that mentions property location, are seldom specific enough to permit exact placement. The secondary materials cite few of their sources, contradict each other at times, and offer vague descriptions.[13] Maps can be used when physical landmarks such as Greasy Cove and Rock Creek are given as end points, but the names of such places may have changed over time or may have been assigned to several different spots.[14] Despite such complications, the roads can be mapped with some accuracy. Whenever possible, two independent sources confirm an individual's location. With internal evidence from the road requests to supplement the sources mentioned above, we may follow a typical resident like David Deaderick on the routes he might have taken during the first decades of settlement.

The Washington County road system may best be described by spatially organizing the myriad routes around the two population centers, Jonesborough and Sycamore Shoals, and the most important physical landmarks surrounding them. In the mountains south of Jonesborough lay the Nolichucky River, which begins at the juncture of North and South Indian Creeks in Greasy Cove and flows westward into Greene County. Big and Little Limestone Creeks, with tributaries spreading throughout western Washington County, also flow into the Nolichucky. The South Fork of the Holston River and the Watauga River form a diagonal boundary northeast of Jonesborough that is perforated by the Choate, Bean, and Dungan Fords. On the route from Jonesborough east to Sycamore Shoals lay houses that would eventually form present-day Johnson City. From Sycamore Shoals, settlements and mills on the Doe River to the southeast, the Watauga and Roan Creek to the east, and Stony Creek to the northeast all served as important focal points for the early road system.

During the Revolutionary War, David Deaderick could travel from his home in Jonesborough to many of the surrounding areas. He could venture north into Sullivan County, south to Greasy Cove, and west to Big Limestone Creek and to Greene County.[15] Many roads linked up with the Great War Path, the region's major trade route.[16] In fact, residents from all over Washington County, not just Jonesborough merchants like Deaderick, could reach the

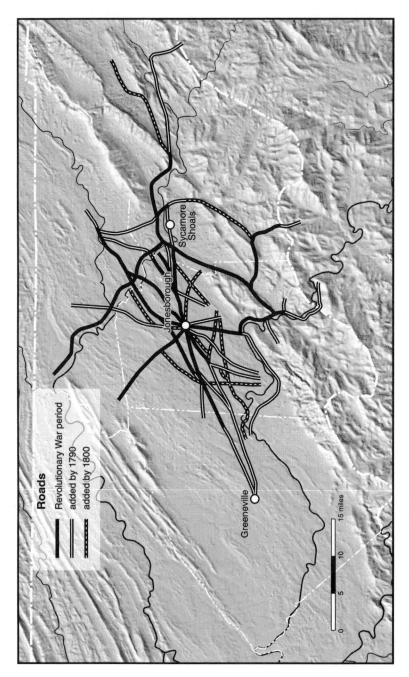

Map 3. Upper East Tennessee Roads

Great War Path and thereby head west and into Virginia. Merchants also attracted customers living in the eastern, more mountainous portions of the country. Roads connected Jonesborough to Sycamore Shoals and then went further into the steep mountain valleys along Doe River, Buffalo Creek, and North Indian Creek.[17] This area contained the one government-ordered road that crossed the Appalachian Mountains to Burke County, North Carolina.[18] Although the court assigned several overseers to the Burke County road, it took little action on other transmontane routes to the North Carolina piedmont. In short, residents like David Deaderick could travel to neighboring counties and could cover about 400 square miles within Washington County. Settlement was unevenly distributed, however, within this area bounded by Greasy Cove and the Nolichucky River on the south, the Greene County line and the Great War Path on the west, the Holston and Watauga Rivers on the northeast, and Sycamore Shoals to the east. With the population concentrated along the principal waterways and at the county seat of Jonesborough, the roads serviced those regions to the exclusion of others.

During the rest of the 1780s, however, the transportation and communication network grew in both scope and depth.[19] Deaderick could travel farther east into the most mountainous portions of the county as well as take new branches off the earlier roads and reach nearby locations more easily. In some cases the court ordered new overseers for existing roads, and at other times it ordered roads to be surveyed because earlier orders were never carried out or because an increase in traffic required expansion of the roads.[20] By the late 1780s, the southern part of the county, watered by the Nolichucky River and its principal tributaries, had acquired new roads to new destinations.[21] The southern part of the county, like the area around the Watauga and Holston Rivers, began to develop an interconnecting series of roads.[22] The spiderweb of roads also began to develop around Sycamore Shoals; residents could travel on new routes that led up the Doe River as well as westward to Gap Creek.[23] By the end of the decade, new routes had penetrated into the eastern, more mountainous regions of Washington County. In 1787, the court ordered a road to run along Boone's Trail, up the Watauga, and to Roan Creek, one of its sources. The work proceeded slowly, however; the court had to request work on the first part of this road, extending about ten miles east of Sycamore Shoals, on three separate occasions.[24] Perhaps the difficulty in completing the road related to problems of terrain (one traveler referred to Roan Creek as "the dismal place")[25] or to an insufficient number of workers.[26] At any rate, the expanding network of roads, which included new routes extending both north (to the Holston River in Sullivan County) and southeast (through the mountains following the Nolichucky to its headwaters), reached into new territory during the late 1780s.[27]

Such expansion did not occur in the 1790s. Although two new roads were surveyed far to the east, near the most northeastern point in the state, no other roads extended the territorial boundaries of the transportation network during the decade. New roads cut across Washington County in different directions, especially south of Jonesborough, but these simply provided new ways to reach familiar destinations.[28] In the vast majority of the cases, the court either assigned new overseers to old roads or ordered new roads to be surveyed along previously requested routes. More than ever before, the court sought to build and maintain roads radiating from Jonesborough and to connect the settled portions of Washington County.[29] The road network had reached a plateau in its development. The court evidently deemed the geographical scope sufficiently extensive and now sought to facilitate movement within the county by maintaining the existing set of roads and gradually supplementing them with interconnecting routes.

Several distinct patterns emerge when we map this road network. Clearly, most of the traffic ran along the valleys in the more open areas of Washington County. Many more roads linked the people to Sullivan County in the north and Greene County to the west than to the North Carolina piedmont. When the locations of all roads are considered, we see a road network consisting of far more external connections leading to the north and west than to the east, and internal connections that linked the population centers to settlements scattered along the county's rivers and streams. By the turn of the nineteenth century, the Appalachian residents had plainly established transportation and communication connections to a wide range of places. We must assess the quality of these connections, however, before the road network can help us understand life within Washington County.

## EASE OF TRAVEL

A simple mapping of the early roads does not indicate how Washington County residents could or could not move about and hence may distort our view of the region's connectedness. The court records describe the road network only imperfectly. On the one hand, the minute books may underestimate the links connecting residents. Many roads are described as running between the farms or mills of two individuals; when these locations cannot be mapped, neither can the road. We suspect that a road has been created without knowing exactly where. In addition, the county court recognized only public roads; a private, informal network of trails and paths was certainly also used. Areas of upper East Tennessee that seem to lie outside the transportation system may therefore actually have been tied in.

On the other hand, we might easily overestimate the connections implied by the roads. The mere existence of such roads does not mean easy travel. The county court occasionally had trouble establishing a road; the court, for example, had to call the same jury repeatedly to survey the same stretch of road.[30] Once surveyed and marked, the roads were often poorly maintained. "We the grand jurymen," Frank Allison reported in 1798, "present the road from Hock Beckens to John Brown's out of repair and Abednego Hail is the overseer." At times, "a tree top and some other impediments" were found blocking roads, and as a result the grand juries typically reported that "the citizens passing and travelling . . . with their horses, carts, carriages, and waggons could not . . . for a long space of time . . . nor yet can go, return, pass, ride, and labour without great damage, to the great damage and common nuisance of all the good citizens passing through, going by, and travelling that way, an ill example to all others in like cases offending and against the peace and dignity of the State of Tennessee."[31] Once fines had been levied, the good citizens, if they were fortunate, would have the road fixed shortly afterward.

Even when roads did not require repairs, travelers had difficulty using them. Francis Asbury, the Methodist bishop who roamed throughout the United States for over forty years, passed through upper East Tennessee on several occasions. By the time he reached the Holston River on 26 September 1801, he had "ridden about

one hundred miles in the last four days; the roads equal to any in
the United States for badness." These words came from a man
who had traveled the length of the United States from Massachusetts to Georgia many times. On another trip to the Sycamore
Shoals area in 1806, he endured "rough roads, and a wild country,
rocks, ruts, and sidelong difficult ways, sometimes much obscured;
it was thus I lost my way, and travelled twenty miles farther than I
needed."[32]

In perhaps the most telling incidents, Asbury had to pass
through forests and over mountains in order to go between upper
East Tennessee and North Carolina. In 1790, his party crossed
Stone Mountain; "those who wish to know how rough it is may
tread in our path." Asbury tells how he, while scanning about for
their guide, was "carried off with full force against a tree that hung
across the road . . . and my head received a very great jar, which,
however, was lessened by my having on a hat that was strong in
the crown." On another trip in the early spring of 1797, the rain
had swollen a branch of the Toe River so that it was "rocky, rolling, and roaring like the sea." After crossing it several times,
Asbury and his companions climbed to the summit of Yellow
Mountain. "We found it so rich and miry that it was with great difficulty we could ride along." It was then "pitch, slide, and drive to
the bottom." When crossing the Great Toe, his horse "locked one
of his feet in a root" but managed to free himself. The next day,
they began "to scale the rocks, hills, and mountains, worming
through pathless woods. . . . I had to step from rock to rock, hands
and feet busy; but my breath was soon gone, and I gave up the
cause, and took my horse again." At last the party made it to the
Doe River and followed it to Sycamore Shoals. "I was much spent
with the labours of this day," he concluded.[33]

François André Michaux also left a detailed account of his journey across these mountains. The Frenchman left Jonesborough on
21 September 1802 and arrived in Limestone Cove "benumbed
with cold by the thick fog that reigns almost habitually in the
vallies of these enormous mountains." Even this route, established
early in the county's history, had its problems. "The road, or rather
the path, begins to be so little cut that one can scarce discern the
track for plants of all kinds that cover the superficies of it."
Michaux had to use an axe to chop through the "twisting and inter-

Fig. 5. François André Michaux. Painting by Rembrandt Peale. Courtesy of the American Philosophical Society.

woven" branches of rhododendron shrubs which towered as high as twenty feet over the path. "The torrents that we had continually to cross added to the difficulty and danger of the journey," Michaux added, for their horses risked slipping on the "loose round flints concealed by the ebullition of the waters with which the bottom of these torrents are filled."[34]

Michaux left Limestone Cove the following morning, "after having made the most minute inquiry with regard to the path I had to take." Given the steep grade of the path, "it is with great difficulty a person can sit upon his horse, and . . . half the time he is obliged to go on foot." By noon he had reached the summit of the mountain, which he "recognized by several trees with '*the road*' marked on each." "Arrived at the bottom of the mountain, I had again, as the evening before, to cross through forests of *rhododendrum*, and a large torrent called Rocky Creek, the winding course of which cut the path in twelve or fifteen directions." Each creek crossing was a trial, as was finding the path on the other bank. "The entrance was frequently concealed by tufts of grass or branches of trees, which have time to grow and extend their foliage, since whole months elapse without its being passed by travellers." Once Michaux emerged from this most mountainous section of the crossing, he could reflect upon his experiences: "I then perceived the imprudence I had committed in having exposed myself without a guide in a road so little frequented, and where a person every moment runs the risk of losing himself on account of the sub-divisions of the road, that ultimately disappear, and which it would be impossible to find again, unless by being perfectly acquainted with the localities and disposition of the county, where obstacle upon obstacle oppose the journey of the traveller, and whose situation would in a short time become very critical from the want of provisions."[35] Such difficulties in physically moving through this region must have been shared by all who traveled this way.

Mountain residents familiar with the "disposition of the county," however, would not have suffered Michaux's confusion about the right path to take. Such "local knowledge" distinguishes the travel experiences of county residents (who have left no surviving accounts) from those of visitors like Asbury and Michaux.[36] We must also consider the visitor's purpose in traveling. Individuals like Asbury, who traveled merely to reach the next destination, would probably have been annoyed by the delays caused by the environment. Such frustration could spill out in the subsequent diary entry and survive to color the historian's view of the experience. Those who moved at a more leisurely pace may not have seen the road in the same way. Although these travelers were certainly interested in reaching their destination, they were also intrigued by what they found along the way. From this perspective, travel does not seem very taxing. The historian must treat published accounts cautiously because of such idiosyncrasies.

## EARLY APPALACHIAN COMMUNITIES

How, then, does the examination of roads speak to the question of isolation and integration in upper East Tennessee during the last decades of the eighteenth century? Clearly, the region was not sealed off from the surrounding counties and states. The external links created by the mere existence of public roads indicate a degree of connectedness that contradicts popular assumptions of extreme isolation. Yet the difficulties encountered while establishing, using, and maintaining the limited set of roads suggests a powerful sense of remoteness. Furthermore, the physical setting of ridges and valleys meant that roads moved along northeast-southwest lines, and it impeded travel in other directions. Crossing the mountains posed such a formidable task that relatively few travelers, using even fewer roads, linked themselves with northwestern North Carolina. Internal road connections radiated from Jonesborough like spokes around a wheel's hub, but steep mountains and narrow valleys discouraged road surveyors from penetrating certain parts of the county. Thus, while the extent and quality of the roads allowed people to enter and move about upper East Tennessee, the convoluted land on which the roads were built made movement difficult. After assessing this geographic dimension, we may place upper East Tennessee somewhere in the middle on the scale of connectedness, perhaps closer to "integration" than to "isolation."

The road network also reveals important patterns in the shape and content of Washington County communities. The court records list fifteen persons at least three times as starting or ending points for roads from 1778 to 1800. We might expect these men to have been prominent landowners and among the region's earliest settlers; as such, they could persuade the court to build roads to their property. Indeed, several of the fifteen men fell into this category. James Stuart, county surveyor and justice of the peace, owned seven tracts of land covering 7,400 acres worth over £7,800. All in all, Stuart's property, which included three slaves, forty-two horses, and thirty-six cattle, was worth about £16,000 in 1779. Robert Young owned three 640-acre tracts near present-day Johnson City, one slave, twenty horses, and thirty-one cattle, worth £5,642 in 1779. John Tipton, militia colonel and clerk of the court, lived nearby on some of his 2,000 acres of land. Abednego Inman, another early settler, owned 450 acres on Big Limestone Creek, two slaves, seven horses, and eight cattle, valued at £2,418 in 1781. Charles Robertson, a justice of the peace who hosted the Washington County court's first session in his home, owned £2,382 worth of property in 1778.[37] In forty-four cases, the court assigned either surveyors or overseers to roads that had property belonging to one of these five men as a terminus.[38]

Yet not all of the fifteen men who frequently appeared in the road requests owned thousands of acres and dozens of livestock. In 1790, William Davis owned 478 acres, Hugh Campbell had 100 acres, and Ninian Hoskins owned no land at all. Even Charles Robertson, who in 1778 had owned considerable property on the Watauga River west of Sycamore Shoals, owned only 200 acres on Cherokee Creek when roads were surveyed through his property in the mid-1790s.[39] In all likelihood, roads ran to these and other people not for their political influence but rather for their geographical location. Roads most frequently began or stopped at waterways; of the 245 times geographical features were mentioned as a road terminus, 57 were rivers and creeks. The total rises to 122 when fords and mills, obviously connected to rivers, are included. Many of the roads that ended at an individual's residence were also located on waterways: William Dovere lived on Buffalo Creek, John Parkson on the Doe River, and Peter French on Cherokee Creek, to name just a few.[40] When we take these into consideration, we see that the majority of the roads in Washington County went where they did because of the local rivers and creeks. These roads did not service water transportation routes; except for the Holston River and, during floods, the Nolichucky and Watauga Rivers, the waterways were unnavigable.[41] The rivers and creeks provided essential sources for power and sustenance and as such became important destinations for county roads.

Fig. 6. "Fording Indian Creek." From "A Winter in the South," *Harper's*, January 1858.

Given the physical characteristics of Washington County and the needs of its residents, a smaller number of roads to these locations would have been surprising.

The road network shaped the communities of Washington County in other important ways. The general costs and difficulties involved in moving individuals and goods over land lead one to conclude that at this time, the mountaineers were not more isolated than their neighbors in other parts of the frontier. The remoteness led some visitors to generalize about characteristics they saw in Westerners. While traveling through Kentucky, Michaux remarked that if a traveler stops, "he is presented with a glass of whiskey and then asked a thousand questions, such as Where do you come from? where are you going? . . . their only object being the gratification of that curiosity so natural to people who live isolated in the woods, and seldom see a stranger." Isaac Weld also noticed that the curiosity of these people "was boundless. Frequently have I been stopped abruptly by one of them in a solitary part of the road, and in such a manner, that . . . I should have imagined it was a highwayman that was going to demand my purse, and without any further preface, asked where I came from? if I was acquainted with any news?"[42] Such inquisitiveness seems plausible, in view of the settlements' remote location, but the ability of individuals like Michaux and Weld to reach such places suggests that they were accessible.

Such observations help us spot the connections that exist in the spiderweb of roads around the county seat of Jonesborough. With ready access to one another, people made face-to-face contacts at the courthouse, the general stores, and the taverns. The roads helped them develop common interests and, as noted earlier, in Thomas Bender's definition, "a network of social relations marked by mutuality and emotional bonds." Furthermore, the difficulty of traveling on the roads, especially when crossing the mountains to North Carolina, fostered a local orientation in upper East Tennessee more generally. The physical barrier of the mountains could shift the residents' economic interests, for example, to the north and west (toward the more open and rolling valleys of Sullivan and Greene Counties) and away from the North Carolina counties to the south and east. At the same time, however, we can also see broader connections at work. The roads allowed Washington County residents to pursue interests that connected them not just with neighbors but to distant places.

Clearly, each individual living in upper East Tennessee at this time was oriented both locally and in a broader geographical sense. The same person whose economic interests pointed him toward the livestock markets in Charleston, South Carolina, also saw himself as a county taxpayer, as a member of the local militia, and as a neighbor. Each of these dimensions—the economic, the political, the social, and the geographical—contributed to the mixture of forces that connected the inhabitants of the region. A community, after all, need not be grounded in a territory of only one size. The Washington County resident lived concurrently in communities the size of his valley, his civil district, his county, and his interstate markets. Most of the residents living within upper East Tennessee established significant connections with others in the immediate locale, but their ties to neighboring counties and states (especially across the mountains to the North Carolina piedmont) were far more tenuous. Appalachia has often been described as geographically isolated, but the early road network prevents us from seeing upper East Tennessee during the late eighteenth century in this light. Nevertheless, the mountain topography compounded the difficulties involved in travel throughout the South and played a vital role in developing a specific regional identity. As the road network continued to develop in the early nineteenth century, so too did the region's economy. This development brought with it not just stronger and more numerous ties to distant locations but also a growing sense of inferiority and backwardness among some inhabitants.

# CHAPTER THREE

# Internal and External Economic Connections

JOHN SEVIER, the first governor of the new state of Tennessee, spoke to the General Assembly in April 1796 about "making a waggon road over what is commonly called the western mountains."[1] The road would serve the region's economic needs by following the French Broad River southeast from Greene County and winding through North and South Carolina, where it would connect with routes leading all the way to Charleston. Nearly twenty years earlier, the North Carolina government (under whose jurisdiction this area fell in 1777) ordered a road built in this area because "the Inhabitants of Washington County would derive great Advantages from a Public Road leading directly through the Mountains into the County of Burke, for Horses, Carts, and Waggons, to pass to the Sea Ports in this State and South Carolina."[2] In the summer of 1796, Sevier informed Governor Nanderhorst of South Carolina that "Charles Robertson, of Greene County (a gentleman of reputation and respect) [was hired] to undertake the clearing and opening of a waggon road" over the mountains to Warm Springs, North Carolina. The road would benefit the general public by contributing to more than just "the convenience of travellers who may have occasion to pass from any of the southern states to [Tennessee]."[3] Sevier emphasized "the great tendency it will have to induce emigrants into the State; besides opening an easy and ready communication with the sea ports and trading towns in the neighboring States, whereby many of the productions of this Country can be transported to market with convenience."[4]

Many upper East Tennessee residents shared Sevier's concern for interregional economic connections. The farmers, iron manufacturers, merchants, and livestock drovers linked themselves with the inhabitants of upper East Tennessee and with residents of regions scattered around the United States. They struggled throughout the late eighteenth and early nineteenth centuries to expand and to consolidate their economic connections. In so doing they moved from a position that was never completely isolated to one that became ever more integrated with the rest of the United States. The residents' perspective broadened as they made connections with the world beyond upper East Tennessee. Yet the region's economy lagged far behind that of nonmountain areas like Middle Tennessee. The disparity, coupled with increasing soil exhaustion and relatively few internal improvements, fostered in upper East Tennessee the belief that the region was indeed a different sort of place and a poorer one. The evolving self-perceptions of upper East Tennessee residents permit us to reexamine the standard interpretations of Appalachia. Local self-perceptions of difference, based in part on external and internal economic connections, played a critical role in causing Appalachian residents to be viewed later on as isolated, poor, and backward.

## A VARIETY OF ECONOMIC CONNECTIONS

Like most Americans, the residents of upper East Tennessee based their economy on agriculture.[5] Of the many crops grown by the 1790s, corn formed the mainstay. It could be ground, grated, roasted, broiled, eaten whole, converted into molasses and whiskey, and fed to livestock. Because it was easy to cultivate and matured quickly, corn became so ubiquitous and so central to people's lives that it could serve as a monetary standard and a form of currency.[6] "Indian wheat forms here also one of the principal branches of agriculture," wrote the French botanist and traveler François André Michaux in 1802. He reported that wheat, which grew seven to eight feet tall and yielded as much as thirty bushels an acre, was raised wherever possible.[7] Other grains, such as oats, rye, timothy, and barley, played a less important role in the economy. Vegetable gardens and fruit trees were also found throughout upper East Tennessee. Although both flax and cotton appeared often in estate inventories, most of the latter probably came from outside the region.[8] Cotton production, Michaux remarks, "is little noticed, on account of the cold weather, which sets in very early."[9]

Corn, wheat, and other crops that needed to be milled provided impetus for the local movement of people and produce. Far from being isolated, Washington County residents built and patronized more than two dozen gristmills during the twenty years following the county's establishment in 1777. Scattered on waterways throughout the county, the mills were relatively accessible for most of the residents. The county court could authorize the building and operation of a public mill and the collection of a tax. Abraham Denton, for example, was "allowed to build a grist mill on Sinking Creek on his own land, and he shall be entitled to toll allowed for public mill." Similarly, Bartholomew Woods, who had already constructed a mill, persuaded the court to designate it a public mill; he was thereby "entitled to take such a toll and have the rights and immunities as other public grist mills within the District."[10] The mill sites, as modest as they were, nevertheless gave residents opportunities to interact with each other on a fairly regular basis during the growing season. A farmer who had settled along a placid stretch of Cherokee Creek, his fields stretching back from its banks, might bring his corn to John Hunter, Jr., or to Charles Robertson, who both operated public mills at points where the creek bed dropped and the flow of the stream increased.[11] Stones turned by the modest waters of Cherokee Creek did not grind corn quickly, and so the miller and his customer had a chance to exchange pleasantries and news. This ritual, repeated throughout the county, encouraged local residents to maintain connections with one another.[12]

The distillation of corn into whiskey provided another opportunity for interaction. In the twelve months preceding July 1796, for example, sixty-four Washington County residents were taxed for distilling over 15,000 gallons of alcohol. In stills ranging in capacity from 40 to 130 gallons, these individuals produced on average 291 gallons per person. William Cobb led all distillers by producing the equivalent of 1,471 gallons during the year.[13] Surely Cobb's family did not consume this quantity by themselves; whether the surplus was sold to local taverns or outside the region, alcohol, like the grains from which it had been produced, helped connect people.[14]

Similarly, animals prompted their owners' integration into networks that extended well beyond the immediate environs. Horses, cattle, sheep, and hogs filled the countryside. Horses in particular played a crucial role in the residents' lives. Although they made up only 11 percent of all the animals found in Washington County estate inventories before 1796 ($N$ = 111), horses, mares, and colts appeared on 89 percent of the estates. Horses, often the most valuable possessions listed in the inventories, not only pulled wagons, carts, plows, and logs but were also used for riding.[15] A horse's value and its central position in its owner's life become evident when we consider the incidents of horse stealing and the punishments meted out for the crime. In a region where even "the poorest man has always one or more horses," François André Michaux noted in 1802 that "at the inns in small towns, [people] are extremely careful in locking the stables, as horse-stealers are by no means uncommon in certain parts of the United States." Local residents were frequently victimized, "as the horses are, in one part of the year, turned out in the forests, and in the spring they frequently stray many miles from home; but on the slightest probability of the road the thief has taken, the plundered inhabitant vigorously pursues him, and frequently succeeds in taking him; upon which he confines him in the county prison, or, which is not uncommon, kills him on the spot."[16] When horse thieves appeared before the court, they sometimes received sentences that appear harsh by today's standards. The Superior Court of Law and Equity met in Jonesborough in 1790 and sentenced Elias Pybourn for horse stealing. "It is therefore ordered that the said Elias Pybourn be confined in the publick Pillory one hour. That he have both his ears nailed to the Pillory and severed from his head. That he receive at the publick Whipping Post thirty nine lashes well laid on; and be branded on the right cheek with the letter H, and on the left cheek with the letter T, and that the Sheriff of Washington County put this sentence in execution between the hours of Twelve and Two this day."[17]

The county court also recognized forms of branding, as when "Jonas Martin came into Court and made Oath that the Ear Mark of his Cattle, sheep, and Hogs is a smooth crop in the Left ear and in the right Ear a half crop on the upper side and the Tail cropt off the hoggs."[18] By registering their marks with the court, Martin and many other residents provided an official means of identifying some of the many kinds of animals that roamed the woods of upper East Tennessee. Cattle accompanied even the first settlers. Evan Shelby, writing to his sons in Maryland, described the ease and inexpensiveness of stock-raising: "Wee sent all our stock to the Kain [cane] . . . so that our Stock will be little cost to us more than salting of them Except halfe a Dozen Cows wee Ceep for milke and four horses wee Ceep To work the others is now [no] Expence To us."[19] Cattle, like horses, appeared in 89 percent of the estate inventories found before 1796. Owners averaged twelve cows, steers, calves, and oxen, with John Carter owning fifty-two, the most on any single list. Sheep were found on 59 percent of the inventories, with an average ownership of eleven animals. Hogs, on the other hand, nearly outnumbered cattle and sheep combined. On average, hog owners had twenty-two creatures; Samuel McQueen, with his seventy-five hogs, was ahead of all the rest.[20] Livestock, especially cattle and hogs, connected upper East Tennessee to markets extending far beyond the Appalachian Mountain region.

William Blount, governor of the Southwest Territory in 1790, before Tennessee statehood, wrote to his brother that on his trip to Washington County through the Shenandoah Valley of Virginia, "it appeared to me that Half the World were in Motion passing to or from Kentuckie or to or from this Territory, I met at least 1000 Head of Cattle from this Territory going to the Northern Marketts."[21] As livestock driving developed, the animals penetrated other farming districts such as the piedmont areas of Maryland, Virginia, and the Carolinas. Farmers in these grain-producing areas, after fattening the cattle further, then drove the animals to markets in Baltimore and Philadelphia.[22] "To consume the superfluity of their corn," Michaux wrote, "the inhabitants rear a great number of cattle, which they take four or five hundred miles to the seaports belonging to the southern states. They lost very few of these animals by the way, although they have to cross several rivers, and travel through an uninterrupted forest, with this disadvantage, of the cattle being extremely wild."[23] Drives in the opposite direction, to the west, might have been even more precarious, given the less developed transportation system in that region. Yet large numbers of livestock reached Nashville and Knoxville, and from Knoxville the animals were further shipped to planting regions in the southeast, to western Georgia, and to Alabama.[24] Through its animals, therefore, upper East Tennessee established early connections with regions in every direction.

Commerce, closely tied to agriculture, also involved extensive forms of economic connectedness.[25] John Sevier often stepped into Samuel May's store in Jonesborough, sometimes buying for himself "8 lbs. sugar, 1 bottle mustard, 2 pr. w. shoes & sundry other things" and at other times settling a tangle of related local debts: "Memo. paid to Mr. Samuell May for Samuell Sherrill in part pay of negro man named Will. Samuel Sherrill's own account with Mr. May £29.10.7 to Mr. May for goods to Josiah Allen on Mr. Sherrill's account £4/.10.0 Virginia money. Memo. pd. Mr. May for Charles Waddell." Furthermore, Sevier patronized several different stores; he acquired one type of fabric from Mr. Harrison's store and another type from David Deaderick's.[26] John Sevier, like many other residents of Washington County and upper East Tennessee, did most of his trading and purchasing in Jonesborough, the economic, political, and legal center of the region. Although in 1799 the German travelers Abraham Steiner and Frederick C. de Schweinitz said the town "consists of one long street [and] has nearly 30 houses," it was thriving, "as are all the towns of the back country." Three years later, Michaux found 150 houses in Jonesborough, "built of wood, and disposed on both sides of the road. Four or five respectable shops are established there." Merchants not only attracted local residents to Jonesborough but also made the town a center for trade and, as a result, a focal point of interconnections both within the region and between it and distant markets.[27]

The general stores in Jonesborough operated in different geographical contexts. Nathaniel and Samuel Cowan, for example, traded on a regional, East Tennessee scale; they sold goods at stores in both Jonesborough and Knoxville and accepted as barter beeswax, crops such as corn, wheat, and rye, and any type of animal skin.[28] David Deaderick also had stores in these towns (as well as in Greeneville), but he seems to have moved among national markets and not just regional ones. His newspaper advertisements proclaimed that "David Deaderick hath just received from Philadelphia and Baltimore, and is now opening for sale . . . a very handsome and general assortment of goods," which ranged from fabrics, combs, locks, and knives to books, spices, saddles, and pewter. He too accepted as payment "skins, furs, beeswax, and flax" and gave cash "for the best otter, black and grey fox, raccoon, wildcat, muskrat, and mink skins."[29] Deaderick also shipped local produce out of the region and paid £48.2.3 for hemp to be taken to Richmond. In 1801 Deaderick paid John Gifford for "hawling 3007 lbs. from Philadelphia to Jonesborough" and John Masengale for "holing 1294 lbs. from Richmond to Jonesborough."[30] Such interregional trade caught the eye of the county court, which "ordered that John and Anacher Belfom in Company David Deaderick and Robert Ligget, Gentlemen merchants in the town of Jonesborough, shall apply at the Clerk's office on Monday next for the perusal of the acts of the General Assembly Respecting Merchants Bringing Goods from another State into this [one], and upon Non Compliance to Risk the Same at their Peril."[31] Within a dozen years of the formation of Washington County, merchants thus made available in Jonesborough manufactured goods from the eastern seaboard and beyond.

The geographical interrelationships between Washington County customers and suppliers on the local, regional, and national levels become even more complicated when we remember that residents could shop at different places. They did not have to buy at the Cowans' or David Deaderick's stores but could go instead to Saltville in Washington County, Virginia, seventy miles away, where William King sold "dry goods, hardware, & groceries, also saddles, bridles, . . . hats, nails, bar-iron, castings, gun-powder, lead, country linen, cotton cloth, &c." Perhaps it was King's "large quantity of Good Dry Salt" and his offer to accept live pork in barter that led him to advertise in the Jonesborough *Washington Newspaper and Advertiser* and to try to attract customers from that location.[32] John Sevier, for example, sent a wagon from Knoxville back to his home on the Nolichucky River. Sevier might conceivably have moved about more than most of his neighbors because of his wealth and political position (in this instance, he had gone to Knoxville to become governor of Tennessee),[33] but as one Jonesborough store account book reveals, customers did come from a variety of places.

John and Robert Allen advertised in 1803 that their general store had received "a large and elegant assortment of merchandise which they have selected with care from among the latest arrivals in the City of Philadelphia, which they are determined to sell on lower terms than heretofore have been usual in this place."[34] An account book for the Allens' store lists 374 customers for the years 1800 and 1801. Of these, 235 (62.8 percent) can be identified from tax lists as residents of Washington County. The remaining 139 customers could not be located with certainty. Twenty-nine of these were women and blacks and would therefore not have appeared on the tax lists. Of the other 110 customers, the account book mentions the homes of three—Edmund Pendleton Gaines of Sullivan County, Robert Allen, Sr., of Greene County, and William Allen of Wythe County, Virginia—but certainly more customers in this group came to the store from beyond the boundaries of Washington County.[35]

Customers identified on the Washington County tax lists came to the Allens' store more frequently than did people whose residence is unknown. Of the 139 unlocated customers, 106 (76.3 percent) visited the store only rarely, between one and five times in 1800 and 1801. Of the 235 located (Washington County) customers, on the other hand, 138 (58.7 percent) came to the store between one and five times. The percentage that paid monthly visits to the store was 2.5 times higher for the Washington County group than for the unlocated customers. Furthermore, the only customers who came to the store more than twice a month were those found on the county tax lists.[36] While some of the unlocated customers probably lived within Washington County, many who visited the Allens' store just once probably lived outside the county.

The geographical distribution of the located customers reveals distinct residential patterns. By dividing them according to their militia company (which was the unit of tax collection in 1800), we can see that the vast majority lived among the more gently rolling hills and valleys surrounding Jonesborough. Six companies each contained over twenty customers of the Allens' store—Calvert, Henry Taylor, Aiken, Lane, Robertson, and William Taylor—and they form a circle around Aiken's company in Jonesborough. Of the thirty most frequent customers, ten came from Jonesborough itself. If one combines Glasscocke's company

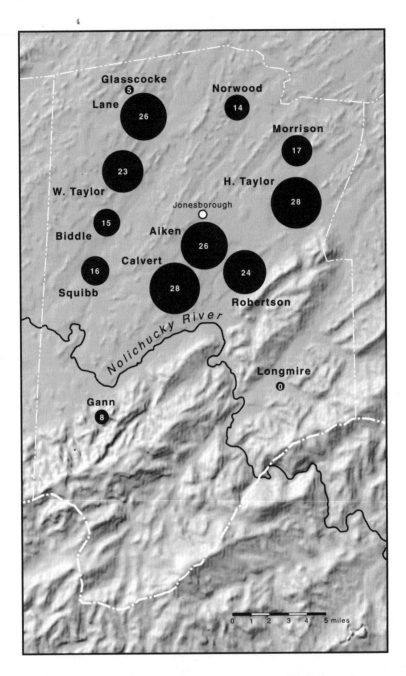

Map 4. Militia Companies and Allens' Store Customers, Washington County, 1800-1807

with Lane's (the two were formed out of a single company that existed before 1800), then the two companies with the fewest customers at the Allens' store (Longmire and Gann) were located in the mountainous regions south and southeast of Jonesborough. Perhaps these residents bought goods at stores in their own immediate communities, in Carter or Greene County, or perhaps at different stores in Jonesborough. Yet the data in the Allens' account book suggest that the environmental setting may have affected the patterns of trade. The 135 people on the Gann and Longmire tax lists, living in the most mountainous portions of Washington County, may have been more isolated economically from others in the county and in the process even further removed from regional and national markets. As we saw in Chapter 2, these inhabitants also had fewer roads at their disposal. The economic and transportation limitations combined may have fostered a more locally oriented perspective in these residents. The emergence of a more inward-looking attitude in this population at a time when residents of Jonesborough were adopting a broader viewpoint would foreshadow a crucial division within the mountain population.

Other nonagricultural enterprises joined commercial efforts to provide additional economic connections in the region. Stonemasons like Seth Smith, Jeremiah Dungan, and Josiah Allen traveled the countryside working on houses. Allen came to John Sevier's home on 23 November 1795 "to work on the kitchen chimney" and the following day "began to haul stones." Two weeks later Allen "began the kitchen Cellar" and by the middle of December had "finished walling and plastering the Cellar of the Kitchen."[37] Hatters sometimes obtained furs from local merchants; Nathaniel and Samuel Cowan, for example, gave James Gordon pelts for twelve hats at ten dollars per hat. Tanners worked not only in Washington County; by 1793, local hides were being sent to tanneries in Abingdon (on the border with Virginia) and Knoxville.[38] Blacksmiths probably lived throughout the county to serve the different settlements, but gold- and silversmiths were located in Jonesborough and other larger towns.[39]

By the second decade of the nineteenth century, Jonesborough's diverse businesses catered to a wide range of needs. William E. Derrick and Thomas Kinnard made cabinets, Flemming Evans tailored clothes, Matthew Aiken sewed hats, Barney

Mackin tanned hides, and O.B. Ross cobbled shoes. New general stores opened as well, with John G. Eason offering "a large and elegant assortment of seasonable and well-selected British, French, and American dry goods."[40] In addition to offering the usual range of merchandise, Elijah & Elihu Embree & James S. Johnson sold bar iron, castings, and nails, accepting "in payment cash, wheat (at one dollar per bushell), bar-iron, at $150 per ton," and other commonly accepted items.[41] As one of the few general stores to trade in bar iron and castings, the Embrees and Johnson combined a mercantile business with iron, a product of the region's most important industry, to make numerous economic connections both within the county and beyond it.

The Embrees operated not only the store in Jonesborough but also "a rolling and sliting mill, and nail factory on the most improved patented plan, at their Ironworks on Holston river, Sullivan County." In constructing the mill and factory, they had hired the holder of the patent and "several other experienced hands from Pennsylvania to carry it on." Such iron goods were typically imported into upper East Tennessee from outside the region, but the Embrees were "well aware of the expensive carriage of these necessary articles to this country." The public, they hoped, "will see the propriety of encouraging the establishment of this kind in our state by favoring the proprietors with their custom. They are determined that their price shall be so regulated that the articles of nails, slits, hoops, and sheet iron shall come at least as low, and on as good terms to the purchaser, at his own house, as he can procure them from any other market."[42]

The Embrees were not alone in trying to capitalize on a vital natural resource. David Ross, who had established an ironworks on the upper James River in Virginia during the Revolutionary War, moved to the south fork of the Holston River in upper East Tennessee and began producing iron in 1790.[43] John Sevier and Walter King set up their ironworks at Pactolus in Sullivan County, and Landon Carter had built the first forge in Elizabethton by the middle of the decade.[44] In 1798, James King produced iron castings at his Kingsport foundry in Sullivan County that Russell Bean shipped (with his own gunsmithing products) down the Tennessee and Mississippi Rivers to Natchez for distribution.[45] Washington County's iron deposits were mined early in the nineteenth century. Nathaniel Taylor and Landon Carter made bar iron at a furnace, or bloomery, on North Indian Creek, carried it overland to the Nolichucky River, and then floated it during high waters to Knoxville and beyond. William P. Chester built a forge in Bumpass Cove on the south side of the Nolichucky by 1812. The Embrees, acquiring it several years later, expanded the works and earned sizable profits.[46] Elijah and Elihu Embree undoubtedly spoke for all of these iron producers when they declared: "As the establishment [of a mill and factory] is an expensive one, and has already involved a considerable capital; and as it will be acknowledged to be of great importance to this country, the proprietors will look for an early patronage from merchants in particular, to enable them to prosecute the business to advantage; and would suggest the propriety of laying in but small supplies of these articles this spring, in foreign markets; and in return they promise they will feel emulous to realize every reasonable expectation."[47] Even as upper East Tennessee imported iron goods from other regions, it also distributed its own products both locally and regionally to markets farther south and west.

Such iron production eventually spurred the development of other local industries. In 1825, David A. Deaderick (the early merchant's son), Henry Marsh, Samuel Crawford, and Thomas Emmerson formed a manufacturing company in Jonesborough. As Deaderick recalled in his diary, they "engaged Ezra Pierce to go to Georgetown, District of Columbia, to procure the patterns [and] learn to make Gideon Davis's patent plough." Construction took place in locations scattered throughout Washington County. "The castings were made at Embree's Furnace in Bumpass Cove . . . and were the first mould boards cast in East Tennessee. Ezra Pierce put the plows together at his own residence, some eight miles northwest of Jonesborough. He and I were much interested about the plow, and were frequently together both at the furnace at Jonesborough and at his house." Distribution, however, was not limited to the county. "I was the agent to sell the plow," Deaderick wrote, "and [was] sent to different places in East Tennessee. I recollect sending some to Knoxville consigned to Robert King, a commission merchant there. They sold slowly at first, but finally were very much used, especially in upper East Tennessee. The plow was a most excellent one."[48]

Fig. 7. David A. Deaderick. Artist unknown, supposedly painted during the winter of 1819-1820. Courtesy of the McClung Historical Collection, Knox County Public Library, Knoxville.

In short, the plow company linked local resources with ideas and customers in different regions. The raw materials and factories available in Washington County produced plows from a pattern found in Georgetown for distribution throughout East Tennessee. The company's success may be due in part to the interplay between economic and physiographic conditions. Ezra Pierce could travel to Georgetown easily enough, just as Deaderick could readily move about the region selling the plow. But the transportation of goods by land was still sufficiently difficult and expensive to discourage people from importing such plows from outside upper East Tennessee. As a result, the mountains actually gave the plow company a regional niche; implements made from local resources cost less. An environment that discouraged one type of economic connection between regions (the importation of finished products) paradoxically also encouraged the development of the same ties at a different level (obtaining the patterns and selling the plows).

Deaderick ardently believed that such local natural resources would bring prosperity to upper East Tennessee. "Our country, however, will never so much flourish as when we become a manufacturing people," he wrote in 1828. "We have water power without end to propel machinery, and in iron manufactures especially, this county and the adjoining one of Carter, will in time become celebrated." Development had already eased the region's dependence on imported iron goods. The nail factory in Sullivan had had "a salutary effect on the counties near it, in creating a market for many of the products of the country and in supplying an article of first necessity, which until the erection of the factory was obtained by land conveyance from Baltimore and Richmond. . . . All heavy articles or iron manufacture will be made in this country, I should think, before many years." Similarly, Deaderick noted that "a cotton spinning factory, on a small scale (84 spindles), was put into operation in Washington county by Charles Cox on the waters of Boone Creek, . . . being the first factory of the kind erected in this part of East Tennessee. Similar factories had been in operation previously in Knoxville, but none before east of that place."[49] By 1830, then, upper East Tennessee had what seemed to be a thriving economy firmly anchored within a broad geographical and commercial context. This economy fostered a general sense of connectedness and an attachment to the world beyond the mountains for most of the inhabitants.

## Middle Tennessee

Despite upper East Tennessee's economic connectedness, by comparison with Middle Tennessee the mountain region was clearly less accessible economically (and for a longer period of time). Nashville, which was founded on the banks of the Cumberland River in 1780, in 1785 had but "two houses, which, in true, merit the name." A dozen years later, the town housed "about sixty or eighty families," whose log and frame houses were scattered over the town's entire site.[50] Yet during the first decades of the nineteenth century, Nashville's population grew far faster than any place in East Tennessee; the residents numbered 3,463 in 1823, increasing to 5,566 in 1830 and to about 7,000 in 1834. Three hundred brick homes joined 80 brick stores and 15 with wood frames, 20 brick warehouses, 50 offices of brick and 25 with wood frames, and 100 workshops.[51]

The region's powerful agricultural economy spurred this remarkable growth.[52] The development of the plantation system and the introduction of the cotton gin in 1799 helped cotton to replace corn as the principal cash crop and to become, very quickly, big business. Lewis Cecil Gray estimates that Middle Tennessee farmers produced 1 million pounds of cotton in 1801. Production jumped to 3 million pounds in 1811, to 20 million in 1821, and finally to 50 million pounds in 1833.[53] Middle Tennessee farmers also continued to diversify their crops, raising flax, hemp, tobacco, oats, wheat, and a variety of fruit trees.[54] These Cumberland farms were also dotted with animals. Small herds of 50 to 100 cattle were common, while increased corn cultivation allowed numbers of hogs to rise quickly. The pages of stock mark registrations in the county court records attest to the widespread ownership of both types of animals. Anne Newport Royall, passing through the Nashville region in 1817, commented that the region was "an open plain of uninterrupted good land; and the farmers raise corn, tobacco, and pumpkins in great abundance. They rear great numbers of hogs and horses, and have a great many distilleries in operation. In this way they convert their surplus produce into cash."[55]

The rapid growth of the Cumberland occurred in part because of the quick prosperity available to individual farmers. François André Michaux, who traveled in both Middle and upper East Tennessee, found much of the land in the latter region "of a middling quality," and he concluded that land there "is in every point inferior in fertility to Cumberland and Kentucky."[56] Fertile land in Middle Tennessee, however, provided the settler with the key to success. Michaux described the process: "There is scarcely a single emigrant but what begins to plant his estate with [cotton] the third year after his settling in the country." He calculated that a family of four or five may "cultivate four acres with the greatest of ease, independent of the Indian wheat necessary for their subsistence." If 350 pounds of cotton were grown per acre, "which is very moderate according to the extreme fertility of the soil," the family would have 1,400 pounds of cotton at season's end. At $18 per hundredweight, "the lowest price to which it had fallen . . . when I was in the country [1802]," the family would gross $252 and net $212 after deducting $40 for expenses. "This light sketch demonstrates with what facility a poor family may acquire speedily, in West Tennessea, a certain degree of independence, particularly after having been settled five or six years, as they procure the means of purchasing one or two negroes, and of annually increasing their number."[57] Such fertility, when combined with easier access to navigable rivers and markets, helped Middle Tennessee prosper.

Despite the agricultural abundance, the settlers had not become self-sufficient. Lead and salt had to be imported, perhaps from upper East Tennessee and southwestern Virginia. Abraham Steiner and Frederick de Schweinitz once lodged with the blacksmith Michael Schneider, who "has a good business, but he is obliged to pay 1 shilling the pound for iron which is brought in from Kentucky on the river."[58] The wheat crop also failed to meet local demand; Daniel and William Constable noted in 1807 that "considerable quantities of flour are brought here [Nashville] from the countries on the Ohio and sells here now for ten dollars the barrel, being three dollars more than the price at New Orleans when we were there."[59] Even mills could be hard to find. "There are but few springs that flow the year round," report Steiner and Schweinitz, "and still fewer water-mills that can grind throughout

the year. Nearly everywhere they are idle half the year; consequently, the people use horse-mills that are to be found everywhere in the country."[60]

Given its lack of self-sufficiency, Middle Tennessee depended
on trade with other regions. From the earliest years of settlement,
trade drawn from an immense area played an important role in the
local economy. "Furs are the sole production of this region, with
which the people supply their wants," noted Lewis Brantz. "The
traders who supply them with merchandise are mostly Frenchmen,
either from Illinois, or the Post Vincennes." Those from Illinois
obtained their goods from Michilimackinac and liquor from New
Orleans, while "the St. Vincennes people purchase their articles of
traffic (which are generally of a substantial character) from Detroit."[61] By the end of the 1780s, farmers in Middle Tennessee had
finally generated sufficient agricultural surplus to ship goods by
flatboat down the Mississippi to New Orleans.[62]

During the early decades of the nineteenth century, Nashville
had connected itself with Pittsburgh, Philadelphia, Baltimore, and
other cities to the northeast. As in Jonesborough, Michaux found
in Nashville shops "which are supplied from Philadelphia and Baltimore, but they did not seem so well stocked as those at Lexington and the articles, though dearer, are of an inferior quality. The
cause of their being so dear may be in some measure attributed to
the expense of carriage, which is much greater on account of the
amazing distance the boats destined for Tennessea have to go up
the Ohio." Philadelphia lay more than 1,500 miles away, of which
about 80 percent could be traveled by water.[63] Nashville also sent
products to the east along this route. During his visit in 1802,
Michaux heard of Nashville residents who had made "the first attempt to send cottons by the Ohio to Pittsburgh, in order to be
thence conveyed to the remote parts of Pennsylvania." As a result,
he proclaimed, "the remotest parts of the western states [are]
united by commercial interests of which cotton is the basis, and
the Ohio the tie of communication, the results of which must give
a high degree of prosperity to this part of Tennessea."[64]

Nashville also traded heavily over a second major route, with
New Orleans to the south. Farms in surrounding counties sent
their products to Nashville, where they were loaded onto flat-
boats. Cotton quickly superseded corn as the principal export

crop, aided by its ability to be stored in bales and shipped the 1,200 miles to New Orleans without damage. At that port, the cotton was then placed aboard ships bound for New York, Philadelphia, and Europe. When the Louisiana Purchase ensured that New Orleans would remain an open port, Middle Tennessee sent even larger amounts of material downriver. At the same time, merchants from New Orleans began to arrive in Nashville with increasing frequency. Although many returned to Nashville on foot via the Natchez Trace, those bringing home goods used keel boats. In the first decade of the nineteenth century, a round-trip journey lasted six months, although the fastest keel boats could cut that time in half.[65] Even with faster boats, however, the distance between Nashville and New Orleans caused difficulties for the farmers.

Some Middle Tennessee cotton planters migrated to the Natchez region in Mississippi because it lay 500 miles closer to New Orleans. Nashville boosters, trying to keep these farmers in Middle Tennessee, vigorously countered by pointing out that "Capt. Caffery, with a public spirit peculiar to himself, proposes carrying any species of produce to New Orleans for the moderate price of one dollar per hundred[weight] which is the price (I understand) from the Natchez."[66] But such offers did not solve every problem caused by distance. Since none but the richest planters could ship their own products downriver, farmers who hired the likes of a Captain Caffery ran the risk that boats would prove unreliable and would sink, that shippers would swindle them, or that commission merchants in New Orleans would cheat them. William Faux saw conditions in 1819 where "produce is surrendered to enterprizing men, as they are called, on the rivers, but who frequently prove to be thieves; for if the boat is stove in, or markets are bad or dull, there are no returns, you hear no more of either produce or the boatmen. . . . To go yourself to market is impossible, for while selling one crop, you would lose the time for raising another."[67] As a result, farmers had to sell their crops to middlemen in Nashville at a heavy discount; cotton that brought fourteen or fifteen cents per pound in New Orleans in 1810 garnered only eight cents in Nashville.[68]

But technological advances during the 1820s helped Middle Tennessee farmers overcome the problem of distance. The first steamboat in Nashville, the *General Jackson*, arrived on 8 March 1818 and inaugurated regular trade between Nashville and New Orleans. Soon, round-trip excursions that had taken the biggest barges five months in 1815 were shortened to thirty days. Steamship traffic became so regular that schedules of arrivals and departures regularly appeared in Nashville newspapers. By the 1830s, steamboat technology had advanced to the point where the fastest boats could finish the trip between New Orleans and Nashville in only five days and eighteen hours.[69] Such shipping was unavailable to most of East Tennessee, and especially upper East Tennessee, because steamboats could not navigate Muscle Shoals on the Tennessee River to reach Knoxville during this period. Such technology, however, plays a minor role in creating this fairly common economic distinction between mountainous and flat regions.[70] In Middle Tennessee, the climate, soil, topography, transportation links, and commercial outlook fueled an economy that dwarfed East Tennessee in both geographical scope and agricultural output.

## The Struggle to Improve Economic Connections

By comparing the eastern tip of Tennessee with the Nashville basin, we see the ways in which the agricultural and commercial trade available in Jonesborough was relatively limited by its topography and location. Despite the advantages of its iron ore, upper East Tennessee was, according to Michaux, "of all parts in the United States that are now inhabited, the most unfavourably situated, being on every side circumscribed by considerable tracts of country that produce the same provisions, and which are either more fertile or nearer to the borders of the sea."[71] To overcome the problem of fertility, some of the area's residents called for improved agricultural practices. Although David Deaderick acknowledged that his family farm just east of Jonesborough was "much worn, as is almost universal with farms which have been long cultivated in this country," he believed "the day not far distant when this part of Tennessee, now considered poor and undesirable, will be the most desirable part of the state." Improvement in the soil could be achieved only by rotating crops, applying manure, and plowing more efficiently.[72] To overcome problems of market accessibility,

other residents called for better transportation and internal improvements throughout the region. While the extent of such support for improvements remains uncertain, many prominent
citizens worked toward this end.[73] Thomas Emmerson and his
monthly newspaper, the *Tennessee Farmer*, advocated both modern agricultural practices and internal improvements. The advice
his readers in Washington County (and throughout the state) received reflects one view during the 1830s of how East Tennessee
could surpass other lands that Michaux described as "more fertile
or nearer to the borders of the sea."

Thomas Emmerson moved from Virginia to Knoxville in 1800
and began to practice law at the age of twenty-seven. He rose
quickly in local circles, became a trustee of local colleges, and
served as a judge for the superior court in 1807. The residents of
Knoxville elected him their first mayor in 1816, and two years
later, the people of Tennessee elected him a justice of the state supreme court. Emmerson resigned in 1821, however, and moved to
Washington County. He practiced law at an office in Jonesborough and conducted different agricultural experiments at his
farm on Cherokee Creek. He began publishing the *Washington
Republican and Farmers Journal* out of Jonesborough in 1832; after
his partners withdrew in 1834, Emmerson continued to pass along
advice and opinions on improving local agriculture in the paper
(now called the *Tennessee Farmer*) until he died in 1837.[74] As
president of the Washington County Agricultural Society and as
newspaper editor, Thomas Emmerson sought "to promote the interests of Agriculture in all its branches, by conveying . . . such information as will enable [the people] to derive the greatest
permanent profit from their labor and capital."[75] In its content and
editorial direction, the *Tennessee Farmer* helped integrate upper
East Tennessee with areas throughout the country. It shows that
these farmers, like their counterparts whom Richard D. Brown describes in New England, were "not in truth insulated from external
affairs either in their consciousness or as a matter of practical fact,
nor were they content to dwell wholly within a local sphere."[76]

"The great and primary object of this paper," wrote Emmerson
in 1836, "is the improvement of Agriculture, by the wide and general diffusion of Agricultural Knowledge."[77] Inasmuch as he received newspaper articles from around the country and letters and

Fig. 8. Thomas Emmerson. Courtesy of the McClung Historical Collection, Knox
County Public Library, Knoxville.

other contributions from areas throughout Tennessee, Emmerson
had many resources on which he could draw to disseminate "Agricultural Knowledge."[78] These far-flung sources of information fostered a broad, outward-looking perspective in readers who already
tended to see their interests as extending beyond the region.
Emmerson supplied information on topics ranging from producing
silk to rotating crops, from raising poultry to harvesting fruit.

Many local farmers needed such information because, as Emmerson declared in 1835, "too many are still to be found, blindly and heedlessly pursuing the same wretched, murderous, land-killing practices to which we are indebted for the great injury, which the country has already sustained in the impoverishment and total exhaustion of so many fields, once fertile."[79]

Emmerson believed that better farming practices would lead to increased production, which in turn would require an improved transportation system that would play an absolutely vital role for the mountain regions of North Carolina, Virginia, and Tennessee. "Internal improvements and the improvement of agriculture are inseparably connected," Emmerson claimed. "The success of either will promote the success of the other. Let internal improvements open a market for agricultural products, and offer to the Farmer a reasonable remuneration of his labor, and agricultural improvement will speedily follow." Conversely, if farmers develop large surpluses by using new techniques, they will demand "that the best and cheapest means of conveying it to market be afforded to them."[80] Emmerson stressed not the market and economic benefits of internal improvements, but instead the ways improvements would fund universal education and lead to "the elevation of the moral and intellectual character of the people . . . and the perpetuation of Free Government."[81] But no matter what one saw as the true worth of such projects, citizens like Emmerson called for internal improvements to connect upper East Tennessee with other regions.

During the 1790s and early 1800s, the Tennessee government had little money with which to fund internal improvements. It relied on private navigation companies to raise money by subscription, lottery, or tolls for river improvements. The state legislature chartered the Nolichucky River Company in 1801 for clearing the river and maintaining a minimum depth of eighteen inches. The company was authorized to establish three tollhouses and to charge one dollar per ton for all boats and rafts, yet little resulted from this charter. Similarly, as a long-term resident recalled a subsequent operation, "the Nolichucky Navigation Company chartered by the Legislature in 1813 caused a great deal of work to be done in removing obstructions from the river from its mouth up to the Sluice hill, but . . . the first works erected were generally washed away and done the navigation more harm than good."[82] Once the state's hopes for federal aid had been dashed by Andrew Jackson's veto of the Maysville Road bill in 1830, the legislators finally appropriated more state funds.[83] They allotted $60,000 to a "Board of Internal Improvements for East Tennessee" (formed in 1831 with David A. Deaderick as one of the three commissioners), and by 1834 workers had removed many obstructions to steam travel around Knoxville. In 1837, the state legislature heeded calls for more improvements. It subsidized a great number of projects throughout the state. East, Middle, and West Tennessee all competed for the same limited funds, and "the adoption and consummation of any logical state system of internal improvements [was] rendered difficult by the differences in sectional interests [and] the jealousies and antagonisms which resulted from the unequal distribution of the benefits."[84] Nashville, designated a port of entry, received $135,000 to improve the Cumberland River. West Tennesee received funding for a road between Memphis and Little Rock, Arkansas. But East Tennessee got very little for any of its river or road projects. In this respect, the mountain residents were frustrated in their attempts to catch up with their rivals to the west.

Low prices brought on by the panic of 1837 and the ensuing depression certainly affected upper East Tennessee. Even with a plentiful harvest on their Greene County farm, Solomon and Catharine Beals told relatives that prices were falling in Indiana. "I have seen some [corn] sold at 62 and a half cents per bushell 9 months credit but corn has fell to forty cents. pork has been a 6 dollars per hundred but now is down at 5 dollars." Hannah Beals wrote to the same relatives in 1840 that "we all have something to weare & something to eat so far. . . . pork last fall five Dollars, wheat 50 cents, corn 25 cents, Money very scarce."[85] George Moore told his sons about "one bay mare that I give fifteen dollars for a few days ago for times is hard, to be sure and money is not to be had and I have seven head of cattle and fourteen head of sheep and nineteen head hogs and I killed seventeen hogs this year for bacon, but times is so hard that bacon is worth only four cents per pound. There is the hardest times ever was in this Country for to git money," he concluded, "but there is other articles a plenty."[86]

Improved transportation would provide the best way to sell

that plentiful grain at higher prices (and thereby get money). William G. Brownlow, editor of the *Tennessee Whig* in Elizabethton, described the situation succinctly:

> For the want of some slight improvements, say in Holston, Watauga, and [Noli]Chucky, we are prevented through the course of the fall and winter from getting off with our produce . . . upon moderate tides which, were those improvements made, would carry us off triumphantly. By failing to get off in due time, the demand for our produce in the lower country ceases, to at least a considerable extent, and the sales made thereafter are limited and dull. Finding no market here at home, we are compelled, on a late spring tide . . . to rush into market all at the same time. The consequence is, as our Boatmen know to their sorrow, that the market is glutted—prices are low—. . . and what little money is obtained in payment, we are kept out of its use, to our great injury.[87]

Manufacturers along the Nolichucky were left with $15,000 to $20,000 worth of nails and iron, "cash articles to all intents and purposes, and articles which are in great demand in the lower country, if the owners could get off with them." If the legislature would appropriate just "a few thousand dollars," Brownlow believed, "those improvements [would] give animation to our whole country. Then would every class of our citizens bear marks of prosperity, and their countenance show forth the smile of contentment."[88]

Yet before the coming of the railroad, upper East Tennessee's economy could not overcome the problems brought on by its location within the Appalachian Mountains. Despite the growth of internal ties and external connections to the eastern seaboard and other parts of the South, the region lagged behind Middle Tennessee decades earlier. Cotton grown in lower East Tennessee had much higher transportation costs when compared with that grown in the rest of the state or in northern Alabama. From corn and other grains farmers in East Tennessee distilled alcohol, which was easier to ship and brought higher prices, but production in East Tennessee dropped between 1820 and 1840 while it rose in the rest of the

state. From 1840 to 1860, East Tennessee's national share of production in corn, hogs, wheat, horses, and mules declined. For this
reason and because of an absolute decline in the numbers of swine,
the region fell behind economically.[89] Calls for internal improvements and the slow development of trade and industry compared
with that in Middle Tennessee signaled this decline. The economic situation in upper East Tennessee, therefore, constantly reminded readers of the *Tennessee Farmer* that although they had
established connections to places throughout the United States,
nothing shaped their fortunes more than the forces that limited
those connections.

## The Economy and Perceptions of the Mountaineers

Upper East Tennessee's economic situation and connectedness
helped shape the images some individuals held of the mountaineers. One observer attributed the region's slower economic development to the characteristics of the residents. "H," writing to the
*Tennessee Farmer,* claimed that "the habits of our laborers present
almost insuperable obstacles to the introduction of any improvement whatever—this argument, however will apply with equal
force to any other department of society, as to the agricultural."
The typical farmer raises a poor and meager unfertilized crop that
exhausts the soil and then,

> while the industrious owner having his crop laid by and
> nothing to do at home, is perhaps a third part of a year, per-
> forming or seeking day labor, at the neighboring villages and
> farms, or failing to procure employment at high wages, he
> may be amusing himself with his gun and dog, in quest of
> game, now become too scarce to afford a successful hunter
> the wages of a day for a week's eager pursuit, or he may be
> found perhaps at the shooting match, or other gatherings for
> *innocent* sport, to pass off agreeably a tedious day, where he
> may have opportunity of wasting pleasantly, in an hour or
> two, the wages of half a month, or of brutalizing himself, by
> an intoxicating draft—to lull to sleep, for a time, a con-
> science grown troublesome by its frequent upbraidings of
> wasted time and improvident contracts.[90]

Similarly but perhaps more charitably, a Knoxville resident believed that the citizens were hampered by ignorance, "yea thick darkness, as to the means of improvement common and familiar in many other parts of our union." He praised Emmerson for his work and added, "if you can but convince our farmers of their ignorance of their own profession, and how far they are behind others not far distant from them, you will do more for them and their posterity, than all the demagogues who have been teaching them to depend on making laws for their relief and prosperity."[91] Images of idleness and drunkenness were attached to poor white farmers throughout the South,[92] but ignorance with its resulting backwardness becomes a peculiarly mountain trait when such a condition is compared with that of "others not far distant from them."

Alongside these statements, however, do appear predictions of a bright future. "H" combined the scathing remarks quoted above with a belief that "East Tennessee is probably destined to be a great manufacturing country. Of course, the home demand for provisions must increase in proportion to the abstraction of labor from agricultural pursuits." And the Knoxville writer had no doubt that "East Tennessee, some day, will be one of the choicest parts of the world. Clover! Clover! Clover! judiciously employed would continue to improve it to an extent, far, very far, beyond the most sanguine tho'ts, perhaps of any of us."[93] If the farmers of Washington County would learn the improved methods, "A Friend of Agriculture" wrote, "I will venture to predict that the mania for emigrating to the 'far west' will at least measurably subside and each one will be satisfied with his old home."[94] In 1826 David Deaderick had considered moving to Fayette County in West Tennessee because "the appearance and prospects of that country, indeed of all West Tennessee, compared with ours seems vastly more flattering to those disposed to accumulate the *good things* of this world." He stayed in Washington County, however, because "the more of moral feeling, less devotion to money making, and less absorption in the business of the world, are, I think, discernible more in East than in West Tennessee."[95]

Upper East Tennessee did have its drawbacks. "Our soil is poor in comparison with the Western District [of Tennessee]," he wrote in 1826, "and we have it not within our reach, as a people, to become rich as they can in the west." Three years later, he noted that "the enterprise, prospect of wealth, and comparative ease of living in those countries [Illinois, Indiana, and Missouri] seem inviting to us of poor East Tennessee, where we are barely living, without a prospect speedily of growing rich."[96] Deaderick nevertheless emphasized the noneconomic benefits of living in the mountains. Even though his region could not grow cotton, "East Tennessee, particularly this part of it, will be in twenty years a much more desirable part of the state, for we cultivate the grain and grass crops which always contribute greatly to the comfort and plenty of a country." Notwithstanding the profit available in the cotton regions, Deaderick believed that for "one who can content himself with a little, and *depend on prosperity far ahead*, East Tennessee is a pleasant country. I doubt whether any one comfortably situated is justifiable in removing to any other country, if contentment be their wish. But if to get wealthy, which is by no means synonymous with happiness, be the sole object, a removal might be advisable."[97] Perhaps those without material riches took solace in virtue:

> Our country will be more desirable as a place of residence than any part of the west, for where there are temptations and opportunity to get wealth men are less apt to be virtuous and happy; and where property is most equally distributed, there is most contentment and peace of mind. . . . Most impartial persons will observe that we are more moral and religious and less absorbed in the business and cares of the world than the people of West Tennessee, or of any cotton country. It is not the ability to get rich alone that makes the difference I believe to exist, but where . . . slaves are found in great numbers and where all the work, or nearly all, is performed by slaves, a consequent inaction and idleness are characteristics of the whites, and any one knows that there is no surer way of vitiating a man, than to leave him with nothing to do.[98]

Deaderick, who owned no slaves and was far from being idle, probably found contentment in his life.

In his description of upper East Tennessee as "a pleasant country" and not an economically and intellectually inferior region,

David A. Deaderick illustrates the delicate and shifting balance of connectedness that existed within each inhabitant. His father's mercantile business brought in goods from outside the region, his own plow manufacturing company exported products and improved the local agriculture, and his service as a commissioner to develop internal improvements helped make these activities possible. Deaderick's pursuits demonstrate that he had forged extensive external connections and had developed a concern for the larger world. Upper East Tennessee, however, could not match the booming growth of Middle and West Tennessee; Deaderick realized that his own region failed to keep pace. All his life Deaderick tried to make money, but if more could be made in the west, then why did he still live in the mountains? Only a person with a strong local sensibility could become attached to upper East Tennessee; the trick was to be, as he writes, "one who can content himself with little" and be "less absorbed in the business and cares of the world." Deaderick turned his back on the planter's lifestyle and took comfort in what he considered moral and social virtue. This particular mountain resident saw that his society had developed differently from that elsewhere. In its development some observers read decline, others progress. How one judged the region depended in part on how one valued the different dimensions of connectedness. Individuals with a broader outlook, like the writer "H," described the inhabitants as lazy and ignorant, while people with a more local orientation saw residents content and assured of their social and moral superiority.

No matter what positive or negative terms came to describe upper East Tennessee, individuals saw the region and its inhabitants as ever more distinctive. Outsiders have viewed the inhabitants as being different ever since the victory at King's Mountain; a half century later, the same perspective began to develop among some of the inhabitants *within* the region as well. The awareness of difference grew with the increasing connections between upper East Tennessee's economy and the world beyond the mountains. Most of the residents sought continuously to increase the connections, especially through internal improvements such as railroads, in an effort to improve their lives and to refute charges that they were inferior. Others, however, made their peace with the situation and focused their efforts more locally, in part by separating

themselves from their neighbors. These broad and local perspectives eventually came into conflict within the community of upper
East Tennessee and created the situation that would give rise to
images of Appalachia.

# CHAPTER FOUR

# Population Persistence in Washington County

BY THE 1830s, RESIDENTS in upper East Tennessee had developed geographic and economic ties both within the South and to other sections of the United States. These connections, however, did not necessarily mean that the population was mobile. Some of the most powerful portraits of the mountaineers emphasize that they stayed in one place. Recalling the metaphor of running water, John Fox, Jr., wrote that "streams of humanity" had penetrated Appalachia, but "the hills have cut it off from the main stream and have held it so stagnant, that, to change the figure, mountains may be said to have kept the records of human history somewhat as fossils held the history of the earth."[1] Modern images of Appalachia depict a static (and hence stagnant) population, the result primarily of geographical isolation, throughout the mountain region. According to William Goodell Frost, the mountaineers were "not only isolated from the great centres and thoroughfares of the world, but also isolated from one another. The families who live along one valley form a community by themselves, and the children grow up with almost no examples or analogies of life outside these petty bounds."[2] John C. Campbell's *The Southern Highlander and His Homeland* contains a letter from a friend who was struck by "the isolation nature has imposed upon those people. You probably know how steep and high as well as how intricately winding the ridges are, and how cabins perched far up in the heads of coves have an isolation that is painful. This tells on the people, and especially on the women who stay at home."[3]

Yet François André Michaux, the intrepid French traveler,

noticed a pattern of population movement in Kentucky and Tennessee at the turn of the nineteenth century that belies the entrenched notions of insularity. "[The first settlers] began to clear those fertile countries, and wrested them from the savages . . . but the long habit of a wandering and idle life has prevented their enjoying the fruit of their labours, and profiting by the very price to which these lands have risen in so short a time. They have emigrated to more remote parts of the country, and formed new settlements." In their place "will succeed fresh emigrants, coming also from the Atlantic states, who will desert their possessions to go in quest of a milder climate and a more fertile soil." Finally, he predicted the arrival of more permanent settlers, who, "instead of log-houses, with which the present inhabitants are contented, will build wooden ones, clear a greater quantity of land, and be as industrious and persevering in the melioration of their new possessions as the former were indolent in every thing, being so fond of hunting."[4] Michaux's description of a steady procession of peoples into and out of regions like upper East Tennessee provides a first-hand account of the larger population movement within and through the mountains.

Such movement traced on a more local geographic level brings an analytical perspective to the popular images of a static population "imprisoned in their mountain fastness," separated "from the main stream," and held "stagnant." The static image implies a particular timing of events: separation must have occurred shortly after the region was first settled and must then have been maintained until the twentieth century, or modern characterizations would not be at all plausible. To determine whether initial high levels of population persistence existed, as indicated by popular images of the Appalachian region, we may begin by examining the evidence for Washington County during the first several decades of settlement. The residents of Washington County were scarcely trapped in a stagnant pool, for they moved into and out of the region with roughly the same frequency as other citizens in the United States. Within this larger phenomenon of population turnover, we can also see that some residents moved into the most remote portions of the county. People who left the region may have sought broader connections with the larger world, while people who stayed in the region's steepest mountains may have sought closer connections to their immediate community. This latter group, rather than the mountain population in general, gave rise to modern Appalachian images.

## MEASURING POPULATION PERSISTENCE

Historians have studied early American persistence and internal migration patterns in great detail, tracking the residents of small towns, cities, counties, and entire states over the decades. Although these studies differ in sample population and methodology, they agree on the general transience of most Americans during the first half of the nineteenth century. Such low persistence rates can suggest "a retardation of class consciousness among workers, an acceleration in the economic and political stratification of society, and/or the creation of a bifurcated society inhabited by movers (failures) and stayers (successes)."[5] Douglas Lamar Jones, summarizing the results of many population studies, finds relatively high persistence rates in seventeenth-century America, rates that dropped steadily through the centuries. He calculates from the secondary literature a mean persistence rate of 67 percent for ten years in the seventeenth century, 60 percent in the eighteenth century, and 41 percent (for rural communities) in the nineteenth century. Jones's own work on the Massachusetts towns of Beverly and Wenham, with 1761-1771 persistence rates of 64 percent and 59 percent, respectively, follows this pattern.[6]

Subsequent work by other historians has generally supported this trend of declining persistence. For 1780, Daniel Scott Smith finds that 75.1 percent of all militiamen "still resided in their state of birth at the time of enlistment into service"; of this group in Massachusetts and Virginia, 73.5 percent also lived in their county of birth.[7] John Shy examines three communities from the 1770s to 1790. The decennial persistence for Lynn, Massachusetts, was 72 percent for individuals and 84 percent for families (surnames); in Pawling, New York, 64 percent for individuals and 88 percent for families; and in Orangeburg, South Carolina, 47 percent for individuals and 68 percent for families.[8] Richard Beeman sees heads of households in Lunenburg County, Virginia, staying at a rate of about 40 percent from 1764 to 1769 and at 48 percent from 1769 to 1782.[9] Similarly, Robert C. Kenzer notes that 52.2 percent of

white men aged twenty and above living in Orange County,
North Carolina, in 1850 could still be found in the county a decade later.[10] Lee Soltow discovers that 47.7 percent of Ohio property holders in 1810 still lived in the state in 1825.[11] Finally, Hal S.
Barron states that 32.1 percent of male heads of household remained in the township of Chelsea, Vermont, from 1840 to
1860.[12] Comparisons and conclusions may be difficult to draw because of differences in methodology (some writers fail to take mortality into account), in populations sampled (whether individuals,
heads of households, or property holders), and in evaluation crite-
ria (the particular level of persistence that should be judged transient). Nevertheless, these studies join a host of earlier works to
provide ample evidence upon which to base an opinion.

   No such detailed literature exists for the Appalachian region.
Few works address the revolutionary and antebellum periods and
examine persistence as thoroughly as do the studies cited above.
For Cades Cove in southeastern Tennessee, Durwood Dunn uses
qualitative evidence to show that "the Cherokee lands in Georgia
during the 1830s, and later, the opening up of new territories in
the West caused periodic fluctuations as older settlers left and new
immigrants entered the cove." Cades Cove was depleted by "mass
migration in the 1850s to the West" and was then stabilized by
"minimal migration into or out of the cove since the Civil War,"
but Dunn does not go into further detail.[13] Phillip Shaw Paludan
describes the inhabitants of Shelton Laurel, in northwestern
North Carolina, in terms that imply population persistence.
"People did not just reside in Shelton Laurel; they were a part of it.
They did not sell the land to strangers. They did not speculate on
it. They kept the land and passed it on to their descendants, who
raised their children on it and gave the land to the children who
had grown up on it. And the children stayed and raised their children within Shelton Laurel, until the place and the people were
almost one." Paludan, however, provides no specific evidence to
support his statements. Instead, he cites the interviews that Robert Coles conducted during the 1960s and applies the results to the
1850s, arguing that "the ideas and culture of past generations still
hold sway in modern times, that the insights of twentieth-century
observers can illuminate the world of a century ago."[14] This argument presumes that mountain society is static in a way that nearby

upper East Tennessee clearly is not. Most recently, Robert Tracy McKenzie has examined geographic persistence as part of a much larger study of the agricultural population in Tennessee from 1850 to 1880. Sampling the population of heads of free farm households in Grainger, Greene, and Johnson Counties (all in upper East Tennessee), he finds that 55.8 percent of the individuals persisted from 1850 to 1860. McKenzie concludes, "It is worth noting that, in the larger American context, it is the extremely high persistence of farmers in eastern Tennessee rather than the extremely low persistence of western farmers that is anomalous."[15]

A lower level of population persistence emerges when we examine Washington County from 1790 to 1845. When created in 1778, Washington County contained about 2,500 persons. In 1800, after the county's boundaries had stabilized, there were 6,379; by 1840, the number had grown to 11,751.[16] One way to measure the persistence or movement of these Washington County residents involves following specific individuals through the tax lists. Three civil districts (Districts 1, 7, and 18 in 1845) lay in the southeastern portion of the county, its most mountainous section; if any people were cut off and trapped by the environment, it would have been these residents. District 1 was bounded by the Nolichucky River to the north and by Greene County to the west. Districts 7 and 18, separated by the Nolichucky River in 1845, were combined as a single district in 1836. For the sake of clarity, I will call the entire area "District 7/18." District 13, located in the northwestern part of Washington County's more open and rolling valleys, serves as a control area. Tax lists for these areas provide lists of names for specific years: 1790 or 1792, 1797, 1805 or 1806, 1814, 1824, 1836, and 1845. By tracking the people on these lists (white males, with an occasional female, who pay a property tax, a poll tax if they are between the ages of twenty-one and fifty, or both), we can determine how many remained in a particular region or left it.[17]

The tax lists by their nature prompt several methodological questions. Taxes were collected according to militia company until 1836, at which point the civil districts came into being. Since no militia company boundaries can be found, we must begin with the civil districts in 1845 (for which maps do exist) and work back to the eighteenth century. By comparing names on each list, we can

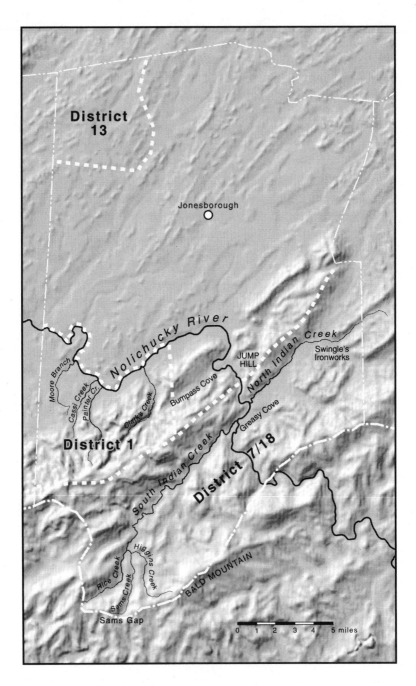

Map 5. Selected Washington County Civil Districts

determine which captain's company corresponded to each civil district.[18] Since the militia company boundaries are unknown, we may be comparing areas of different size. For example, the area covered by Captain Greer in 1806 (and hence the number of individuals included on the tax list) may not be the area that was covered by District 1 in 1836. By matching names between lists we can identify areas that are roughly comparable, however, and inasmuch as the total number of militia companies and civil districts remains fairly consistent over the decades, we may still draw preliminary conclusions about persistence. We may also compare the mountainous areas and the rolling valleys, because both regions are affected in similar ways by the uncertain boundaries.

A second problem concerns the types of taxpayers included on the lists. Those paying a poll tax who fall between the ages of twenty-one and fifty are listed with those paying a property tax; those who are older than fifty or who lose their property necessarily vanish from the list even if they stayed in their district. Therefore, individuals are tracked for a period of thirty years (the span between the ages of twenty-one and fifty) even though some may remain longer. Furthermore, the absence of any adequate means of accounting for the taxpayers who die complicates the issue. The surviving records do not permit the type of reconstituted census that Lorena S. Walsh has produced for coastal Maryland.[19] As a result, mortality has not been factored into the calculations for any of the districts.

Third, the tax lists ignore a section of the population—adult males who own no property and pay no poll tax—that might affect the overall persistence rates in the county. We might expect tenants, day laborers, and other agricultural workers without real estate property to compose the more mobile population of Washington County. Hal S. Barron argues that "property ownership was a distinguishing feature of those who remained" in Chelsea, Vermont.[20] Similarly, Robert Tracy McKenzie concludes that "when farmers owned the land they worked, they were much less likely to leave."[21] By using tax lists to measure persistence, then, we omit some individuals and slant the resulting calculations toward higher levels of persistence. As the following Washington County data show, however, the population persisted at rates lower than the estimates stated by the likes of Fox, Frost, Campbell, Paludan, and McKenzie. The tax lists' bias thus makes the conclusions drawn from the data even more startling and revealing. The federal manuscript censuses might conceivably afford a means of tracking people who own no land, but for Tennessee the censuses of 1800-1820 were destroyed in a fire, and only in 1850 does the census reveal an individual's occupation and real estate ownership. The tax lists thus provide one way of moving beyond the limitations of these particular census records.

Finally, we must evaluate the appropriateness of using tax lists and the linking of names as a way of measuring persistence. A comparison between the census and tax lists for 1830 shows that the tax lists surveyed the county's population thoroughly. They record 1,053 white polls for 1830. The census reports 1,503 white males between the ages of twenty and fifty. Apparently, the tax lists capture only 70 percent of the population; the census, however, listed 239 families with more than one adult male between the ages of twenty and fifty, while the tax lists recorded only six families with more than one white poll. Nearly all of these 239 families appear on the tax list, either as property owners or as a single white poll. The undercounting of white polls remains to be explained, but more important for this study, all areas of the civil districts were included on the tax lists: no pockets of geographically isolated mountaineers seem to have been omitted. As for the procedure of tracing the names that do appear on successive tax lists, Donald H. Parkerson concedes that although direct estimates of persistence are more accurate than this type of record linkage, "the two methods yielded relatively small persistence differentials" (about 2 percent) in places (like Washington County) that grow less than 25 percent over ten years.[22] In short, tracing names through the tax lists should provide reliable estimates of population persistence.

## Population Movement

The tables for Districts 1, 7/18, and 13 show, for each year, the number of individuals on the tax lists and how many individuals from one year's list remain during subsequent years (see tables 1-6). The tables also provide these data as the percentage of the individuals who remain. In District 1, for example, eighty-five

Table 1. Individuals from One Tax List for District 1 Who Appear on Subsequent Lists, 1790–1845

| YEAR | 1790 No. | % | 1797 No. | % | 1806 No. | % | 1814 No. | % | 1824 No. | % | 1836 No. | % | 1845 No. | % |
|------|------|------|------|------|------|------|------|------|------|------|------|------|------|------|
| 1790 | 48 | 100 | 20 | 41.6 | 15 | 31.3 | 12 | 25.0 | | | | | | |
| 1797 | | | 62 | 100 | 22 | 35.5 | 17 | 27.4 | 12 | 19.4 | | | | |
| 1806 | | | | | 85 | 100 | 35 | 41.2 | 29 | 34.1 | 13 | 15.3 | | |
| 1814 | | | | | | | 88 | 100 | 37 | 42.0 | 21 | 23.9 | 15 | 17.0 |
| 1824 | | | | | | | | | 101 | 100 | 29 | 28.7 | 20 | 19.8 |
| 1836 | | | | | | | | | | | 116 | 100 | 44 | 37.9 |
| 1845 | | | | | | | | | | | | | 169 | 100 |

Data compiled from Washington County, Trustee's Office, Tax Books.

Read data by following each row. Of the 48 indiviudals found on the 1790 list, 20 remained in 1797, for a persistence rate of 41.6%. Only 15 remained in 1806, for a persistence rate of 31.3%.

Table 2. Surnames from One Tax List for District 1 That Appear on Subsequent Lists, 1790–1845

| YEAR | 1790 | | 1797 | | 1806 | | 1814 | | 1824 | | 1836 | | 1845 | |
|---|---|---|---|---|---|---|---|---|---|---|---|---|---|---|
| | No. | % | No. | % | No. | % | No. | % | No. | % | No. | % | No. | % |
| 1790 | 31 | 100 | 16 | 51.6 | 14 | 45.2 | 12 | 38.7 | 12 | 38.7 | 13 | 41.9 | 11 | 35.5 |
| 1797 | | | 42 | 100 | 20 | 47.6 | 18 | 42.9 | 16 | 38.1 | 14 | 33.3 | 12 | 28.6 |
| 1806 | | | | | 48 | 100 | 27 | 56.3 | 27 | 56.3 | 20 | 41.7 | 18 | 37.5 |
| 1814 | | | | | | | 53 | 100 | 29 | 54.7 | 17 | 32.1 | 18 | 34.0 |
| 1824 | | | | | | | | | 50 | 100 | 19 | 38.0 | 19 | 38.0 |
| 1836 | | | | | | | | | | | 51 | 100 | 30 | 58.8 |
| 1845 | | | | | | | | | | | | | 52 | 100 |

Data compiled from Washington County, Trustee's Office, Tax Books.

Read data by following each row. Of the 31 surnames found on the 1790 list, 16 remained in 1797, for a persistence rate of 51.6%. Only 14 remained in 1806, for a persistence rate of 45.2%.

Table 3. Individuals from One Tax List for District 7/18 Who Appear on Subsequent Lists, 1792–1845

| YEAR | 1792 | | 1797 | | 1806 | | 1814 | | 1824 | | 1836 | | 1845 | |
|---|---|---|---|---|---|---|---|---|---|---|---|---|---|---|
| | No. | % | No. | % | No. | % | No. | % | No. | % | No. | % | No. | % |
| 1792 | 43 | 100 | | | | | | | | | | | | |
| 1797 | 16 | 37.2 | 49 | 100 | | | | | | | | | | |
| 1806 | 6 | 13.9 | 17 | 34.7 | 71 | 100 | | | | | | | | |
| 1814 | 2 | 4.7 | 7 | 14.3 | 27 | 38.0 | 58 | 100 | | | | | | |
| 1824 | | | 6 | 12.2 | 21 | 29.6 | 29 | 50.0 | 82 | 100 | | | | |
| 1836 | | | | | 9 | 12.7 | 16 | 27.6 | 31 | 37.8 | 136 | 100 | | |
| 1845 | | | | | | | 17 | 29.3 | 31 | 37.8 | 60 | 44.1 | 150 | 100 |

Data compiled from Washington County, Trustee's Office, Tax Books.

Read data by following each row. Of the 43 indiviudals found on the 1792 list, 16 remained in 1797, for a persistence rate of 37.2%. Only 6 remained in 1806, for a persistence rate of 13.9%.

Table 4. Surnames from One Tax List for District 7/18 That Appear on Subsequent Lists, 1792–1845

| YEAR | 1792 | | 1797 | | 1806 | | 1814 | | 1824 | | 1836 | | 1845 | |
|---|---|---|---|---|---|---|---|---|---|---|---|---|---|---|
| | No. | % | No. | % | No. | % | No. | % | No. | % | No. | % | No. | % |
| 1792 | 34 | 100 | | | | | | | | | | | | |
| 1797 | 15 | 44.1 | 33 | 100 | | | | | | | | | | |
| 1806 | 10 | 29.4 | 17 | 51.5 | 40 | 100 | | | | | | | | |
| 1814 | 5 | 14.7 | 9 | 27.3 | 24 | 60.0 | 39 | 100 | | | | | | |
| 1824 | 4 | 11.8 | 8 | 24.2 | 20 | 50.0 | 24 | 61.5 | 46 | 100 | | | | |
| 1836 | 3 | 8.8 | 10 | 30.3 | 17 | 42.5 | 20 | 51.3 | 26 | 56.5 | 63 | 100 | | |
| 1845 | 5 | 14.7 | 12 | 36.4 | 17 | 42.5 | 18 | 46.2 | 23 | 50.0 | 41 | 65.1 | 82 | 100 |

Data compiled from Washington County, Trustee's Office, Tax Books.

Read data by following each row. Of the 34 surnames found on the 1792 list, 15 remained in 1797, for a persistence rate of 44.1%. Only 10 remained in 1806, for a persistence rate of 29.4%.

Table 5. Individuals from One Tax List for District 13 Who Appear on Subsequent Lists, 1790–1845

| YEAR | 1790 No. | % | 1797 No. | % | 1806 No. | % | 1814 No. | % | 1824 No. | % | 1836 No. | % | 1845 No. | % |
|---|---|---|---|---|---|---|---|---|---|---|---|---|---|---|
| 1790 | 46 | 100 | 23 | 50.0 | 1 | 2.2 | 2 | 4.3 | | | | | | |
| 1797 | | | 106 | 100 | 22 | 20.8 | 20 | 18.9 | 20 | 18.9 | | | | |
| 1806 | | | | | 79 | 100 | 43 | 54.4 | 34 | 43.0 | 23 | 29.1 | | |
| 1814 | | | | | | | 93 | 100 | 48 | 51.6 | 29 | 31.2 | 21 | 22.6 |
| 1824 | | | | | | | | | 108 | 100 | 47 | 43.5 | 34 | 31.5 |
| 1836 | | | | | | | | | | | 140 | 100 | 61 | 43.6 |
| 1845 | | | | | | | | | | | | | 147 | 100 |

Data compiled from Washington County, Trustee's Office, Tax Books.

Read data by following each row. Of the 46 individuals found on the 1790 list, 23 remained in 1797, for a persistence rate of 50.0%. Only 1 remained in 1805, for a persistence rate of 2.2%.

Table 6. Surnames from One Tax List for District 13 That Appear on Subsequent Lists, 1790–1845

| YEAR | 1790 | | 1797 | | 1806 | | 1814 | | 1824 | | 1836 | | 1845 | |
|---|---|---|---|---|---|---|---|---|---|---|---|---|---|---|
| | No. | % | No. | % | No. | % | No. | % | No. | % | No. | % | No. | % |
| 1790 | 36 | 100 | 20 | 55.5 | 5 | 13.8 | 5 | 13.8 | 4 | 11.1 | 6 | 16.7 | 5 | 13.8 |
| 1797 | | | 57 | 100 | 16 | 28.1 | 17 | 29.8 | 17 | 29.8 | 16 | 28.1 | 17 | 29.8 |
| 1806 | | | | | 49 | 100 | 31 | 63.3 | 28 | 57.1 | 23 | 46.9 | 21 | 42.9 |
| 1814 | | | | | | | 53 | 100 | 35 | 66.0 | 26 | 49.1 | 24 | 45.3 |
| 1824 | | | | | | | | | 53 | 100 | 35 | 66.0 | 27 | 50.9 |
| 1836 | | | | | | | | | | | 75 | 100 | 39 | 52.0 |
| 1845 | | | | | | | | | | | | | 73 | 100 |

Data compiled from Washington County, Trustee's Office, Tax Books.

Read data by following each row. Of the 36 surnames found on the 1790 list, 20 remained in 1797, for a persistence rate of 55.5%. Only 5 remained in 1805, for a persistence rate of 13.8%.

individuals appeared on the 1806 tax list, thirty-five of whom re-appeared on the 1814 list, twenty-nine on the 1824 list, and only thirteen for the 1836 list. Two broad generalizations emerge regarding persistence. First, the total number of individuals in each region more than tripled from 1790 to 1845. This growth cannot be explained by natural increase alone; surely immigration plays a significant role. Second, in almost every case, over half of the individuals from the first tax list do not appear on the subsequent list. Even if we consider possible deaths, the results suggest that people readily left their particular region, often within ten years or less.

Examination of the persistence of surnames reinforces these conclusions. Family persistence figures importantly in the traditional view of the mountaineer. According to John Fox, Jr., the mountaineer "has lived in the cabin in which his grandfather was born, and in life, habit, and thought he has merely been his grandfather born over again."[23] By analyzing surnames we avoid the problem of not knowing who has died (which slants the results toward transience) and focus instead on a family's continuing residence. The number of surnames doubles from 1790 to 1845, and between 40 percent and 50 percent of the surnames on one tax list are absent from its successor. Of the forty-eight surnames listed for District 1 in 1806, only twenty-seven remained on the 1814 tax list. Although some surnames may disappear because a family had no male children, the evidence conflicts with notions of a stagnant population in an isolated location during this time period.

Some of the emigrants sought fertile land and economic opportunity in the Midwest. John Gregg left upper East Tennessee in late October 1813 and wrote from Indiana two months later: "I find none [of the good land] here worth entering in my oppinion, I in tend going out to White River shortly in search of land, where I'm told there is some tolerable land unlocated yet[.]"[24] Similarly, Benjamin Hyder wrote from Park County, Indiana, in December 1830, "I like the face of the country verry well as much as I have seen[.] I purpose going over to the State of Illinois not verry far from here[.] I am respectably informed that if a person will go there they may get excellent entry of land, good water and pick of situations[.]"[25] Many such emigrants probably never returned to upper East Tennessee. Note how desperately one Washington County resident wanted to see her daughter and her son-in-law:

You that live at a Distance I see nothing to hinder you or some of you from coming to see me if you want to come, you have plenty of land plenty of stock plenty of money & a little wagon. Your children all living near you now what is to hinder you[?] You enjouy tollerable good health[.] Start before the sickley Season comes on and spend the Sumer in seeing your friends & relations in Tenessee. You seeme some times to pore warm water & sometimes cold[.] You thought some years ago to be here in 1827 but now think it Doubtful wheather you ever will or not.[26]

Although cyclical migration certainly occurred, most of the out-migration remained permanent.

Some might object that militia companies and civil districts form too small a unit of measure for estimating this type of movement. A resident may leave a district yet remain in the county and in the mountains. In order to estimate the degree of this local, short-range migration, we might compare the 1814 and 1845 Washington County tax lists, looking for individuals who had left Districts 1, 7/18, and 13. For 1814, the resulting adjustment increased persistence by about 8 percent in District 1, between 4 percent and 9 percent in District 7/18, and between 5 percent and 35 percent in District 13. The large increase for District 13 probably comes from a shifting of the militia company boundaries near the turn of the nineteenth century.[27] For 1845, the persistence of individuals increased between 3 percent and 10 percent in District 1, between 2 percent and 5 percent in District 7/18, and between 5 percent and 12 percent in District 13. Despite these increases, the general conclusions remain unchanged. In both Districts 1 and 7/18, the most mountainous districts, over half of the individuals from the 1806 and 1836 tax lists were not found in Washington County less than a decade later. In District 13, between 40 percent and 50 percent of the individuals had departed during these same years. Similarly, the number of surnames found outside Districts 1 and 13 increased by comparable percentages; District 7/18 remains the anomaly, inasmuch as more surnames are found in the district than in the rest of the county.[28]

The movement of peoples out of both district and county indicates not only low levels of persistence for the residents but also, surprisingly, greater movement of people out of the mountainous districts than out of the control area. We cannot attribute persistence to the mountain environment when higher percentages of both individuals and surnames are found staying in the rolling valleys. After 1805 a consistently higher percentage of surnames remains in District 13 than in District 1. A higher percentage of surnames for District 1 exists at only a single point: family names on the 1836 list that appear in 1845. Although physiographical features cannot be responsible for such population movement, the environment can still offer, in the form of land values, a promising explanation for the greater persistence in District 13.

The 1836 and 1845 tax lists record not only the amount of land each person owned but also the value of the property. In 1845, the county court valued the 26,270 acres in District 1 at $51,678 ($1.97 per acre). The 53,085 acres in District 7/18 had a value of $32,163 ($0.61 per acre). District 13 was the richest; its 15,219 acres had a value of $60,273 ($3.96 per acre). The discrepancy in land value suggests an alternative explanation for persistence: the better land in District 13 encouraged residents to stay. People living in this district felt less pressure to leave the area in search of fertile soil than did those living in the more mountainous areas. The higher percentages of individual and surname persistence might reflect the land's differential ability to support families and their relations. A glance at the landowners who persist over four successive tax lists supports this hypothesis. The sixteen persisters in District 7/18 owned on average 174 acres; the twenty individuals in District 1 averaged 207 acres; the thirty persisters in District 13 owned 243 acres on average. Perhaps the larger average landholdings and their higher average value in District 13 accounts for the greater persistence of its inhabitants during the early nineteenth century. Similarly, smaller holdings of less valuable land might be associated with a decision by adult men to leave the mountainous parts of Washington County.

Land values, however, cannot account for persistence in District 7/18. The percentages of individuals and surnames remaining in this mountainous area reach about the same levels as those for the control region. In the nineteenth century, the persistence of surnames in both districts drops to 60 percent, then to 50 percent and 40 percent on successive tax lists. Yet the land in District 7/18 was worth less than one-sixth of the value of land in District 13. If good land might explain relatively higher rates of persistence in District 13, surely poor land cannot explain the same phenomenon in District 7/18. Land that is poor in the agricultural sense, however, may nevertheless have bountiful natural resources. The iron mines in and around Greasy Cove may be responsible for the higher levels of persistence in District 7/18.

In the first decades of the nineteenth century, residents in Greasy Cove had access to several iron mines. Iron manufacture played so important a role that the territorial Legislative Council passed resolutions allowing the work to continue unhindered. "Resolved, that fourteen of the principal artists belonging to any furnace for the manufactory of iron in this Territory be exempted from military duty, who shall not be called into service in case of insurrection or invasion unless his Excellency the Governor shall deem their services necessary."[29] From Greasy Cove, where the Nolichucky divides North and South Indian Creek, one could travel five miles up North Indian Creek to Swingle's Ironworks. This furnace, or bloomery, was probably located on George Swingle's 142-acre holding.[30] One could also leave the district and follow the Nolichucky River downriver for about six miles to Bumpass Cove. Since the 1780s, when William Colyer operated a mine, the cove served as a center of economic activity. In 1812, William P. Chester bought 260 acres at the mouth of the cove and built a forge. Later that year, the Washington County Court of Pleas and Quarter Sessions instructed a jury to set aside 3,000 acres for his ironworks' use. For at least twenty years, the court had encouraged such enterprises by reserving "three thousand acres of land not fit for cultivation for the purpose of building Iron works."[31] The Tennessee legislature supported such county initiatives for ironworks by passing legislation in 1809 that provided for the condemnation of public lands. Elijah Embree, who bought Swingle's operation around 1808, also purchased Chester's ironworks in 1819 for $4,500. Embree, with his brother and other partners, expanded the operations and eventually formed the Washington Iron Manufacturing Company in 1839. The mines, forges, bloomeries, mills, and furnaces belonging to Embree and

his associates used timber and ore from about 30,000 acres surrounding Bumpass Cove and supplied products for both local and
regional markets.[32]

Furthermore, the residents of Greasy Cove could reach these
mines by using the road network described in Chapter 2. A road to
Swingle's Ironworks on North Indian Creek existed as early as
1783.[33] One of the court's first road orders probably included
Bumpass Cove, given that "a Road be Laid off from first [forks?] of
Indian Creek Near Jacob Brown's as may be most convenient."[34]
At the time, Brown lived on the Nolichucky River even farther
downriver than Bumpass Cove. The imprecise wording, however,
makes the exact route unclear. The earliest evidence of a definite
road between Bumpass and Greasy Coves appears in August 1810,
when Benjamin Dillard was named overseer of the road from "the
Jump hill to the red bank foard on nolachucky river."[35] Clearly, the
ironworks provided a nonagricultural means of support for people,
and roads allowed the residents to reach these places (although
travel upon these roads was seldom easy). Given such economic
and geographic connections, David A. Deaderick predicted the
county "will never so much flourish as when we become a manufacturing people. We have water power without end to propel machinery, and in iron manufactures especially, this county . . . will in
time become celebrated."[36] Such opportunities in the mountains,
rather than the mountains themselves, might explain the relatively high levels of persistence for this district.

Although long-term persisters may have stayed for different
reasons (because of mineral resources rather than because of agricultural goods), nearly all of them lived on the county's principal
waterways. In the mountainous districts, the most valuable land
was located on the banks of the Nolichucky River or its principal
tributaries. Some of the residents lived at such locations for several
decades. In District 1, Simeon Broyles, Sr., lived near Cassi Creek
and Henderson Clark lived on Clark's Creek; both creeks feed into
the Nolichucky River. Lawrence Glaze and John Winkle, Sr., both
lived off Moore Branch, which joins the Nolichucky a bit farther
downriver.[37] In District 7/18, Joseph Longmire served as the postmaster of what is now the town of Erwin, where the Nolichucky
splits the Indian Creeks. John Edwards and Robert Love resided in
this area as well. Thomas Tilson most likely lived near where Rice

and Sams Creeks join to form South Indian Creek. George
Swingle, as mentioned above, lived on North Indian Creek.[38]

Other longtime residents lived on waterways that still bear
their families' names. For example, the Clarks who settled near
Clark's Creek appear on the 1790 (and each subsequent) tax list.
The Painters lived along Painter Creek and were similarly persistent. Surely many of the creeks received their names from families
that lived along them for generations. If so, we might be able to
trace the spread of the population in a rudimentary way. By noting
when specific surnames appear in the court records and then lo-
cating the names on a map, we might be able to tell when certain
residents (who left very few records otherwise) moved into a particular region. By applying this method to Rice, Sams, and Higgins
Creeks in the far southwestern portion of District 7/18, we see why
the Rice, Sams, and Higgins families may have chosen to move
into that area when they did. As we trace and examine this movement, we can begin to understand how certain groups of people in
upper East Tennessee may have been separated from the majority
of the population and may have come to be regarded as different.

## Persistence in the Most Mountainous Areas

Rice, Sams, and Higgins Creeks, which join to form South Indian
Creek, apparently saw no settlement along their banks for many
years. Few records of early settlement exist in this most mountainous portion of both the district and the county. The court documents reveal no roads built in this area before 1800. Neither
"Rice" nor "Higgins" appears on the early tax lists. "Sams" does
show up as early as 1792 but not in this area; James and John Sams
are listed in the Greasy Cove tax district. The deed books, however, mention only Edmond Sams, who bought 100 acres from
Martin Webb on 25 September 1784. This land lay next to Webb's
1782 North Carolina grant, which was located "on the Greasy
Cove on the Nolichucky."[39] It seems unlikely that any of these
Samses lived on what came to be called Sams Creek. This conclusion gains support from a contemporary diary. John Strother, chief
surveyor of the team that marked the Tennessee–North Carolina
boundary in the summer of 1799, recorded their progress on June

18: "Set out early this morning on ye line. Col. Robt. Love our pilot continued it along in the extreme height of the Mt. about 5 m to a low gap between the head of Indian Creek & the waters of ye S. fork of Laurel where we encamped & called it Vance Camp."[40] This spot, now called Sams Gap, was evidently unnamed and unoccupied in 1799. Perhaps the area's remoteness or the opportunities available in Greasy Cove discouraged settlement until later decades.

The surname "Sams," absent from the 1806, 1814, and 1824 tax lists, resurfaces in 1836 and continues in 1845. "Higgins" also appears in 1836 and 1845. "Rice" first shows up in 1845. Noting the low value of their property, we would suspect that these people lived in the extreme southwestern part of the district. Given that District 7/18's eleven longtime residents generally owned land of greater value along the Nolichucky or other principal waterways, the poorer land of the Rice, Higgins, and Sams families suggests that they did not live near the longtime residents. The eleven long-term persisters owned 2,993 acres, worth an average of $2.11 per acre. Spencer and William Rice owned 112 acres, worth $1.12 per acre. Ellis and Barbara Higgins owned 450 acres, valued at $0.66 per acre. Finally, Jacob C., Mary, and William H. Sams owned 225 acres, worth only $0.55 per acre. In a district where the best land lay near the larger creeks and rivers and where land unfit for cultivation was made available to the iron companies, the Rice, Higgins, and Sams properties fell into the poorer category.[41] As newcomers to a district in which the better land was already occupied, these people were probably forced to occupy more marginal areas located farther away from the first settlements.

The Higgins, Rice, and Sams families continued to acquire property on South Indian Creek and its tributaries during the 1840s and 1850s. While no deed records have been found to correspond with the earliest appearances of the Sams and Rice families in the tax lists, fairly complete records exist for the later period. From these deeds, we can draw several conclusions about the pattern of settlement in the southernmost portion of District 7/18. First, the deeds show not only that the three families owned numerous tracts of land throughout the area but also that (unlike some property holders) they lived on the land. For example, James Sams lived on "the road fork of Indian Creek" at the time of his death in 1842. William S. Erwin then bought the property at a public sale the following year, the proceeds of which paid Sams's outstanding debts. Erwin lived in Greasy Cove, however, not on this property. In the summer of 1849, Erwin transferred this land for an unknown sum, if any, to Jacob C. Sams (son of the deceased James Sams) and his wife Mary. A deed in 1850 from Mary to Josiah B. Sams, her son, shows that the family was well established at the site. The son acquired the 123 acres from Mary on condition that he "doth fine me his Mother with grain and meat a plenty for the support of herself and daughter Catharine and Eliza during their being single or as long as they live on the place with the liberty of the houses and stables and other out houses where she the said Mary Sams here lives."[42]

The deed records also show the three families with land fairly close to one another. The three creeks bearing the family names all feed the same stream, so one would expect these families to be neighbors. The parcels of land in the various deeds are described in metes and bounds (for example, from "a sugar tree" to "a chestnut oak on the top of a ridge"), but many of them include references to the same identifying features, such as the Walnut Mountain road, the state line with North Carolina, and the Middle Ridge.[43] Certain tracts were located so close to one another that the two parties resolved their disputes by registering legal boundaries with the county court.[44] Yet the Sams, Rice, and Higgins families did not live alone in this area. They regularly sold land to other residents of Washington County and to their neighbors in North Carolina. In all likelihood, some of these purchasers also came to live in the region.[45]

The data on the Rice, Higgins, and Sams families indicate that they went "up the coves" and into the more remote regions. Such movement suggests how different groups in upper East Tennessee may have diverged socially by the middle of the nineteenth century. If settlers chose not to migrate westward, the unavailability of level, more fertile land along the larger rivers would have forced them into some of the most physiographically extreme areas in the eastern United States. The requisite conditions existed, then, for the development of characteristics that eventually came to be seen in stereotypical terms. Consider the following incident, which David A. Deaderick recorded in his diary:

On the 27th of Nov. [1824] David Greer killed Holland
Higgins. Higgins was at the time in custody of Wm. S.
Erwin, constable in the Greasy Cove. On the 26th Greer
had shot at Higgins and missed him. On the following day,
Greer getting ahead waited in a waste house, on Indian
Creek, directly on the road, 3 or 4 miles from the mouth of
the creek, from which he shot and killed Higgins on the
spot. Erwin succeeded after a hazardous encounter in securing Greer. This he would not in all probability have effected,
had not he directly ordered Cooper, a young man who was
with him, to shoot Greer, which he did and wounded him in
the hand. Greer is a man above the ordinary size and of great
strength. He has lived for 20 or 30 years past near the top of
the Bald Mountain, (the pinnacle of which he had ditched
for the purpose of cultivation) entirely alone. He is thought
to be somewhat deranged.[46]

According to the editor of this diary, Greer came from South
Carolina to western North Carolina in 1798. He worked for Colonel David Vance (perhaps on the Tennessee-North Carolina
boundary survey mentioned above) and fell in love with Vance's
daughter but was not allowed to marry her. Therefore, in 1802, he
moved to Bald Mountain (on the Tennessee-North Carolina border in District 7/18), cleared nine acres, and separated himself
from the rest of the population. The incident with Higgins began
when Greer believed Higgins to have encroached on his land. The
state charged Greer with murder, but he was acquitted on a plea of
insanity. Several years later, a friend of Higgins's killed Greer.[47]

The David Greer incident evokes many stereotypical Appalachian attributes, including violence, lawlessness, physical
strength, and derangement. Greer seems to have had a quick tem-
per that was readily aroused when he thought his property was being threatened. He apparently died as a result of an act of revenge.
Finally, he was isolated, both socially and geographically, from the
other residents of the county. But his isolation differed from the
sort described by Fox and Frost, for Greer chose to live on Bald
Mountain and to separate himself from society. The initiative he
took in this regard allows us to see him and the Sams, Rice, and
Higgins families in a new light. These people should be viewed not

as having passively accepted the conditions imposed by the mountains but as having decided for themselves where to live. As a result, the data on persistence and the spread of the population raise questions about the David Greer incident that Fox and Frost would not have asked. Was Holland Higgins a recent immigrant to Washington County and to Higgins Creek? Did he "encroach" upon Greer's property because no other land was available? Why did Greer and Holland Higgins live in the Bald Mountain area rather than somewhere outside District 7/18? Although residents such as these have left hardly any documentary record, the search for land (however unproductive), together with other possible reasons for leaving or for staying, may demand our attention if we are to understand Appalachian characterizations. These people, when located on extremely difficult terrain, could prevent their contemporaries from seeing them accurately. Historians suffer a similar blindness, for neither Greer nor Higgins appears on the 1824 tax list. And given that the entire county was late tying into wider transportation networks, outsiders would have found it even more difficult to obtain reliable accounts.

Perhaps the residents, deranged or otherwise, who chose to separate themselves from society afford the raw material for images of Appalachia. The distance between newly settled places like Sams Creek and towns like Jonesborough cannot be measured simply in miles; problems of travel make even incidental contact with other county residents unlikely. The physical setting helped David Greer keep himself apart from society; at his home on Bald Mountain, few passers-by would simply drop in for a visit. As a result, perhaps the settlement of these remote areas encouraged people to turn in on themselves, to focus on their immediate surroundings and circumstances. The District 7/18 surname data reveal that family names concentrated in the district and that fewer of these surnames appeared in the rest of the county. Most of Washington County's residents had reasons for staying in or leaving upper East Tennessee that differed little from those of people living in other frontier regions. Fertile land and natural resources more plausibly explain why people remained in the county than does isolation imposed by the mountains. For a few residents, however, Washington County's mountains offered something unavailable in the more open areas of Tennessee or the Old Northwest:

seclusion or land that was nearby although poor. As the rest of the United States shifted from a frontier society to an industrial one, outsiders may have seen in the Higgins, Rice, and Sams families the development of a uniquely Appalachian society. Eventually, certain residents within upper East Tennessee came to share this perspective on their neighbors living in the mountains.

# CHAPTER FIVE

# Railroads in Upper East Tennessee

WHILE THE HIGGINS, Rice, and Sams families acquired and sold land in the southern, most mountainous portion of Washington County, other residents tried to plug into the national network for commerce and communication. Starting in the 1830s with the momentum generated by early efforts at internal improvements, a dedicated group of upper East Tennessee residents organized, promoted, and built the East Tennessee and Virginia Rail Road. Through such efforts, the region established links with the Atlantic coast to the east and with the Mississippi River valley to the west. The effects of such connections, however, were not felt uniformly throughout the region. The railroad benefited residents who lived along the route far more than it did those who lived in the mountains no more than a dozen miles away. This latter group, with its largely local perspective, remained to a large degree disconnected not only from outside regions but also from the townspeople within upper East Tennessee. Promoters of the railroad, with their broader perspective, described the region and its more locally oriented inhabitants in terms that signal the beginnings of modern characterizations of Appalachian Mountain people.

## THE PERCEIVED BENEFITS OF INTERNAL IMPROVEMENTS

The promotion of internal improvements on the national and state levels during the 1830s gives us one way of seeing local conditions and social distinctions through the eyes of the participants.[1] William B. Carter, upper East Tennessee's representative to

Congress, frequently submitted resolutions to improve the area's water transportation. He sought to fund the removal of obstructions in the Tennessee and Holston Rivers and to survey those rivers from Muscle Shoals to Kingsport (which he also hoped to make a port of entry).[2] With the federal government already at work at Muscle Shoals in 1836, Carter sought an appropriation of $100,000 to extend the improvements to Kingsport. While Carter emphasized the national character of the project (and thereby adhered to the strict constructionist mood of the day), he presented conditions in his district in a rather rosy light. "[The work] opens a free, safe, and direct communication between the interior of the fertile and valuable country of East Tennessee, possessing an inexhaustible treasure of natural wealth and national resources, of indispensable materials for national defence, as well as an abundance of provision stuffs; and, sir, it communicates with a hardy, industrious, and patriotic people who . . . are always ready to pour out their blood and expend their treasure in defence of the honor and free institutions of their country." While glowing remarks of this sort are to be expected of a politician seeking funds for his district, we may also sense that this natural bounty desperately needed to be freed. The region had iron "of a better quality than afforded any where else" and was "capable of supplying the world" if appropriate improvements were funded. "East Tennessee seems," Carter concluded, ". . . to be designed by nature for a manufacturing country, as well as for agriculture, and only needs a market to secure the independence and happiness of the people."[3]

Carter further emphasized how upper East Tennessee iron could "supply the Government with ordinance and munitions of war, of every character and description, upon much better terms and of superior quality to any she has been heretofore in the use of, all of which can be transported by means of this improvement to any part of the United States that the Government might require."[4] In 1830, a group of upper East Tennessee residents led by Thomas Emmerson, John Kennedy, John G. Eason, and J. Howard (all of Jonesborough) sent a memorial to Congress promoting Pactolus as the site for a western armory. The location was well endowed with water power, iron, timber, and coal, but the memorialists emphasized how internal improvements would be required before the armory could reach its full potential. "There is no doubt if the beds of [coal] were worked and roads from them opened, it could be supplied on moderate terms to any required extent." Similarly, they claimed that "for a sum not exceeding 20,000 dollars this river [the Holston] could be made navigable [between Pactolus and Knoxville] for steamboats at least six months in the year, and for keelboats the whole year round."[5]

Pactolus had "equal if not superior advantages to any other [site] which can be selected on the western waters," this group of citizens argued, because it had all "the facilities for transporting Arms to the various points at which they may be required for the public service." The weapons "may be conveyed by land in waggons to the State of Virginia in one day, into the States of North Carolina and Kentucky in two or three days, into South Carolina in four or five days; and into Georgia in seven or eight days." The western states could be reached by water, "either by flat bottom boats descending the Holston and Tennessee to the mouth of the latter river" or by land eighty-seven miles to the Sandy River "and there put on board steam boats [that] descend that river to the Ohio."[6] We may wonder whether Congress regarded such access as adequate; in a national emergency, would it be acceptable to take a week to send rifles to Georgia? Still, the memorialists stressed that all parts of the west could be reached if the internal improvements were completed.

The residents who supported the armory believed that its establishment would promote change in upper East Tennessee. "Should the Armory be located at Pactolus," the memorialists proclaimed, "the river will be at once improved by the enterprise of our own citizens" and added, with a telling perspective on local conditions, "compared with what we are now, we shall be a prosperous and happy people."[7] An editorial in the *Farmers' Journal* echoed such predictions. With the armory, "this district of country will assume a very different appearance for the better from what it now presents. Our population will rapidly increase both as to number and respectability. Agriculture will be much improved, and Manufacturing establishments of various kinds will be speedily erected." Similar to David A. Deaderick's prediction that East Tennessee would attract emigrants, the *Farmers' Journal* believed that "industry would . . . be so amply rewarded that our enterprising citizens would not be driven, by that arbitrary tyrant *necessity*, from the 'graves of their fathers,' to seek new homes in the fertile regions of the west—so far from this, hundreds of capitalists and men of industry, intelligence, and moral worth would be found seeking a home among *us*."[8] Bound with such convictions, however, one finds the undeniable reality that much of life in upper East Tennessee could be improved.

Colonel Solomon D. Jacobs put the situation even more plainly in an address before the Lyceum in Jonesborough late in 1831. The region was "labouring under all the disadvantages of a want of proper communications to and from market; having to transport our goods over a land carriage of from three to five hundred miles, and aided only by a precarious flood tide to convey our produce to market." He calculated East Tennessee's annual imports to be 4,617 tons and its exports at least 7,200 tons. Although the land could support 2 million people and ten times the current level of imports and exports, Jacobs warned that "unless the wanted facilities to place us on an equality with other countries are early afforded us, our population must cease to increase and our productions will inevitably decrease."[9] Internal improvements provided the only answer.

Other states had taken the necessary step of funding such improvements, but as Jacobs continued, for many years "the State of Tennessee has stood almost alone, with her arms folded and apparently indifferent to the interest and prosperity of her citizens." The state had finally taken some steps: "the removal of the obstructions in the Muscle Shoals now in progression will open for us a market with the great and growing valley of the Mississippi." Rather than looking to the West, however, Jacobs stressed that the region's future was tied to the East. "But to the projected rail road to the east, by which it is contemplated to unite the waters of Virginia with those of Tennessee, we must look, as the most expeditious as well as the most advantageous road to market for a large portion of our productions." Given the "cheapness and celerity with which we shall be enabled to transport our productions on this rail way," Jacobs felt the state legislature could not ignore this project.[10]

By the end of the year, the government had indeed considered the benefits of a railroad crossing through upper East Tennessee. The Committee of Internal Improvements in the House of

Representatives proposed a line connecting with the Lynchburg and New River Rail Road in Virginia. Given the "abundance of materials in East Tennessee and Virginia, together with the smooth and level valleys through which it would pass," the railroad could be built "at a much less price than heretofore conjectured [about $6,000 per mile]." Enormous benefits would accrue from such a road, according to the committee. "Many heavy articles, which this railway will raise from the rich bowels of the high lands of East Tennessee, will find a market. The low rate of transportation is the only means which can develop the mineral wealth, the inexhaustible mines, which cannot now be worked for the want of improved highways to trade." At present, the "tedious journies to market . . . [and] the loss of time is the loss of so much wealth to the citizens and, consequently, to the state. . . . it will be about twenty days from Knoxville to Richmond for a waggon on a turnpike, allowing twenty miles per day. On the rail road, it would not exceed two days." The railroad would form "an important link in the grand chain of communication from the south west to the Atlantic" and would transform upper East Tennessee into "one of the most desirable and valuable portions of the interior of the Union."[11]

Similar sentiments were voiced just to the north. The Virginia legislature had already authorized the construction of the Lynchburg and New River Rail Road when a convention met at Abingdon on 25 August 1831 to try to arrange for the road's extension to Knoxville. The convention confidently stated that "a double track of rails laid upon stone, in the most durable manner, will not exceed fourteen thousand dollars per mile." Nor did it expect much difficulty in laying the rails. From Lynchburg to Knoxville, "the nature of the surface, and the character of the country, were so perfectly known to a majority of the convention, that they are satisfied every serious obstacle and difficulty would be surmounted after passing the Alleghany, and the region between that height and the head waters of the Holston or Tennessee River." For the remainder of the way to Knoxville, "there is generally a descent, and a good rail road may be obtained along vallies parallel to the course of the streams flowing westwardly."[12]

In the process of setting out the changes that the railroad would bring, the Abingdon Convention first described the type of people in southwestern Virginia and upper East Tennessee in

terms that have been applied to Appalachia more recently. The
railroad would "induce many to visit distant points, and to super-
intend their own business far from home, who without such a convenience would never have left their own firesides. Intercourse,
the parent of improvement, is promoted. Refinement of manners
and character is produced, and the moral, as well as the commercial results, are incalculable." The convention echoed the feeling
in East Tennessee that the region was falling behind other parts of
the nation. "Let us not supinely delay to avail ourselves of the examples of other States," it pleaded, "and of the advantages with
which God & nature have blessed us, in as high a degree as any
other portion of the Union. Let us not permit our lands to lie ne-
glected and unimproved, and our trade to languish, while other
members of the American confederacy are pointing out to us our
true interests, and are on the sure march to wealth and power."[13]
On the eve of railroad construction in the mountains, residents
were invited to contemplate both a sorry past and a happy future.
Internal improvements, according to one editorial, like the "fabled
wand of the magician, [would] change the now dark and gloomy
aspect of our country into joy and brightness and prosperity." For
every prediction that East Tennessee would eventually "be distinguished for its industry, its enterprise, its virtue, and its intelligence," there surfaced a belief that the present situation was
inadequate, a conviction that "the emigrant will not then, as now,
pass by our country as unworthy of his notice."[14]

## ORGANIZING AND PROMOTING THE RAILROAD

Railroad construction in upper East Tennessee and southwestern
Virginia took place within the context of a national craze for railroads. The length of track grew from 23 miles in 1830, to about
2,800 in 1840, to nearly 8,000 miles in 1850. Fueled by a surge of
construction between 1849 and 1854, the foundation for the modern rail network east of the Mississippi River was complete by the
beginning of the Civil War.[15] Yet little construction occurred in
East Tennessee. The state legislature chartered a railroad from Knoxville to the Virginia line in December 1831 but provided no financial assistance. Virginia had authorized the Lynchburg and New
River Railroad extension to the Tennessee line, but the legislature

refused to subscribe 40 percent of the stock. As a result, the company abandoned the enterprise on 25 May 1832.[16] The *Railroad Advocate*, a biweekly newspaper that had begun publication in Rogersville, Tennessee, during the peak of railroad excitement in the summer of 1831, also suffered from the waning interest and folded less than one year later. In its final issue, the newspaper bemoaned the lack of support for railroads and proclaimed: "Railroads are the *only hope* of East Tennessee. With them, she would be everything the patriot would desire;—without them, she will continue to be what she is and what she has been, a depressed and languishing region—too unpromising to invite capital or enterprise from abroad, or to retain that which may grow up in her own bosom. They are the only improvements at all suited to her condition."[17]

Two other railroads attracted some attention during the 1830s for their proposed connections to East Tennessee. The Charleston and Hamburg Rail Road, connecting the South Carolina capital to the Savannah River in 1833, considered expanding all the way to the Ohio River. This company became the Louisville, Cincinnati, and Charleston Railroad and received its charter in 1835.[18] The line sparked enough interest in East Tennessee to prompt Congressman William B. Carter in 1836 to seek authorization from the House Committee on Roads and Canals for "a reconnaissance and survey of the route of the Cincinnati and Charleston railroad" through the region.[19] At the state level, Senator Joseph Powell told his constituents that "by some begging . . . we have made an appropriation to survey the route for the Cincinnati and Charleston Rail Road, and a route from the Virginia line passing as near as practicable through the center of the State to the Mississippi River—little else of importance can or will be effected at the present session."[20] In November 1836, local newspapers reported that of the 13,681 shares of the railroad that had been subscribed, Charleston had taken 8,631 shares, Knoxville had 2,538, and Jonesborough had 122. In a public notice announcing the availability of shares, John G. Eason, Nathan Gammon, and Thomas Emmerson (the Jonesborough commissioners for this railroad) insisted that "both patriotism and self-interest loudly call on every citizen of East Tennessee cordially and zealously to lend his aid" to the completion of this "grand and magnificent enterprise."[21] De-

spite the support in East Tennessee, financial difficulties triggered
by a sharp drop in cotton prices in South Carolina forced the railroad to retrench in 1839 and to abandon its plans to cross upper
East Tennessee.[22]

The Hiwassee Rail Road also generated some interest in East
Tennessee. Begun in 1836, it sought to connect Knoxville with
the Georgia state line, Atlanta, and finally the Atlantic coast.
Strong interest in lower East Tennessee for the Hiwassee supported the construction of the line; by 1839, sixty-six miles had
been graded and one bridge had been constructed over the
Hiwassee River.[23] That year, some Jonesborough residents sought
to have the line extended north from Knoxville and tried to persuade the state legislature to amend the company's charter to allow a spur to be built through upper East Tennessee to the Virginia
line. Although the legislature denied this request, the continued
interest in a railroad link between Knoxville and the Virginia line
eventually led to what would become the East Tennessee and Virginia Rail Road. After seven years of fiscal disaster, in which all
construction on the railroad had been suspended, the company re-
organized the Hiwassee Rail Road in 1847 and renamed it the East
Tennessee and Georgia Rail Road. Its new officers promised re-
newed efforts in raising money, liquidating debt, and resuming
construction. With roads planned from Chattanooga to both
Nashville and Memphis, combined with Virginia's fresh interest in
extending the Virginia and Tennessee Rail Road to the Tennessee
state line, the rail network missed only the 130-mile segment between Knoxville and the Virginia state line.[24] By the late 1840s,
then, the planning for such a road had begun once again.

Early efforts to organize the railroad make it possible to gauge
popular support for the project. During the spring of 1847, organizers held a series of conventions to rally public interest and to draft
a proposal to send to the Tennessee legislature. At the main convention in Greeneville on 5 July 1847, delegates from ten counties
in East Tennessee and three in Virginia split into two factions. A
conservative group sought just river improvements, especially for
the Holston and French Broad Rivers, while the other group demanded a railroad. In their compromise, the delegates asked the
legislature for money to support both projects. Although the state
failed to appropriate funds for either one, it did incorporate the

East Tennessee and Virginia Rail Road Company on 27 January 1848. The company set its capital stock at $1.5 million, with 60,000 shares at $25 each. These shares could be purchased beginning on the first Monday in April; if at least 500 shares were subscribed in one month's time, then the company would be considered formed, and the board of commissioners could have the route surveyed and could estimate costs. The route could not be finalized, however, until at least 25,000 shares had been subscribed and a board of directors had been elected. If such conditions were not met by the first of January 1850, the company's charter would be annulled.[25] Advocates of the railroad therefore had two years to persuade their neighbors to invest in the project. The task proved difficult.

The company struggled to get fully organized. The books did not open for subscription until February 1849, ten months behind schedule. A second board of commissioners decided to waive the initial payment of fifty cents per share in order to attract more subscriptions.[26] By April, about $75,000 had been subscribed in Washington County, but little interest was shown in the neighboring areas.[27] Disagreements within upper East Tennessee over the route of the railroad probably fractured support for the company. Andrew Johnson, the region's representative in Congress, mentioned to Samuel B. Cunningham, president of the railroad, that "we ought to be exceedingly conciliatory and circumspect in all our moves, and be sure to adopt that mode of procedure which would be best calculated to bring about harmony and concert of action in all the upper counties in East Tennessee." Johnson believed that "if we went into the Legislature with the two leading valleys containing all the wealth or nearly so, arrayed against each other, and quarreling about the location of the road, . . . presenting a divided and broken front, we would come out of it disappointed and defeated, failing wholly to accomplish the object so much desired."[28] Such factionalism, disastrous to any project seeking state aid, undoubtedly also hurt efforts at raising private subscriptions.

By November 1849, less than $200,000 had been subscribed to the East Tennessee and Virginia Rail Road Company. The company fell far short of the 25,000 shares needed to retain its charter and struggled to raise more than $175,000 within two months. Faced with the possibility of the railroad's dissolution, thirty-one

Fig. 9. Jonesborough, ca. 1849. Photograph by L.W. Keene. Courtesy of Archives and Special Collections, Sherrod Library, East Tennessee State University, Johnson City, Tennessee.

men formed a joint stock company that subscribed the rest of the shares not to exceed half a million dollars. All but six of the men owned property in Washington County. With the financial pre-requisite met and the project's immediate future assured, the stockholders elected the board of directors on 21 November 1849. All fifteen members of the board were, not surprisingly, members of the joint stock company.[29] This group of wealthy Jonesborough men therefore controlled the future of the railroad.

That the company became operational in 1850 serves as one measure of upper East Tennessee's devotion to a railroad. But given that the majority of the company was owned by just thirty-one individuals in the joint stock company, such a measure means little. In order to gauge the degree of popular support for railroads and regional integration, we must resort to more impressionistic methods. The *Rail Road Journal*, a weekly newspaper published in Jonesborough beginning in April 1850, was "devoted to internal improvements, agriculture, education, mechanical news, and general intelligence—neutral in politics and religion." Samuel Greer and James L. Sparks, the editor and printer of the newspaper, proclaimed that "the great object of the Journal will be to advocate the cause of the E.T. & Va. R.R. and this shall engage our attention until the work is under full way. . . . *The road must be built*, or we may as well shut up East Tennessee and move West and settle on some of the public lands."[30] The *Rail Road Journal* constantly engaged itself in raising money and in persuading people of the railroad's many benefits. The number and types of appeals appearing in the newspaper afford one index of local enthusiasm (or the lack thereof) for the East Tennessee and Virginia Rail Road.[31]

The newspaper went to great efforts to show that every citizen could afford to subscribe to the railroad. One writer calculated that $2 million would be needed to build the railroad. In the eleven counties east of Knoxville, he estimated aggregate taxable wealth to be $12,334,931; when divided among the 17,971 families assumed to be living in the region, the average taxable property per family came to $686. To support the railroad each family would need to pay $111, and even this sum would not be required in one payment. "The work must be progressive, and it is enough if the payments keep pace with the work." Over the five-year span thought necessary to build the railroad, the $111, further broken into monthly installments, came to payments of only $1.85 a month. "Will any one say it can not be met? The will to do it is all that is required—the means are abundant." Furthermore, part of the $111 could be paid in produce and labor. With only one-quarter of the subscription required in cash, the monthly payment becomes minute. "We then have for each month $1.38³/₄ in produce and labor, and 16¹/₄ cents in cash to be raised for five years by every family of seven in Upper East Tennessee, and that builds the road. How small the sum!"[32]

Yet the company had great difficulty raising more money. In September 1850, Samuel Cunningham and Lloyd Tilghman, president and chief engineer of the railroad, together with Landon C. Haynes (speaker of the house in the Tennessee General Assembly), tried to raise subscriptions in Knoxville, the southern terminus and largest community on the East Tennessee and Virginia route. The *Rail Road Journal* reported that "an appointment for speaking and consultation on the subject of the road having previously been published—and so little interest was felt among the people of that city and county that they neither turned out to hear the speaking nor, as we learn, subscribed any stock. This we did not expect, yet it is even so."[33] By the second annual stockholders' meeting on 29 November 1850, only $250,000 had been subscribed apart from the joint stock company, and little of this had been paid.[34] As a result, the railroad had to direct its appeals to the wealthy in order for construction to begin. The *Rail Road Journal* reported that engineers could start grading the road at McBee's Ferry in the autumn of 1850, but "by the decision of the Board a certain amount of stock must be raised before commencing the work. This can soon be done if an interest paramount with the importance of the work could be infused in the minds of the people." For such an infusion, the company now depended upon "gentlemen of influence." "Suppose for example, the amount necessary to be raised in Jefferson [County] be $50,000, more or less, in cash subscriptions. Now there is certainly ten men in that county who can, if they will, step forward and take that amount at once, and thus give the work a start. If they would do this it seems to us that by conversing with their neighbors and getting them interested on the subject they could reduce the sum until it would come within their means, should the amount be more than they can easily manage." With obvious frustration, the newspaper concluded, "Let some plan at least be devised by which the requirements of the board can be met. There is too much apathy on the subject. Let gentlemen of influence rouse themselves and go to work in their respective counties, make it their business to raise the amount necessary, and it will soon be done."[35] The paper had evidently forgotten that such calls were easier to make than to fulfill, for board members themselves had made it "their business to raise the amount necessary," and they had come up short.

Perhaps the local residents hesitated to subscribe because they knew little of the potential benefits offered by the railroad. Many in East Tennessee, according to Chief Engineer Lloyd Tilghman, "are now famishing for information which will guide them aright in their desire to see successfully carried out the grand scheme we now have before us." Tilghman, a graduate of West Point who participated in the recent war against Mexico, had worked on the New York and Erie Rail Road before arriving in Jonesborough on 20 March 1850. He believed that "it is the misfortune, rather than the fault, of most of the inhabitants of East Tennessee that they are so wanting in information on the vast importance of a proper communication with the great depots of wealth and commerce upon our Atlantic and Gulf coast. Nature has placed around and about you barriers, that to your primitive tastes and ideas have seemed insurmountable." The people had forgotten "the vast strides that are being made by your sister states," and Tilghman argued that this "want of information, and I speak it respectfully, is manifested by many of you in the timidity you show in making investments in the stock of your company; a still more lamentable degree of it is seen among the thousands of your citizens who have not yet subscribed one dollar to the stock of the East Tennessee and Virginia R.R. Company."[36]

While traveling throughout upper East Tennessee surveying the possible routes for the railroad, Tilghman encountered many people interested in the project. He would ask, "Are you opposed to the Railroad? No sir, so far from it," was the answer, "only *convince* us that it will be of advantage to us as a community, and we will aid with our means to build it.—We have some money, an abundance of labor, granaries full of corn, smoke houses filled, timber unsurpassed in our woods, all shall be turned in to carry it through."[37] The problem seems to have been not insufficient liquid capital to subscribe shares but insufficient knowledge of the railroad's benefits. Citizens with the broader, more worldly perspective had to convince the more locally oriented residents that the railroad would improve the lives of all. Local speakers and newspaper writers worked tirelessly to educate the public during this critical early phase of railroad construction.

The benefits mentioned by railroad advocates may be classified into three categories. First, daily activities could be made more efficient by using railroads. Second, the railroad would bring new possibilities and profits to local residents. Finally, the railroad would catalyze large-scale societal transformations.[38] By comparing this railroad line with others, and by identifying what the other lines considered to be problems within the region, we may analyze these efforts at describing the benefits of a railroad in upper East Tennessee as they illuminate the view that some residents of Appalachia took of their situation.

East Tennesseans involved in mining, manufacturing, and shipping would all benefit from a railroad. Lloyd Tilghman felt that people underutilized iron ore in Carter and Johnson counties. "The want of an outlet to market has been the sole cause of the backwardness in the manufacture of even the roughest articles made from that ore," he explained. "The precarious and costly transportation by way of the rivers has, as it ever would have done but for this road, made the mere home market the measure of their product." With iron so plentiful—"whole mountains of this ore exist there"—the railroads would produce from this single item "an amount of freight annually equal to the combined freight of all other productions of any one county in East Tennessee."[39]

The construction of the railroad itself would directly support the local iron industry and would trigger a manufacturing boom. Tilghman singled out the ironworks in Bumpass Cove as being especially able to supply the company. It had water power "not only greater but more available than any other establishment in the U. States" and its "ore banks are capable of yielding 20,000,000 of Tons of Shot ore yielding 75 per cent, that is delivered a distance of two miles by water at the furnace mouth for fifty cents per Ton." Tilghman regretted that "the want of means alone will prevent these gentlemen from manufacturing our Iron" and concluded that "this is unquestionably the most valuable tract of land in E. Tennessee and deserves the patronage of this road."[40] Local iron, furthermore, would save the railroad companies thousands of dollars. "A Stockholder" calculated in the *Rail Road Journal* that local iron would cost $18.27 per ton less than iron from England or Pennsylvania, with a total savings of $200,970. The writer told the company's directors that with a policy of using local resources, "you would be, while building your respective roads, giving employment to hundreds of men and an impetus to manufacturing which when your roads were built would forever feed them."[41] "Thousands of men," according to another writer, "will be required to work the mines of coal, iron, copper, lead, plaster, and salt." Ideal local conditions would foster sheep raising and the spinning of both wool and cotton (which would be brought in by rail).

"Thus it may be seen that the various branches of mining and manufacturing, which must grow up on the line of the road, will afford profitable employment in every man, woman, and child in the country. Then the maintenance of these operatives will furnish a large home market for the products of the soil."[42]

Most obviously, the railroad cut the time and costs involved in transporting these goods to market. Moving one ton of dry goods the 200 miles from Abingdon to Lynchburg cost twenty dollars by carriage and would cost only seven dollars by rail. "For 2000 lbs. of domestics, sugar, coffee, queensware, hardware, &c., at present rates, . . . we pay $40. By railroad, the cost would be but $9.50." One person estimated that "merchants of Abingdon, no doubt, pay from $1500 to $2000 a year more for present rates of carriage than they would by Railroad transportation. . . . It is an improvement that every man in these mountains should make it a matter of conscience to push on."[43] Similarly, Tilghman calculated that East Tennessee now spent $0.55 per bushel for 225,000 bushels of salt each year. The railroad could deliver salt at $0.25 per bushel, for a yearly savings of $67,500 by the inhabitants of the region. "And thus it is that it operates," he concluded. "Access will be had to the best markets of the world for your produce at cheap rates and a quick return. Your annual expenditures for the comforts and luxuries of life, to say nothing of the necessaries, will come unburthened by these enormous charges that you are now paying and a total revolution take place in your agricultural and commercial condition."[44]

One of the most astonishing aspects of this "total revolution" involved the expected growth in tourism in the region. For a land that, according to the *Farmers' Journal,* emigrants had once deemed "unworthy of his notice," people would now "leave the warmer and less healthy parts of the Country and seek the salubrious climate and beautiful scenery of this mountain region."[45] Echoing David Deaderick's earlier prediction that people would be attracted by the mountains of upper East Tennessee, the members of the Wytheville Convention in Virginia foresaw a thriving tourist industry generated by local railroads.

When the line is connected between the mountains of Virginia and the Georgia roads, it will be little more than a day's ride from the warm climate of South Carolina, Georgia, and Alabama to the cool breezes of Washington, Sullivan, Wythe, and Montgomery. With this easy, cheap, and expeditious mode of conveyance, there will be a number of visitors sufficient to fill all your villages and every spot offering any inducements to persons seeking recreation or health. . . . A merchant may leave his desk in Charleston . . . and in 35 hours, traveling 20 miles per hour, he may be in Wytheville and return to Charleston almost before his absence is known. This wonderful facility of locomotion will make the mountains of Virginia the favorite summer retreat for an immense region of country.

Since many of these visitors "will purchase summer residences in the counties along this road,"[46] the members of the convention identified the dual nature of the railroad's effect on manufacturing and transportation; not only could the region's goods more easily reach distant markets, but with tourism and in-migration the markets would also come directly to the region.

The advantages brought on by the railroads extended into other areas as well. The railroads would not only increase the profits of existing businesses but would also create new opportunities for making money. Lloyd Tilghman assured the local residents that the East Tennessee and Virginia Rail Road would generate profits. He cited railroads in Massachusetts that yielded an annual interest of 8.25 percent and lines in New York that returned 11 percent in 1845, 11.6 percent in 1846, and 15 percent in 1847. The number of riders on eleven railroads he selected all showed huge increases, which also helped boost the net revenue for some railroads as much as 300 percent in five years. He wondered, "Can it be that there is any one in your community so sceptical upon this subject as to ask more conclusive proofs than are here placed before him of a handsome interest on any investment he may wish to make in the stock of any of the thousand miles of Railroad that are in progress in the United States?"[47] Tilghman guaranteed profit for the East Tennessee and Virginia Rail Road because it resembled, to use Landon C. Haynes's metaphor, "the neck of a great double Funnel which opening one mouth to the north and east draws in all the trade and travel from that direction and empties it at your western terminus, . . . [and] receives in return a vast supply from the currents flowing from the Georgia and Alabama roads, the Nashville and Chattanooga, Nashville and Memphis, and Tennessee and Georgia road." Since the railroad was the "link in the great channel of communication between the north and south," it was "the shortest, cheapest and most certain means by which merchandise can pass between the great Northern and Southern depots of commerce or passengers."[48]

The railroad could also make profits in the almost magical way that it could increase the value of the surrounding lands. Tilghman calculated that land worth ten dollars an acre before the railroad, paying two dollars of profit, could "with Rail Road transportation to reduce the cost of exportation and at the same time carry it to better markets," produce four dollars of profit, and "of course that acre would be worth just double, or twenty dollars per acre." To support such a theory he provided statistics culled from the South Carolina Rail Road comptroller's reports of 1830 and 1846. For example, lots shot up in value over the sixteen years in the districts of Barnwell (from $16,550 to $79,396), Richmond (from $787,824 to $1,234,565), and Edgefield (from $48,628 to $251,870).[49] Somewhat closer to home, one traveler along the East Tennessee and Georgia Rail Road wrote back to Jonesborough inviting skeptics to "ask the farmers the value of their lands before the Road was made and compare the value of land now. Lands that would not sell for $3 per acre are now commanding readily $10 per acre. This is no false pretense; it is so all along the line." The writer noted one farm along the line that had originally sold for $500 and had recently resold at a public auction for $1,850. "If the Rail road will increase the value of the lands through Georgia and that portion of Tennessee where it has already been made, does it not stand to reason that it must enhance the value of all the land through East Tennessee when that road is completed?"[50] Railroad advocates therefore enticed reluctant investors with the vision of profits to be made not only in business but also in doing nothing more than watching their stocks and lands rise in value.

The vision of a transformed society, however, presented the most startling (and perhaps most easily dismissed) benefit attributed to the railroad. According to the writer "X," locations that "once seemed to be cursed of . . . and deserted by man have been made flourishing places. Scenes, where once reigned a dreary solitude, broken only by the cries of birds of ill-omen and the savage howl of beasts of prey, now resound with the hum of a busy city engaged in all the various pursuits which make a nation rich, prosperous, and powerful."[51] Railroads civilized the wilderness and, by implication, the inhabitants. Wyndham Robertson, chairman of the Abingdon Rail Road convention, submitted a resolution proclaiming that "an easy and convenient means of intercourse among men, and of a ready interchange of the products of labor, if not the mainspring, is yet the indispensable condition of Human Progress and National Power, and of all the amelioration, social, moral, political, and material, that follow in their train." Considering all of the evidence before the convention, it felt "authorized to declare that in our opinion the value of the railroad is no more than that of the value of Light and Heat, of the Steamboat or Mariner's compass, open to question."[52] The railroad will "open out the hidden treasures of East Tennessee that have so long been buried for want of an outlet—and then will her citizens who have so long been bowed down, have all the facilities necessary to make them a happy and prosperous people."[53] As "X" put it so emphatically, "Influence of Railroads upon a people! Is commerce dead? they revive it. Is Agriculture dying? they restore it. Are Manufactures defunct? they bring them to life. In short, they stir up the spark of life . . . beneath the ribs of Death."[54]

These claims, like all of the others identifying advantages associated with the railroads, can be understood at several different levels. Most basically, the writers hoped to persuade others to subscribe to railroad stock. The points they chose to emphasize, however, reveal the values and qualities of the project they felt to be most important. They were attracted by promises of increased production, faster and easier communication with distant regions, and profits to be gained. They sought not only what they considered certain financial success but also the lifestyle made possible by such good fortune. Railroads, in the eyes of the Wytheville convention, "will enable every poor man to earn an ample support from the soil, or from the products of his own labor and skill, [and] will bring to his door all the necessaries, and many of the luxurys of life at a cost little over half what he now pays." With the savings, efficiencies, and added income produced by the railroad, the individual "can afford to pay good wages to others to work for him and no man in the country need be idle but by his own choice."[55] Who could resist so good a life? Certainly not the local leaders of the railroad movement, the company (as represented by Lloyd Tilghman, even though he was a New Yorker), or the other writers.

## PLANNING THE ROUTE

Speaking to the inhabitants of East Tennessee, and especially those who had not yet subscribed to the railroad, Lloyd Tilghman announced that "Nature has placed around and about you barriers, that to your primitive tastes and ideas have seemed insurmountable."[56] Precisely because the railroad interests sought efficiency and cheaper economic connections, they focused on the existing costs and difficulties inherent in doing business in the mountains. Yet for some reason the railroad company had great difficulty generating support for the project. Perhaps the arguments that were advanced failed to resonate with the people's concerns. While we may never know exactly why individuals did not subscribe to the railroad, the early financial troubles and sheer number of newspaper articles pleading for support indicate that the majority of upper East Tennessee residents were relatively unenthusiastic about it. Failing to see how precarious the situation was, one writer asked, "But where indeed is the use of discanting on this subject? we are all convinced already."[57] Clearly, many felt differently.

Some of the people's reluctance to subscribe may have reflected dissatisfaction over the proposed route of the East Tennessee and Virginia Rail Road. By September 1850, Lloyd Tilghman and his assistants had made 476 miles of experimental surveys.[58] Throughout these months, the newspapers discussed various perspectives on the principles that individuals felt should govern the selection of the route. Every consideration was colored by the characteristics of the physical environment and the distribution of the population within that setting. The single-mindedness of some individuals about the railroad's location alarmed Andrew Johnson in 1849. He believed that the emphasis on location, "if persisted in would produce division, and that division might result in defeat." He urged instead that the specific route be relegated to the

third priority, after building the railroad as a public good and en-
suring that both the state and private citizens subscribe to it. If the
location was determined "with an eye single to the public good . . .
[and] the cheapest and most practicable route," Johnson concluded, "those that are disappointed cannot defeat it, for it will
then be too late, and the public weal will be promoted regardless
of private interest."[59] Nonetheless, different groups persisted in
trying to influence the final path of the East Tennessee and Virginia Rail Road.

Even before any stock had been subscribed in the company,
some groups accused Jonesborough residents of trying to direct the
route through their own town. According to one writer, "We have
no hesitation in declaring that we are not so destitute of self-interest that we would not be particularly delighted to see a railroad
constructed directly through the town of Jonesborough, if it be
practicable to do so." But since the Board of Directors, elected by
the stockholders, had final responsibility for selecting the route,
this writer told his critics, "If it is regarded as a public calamity that
the road should pass through Jonesborough, we respectfully submit
that the best method of preventing it will be for the other counties
to take stock to the utmost of their ability and thus have a controlling vote in the selection of the Board."[60] One year later, the *Rail
Road Journal* answered accusations that "we cannot be sincere advocates of railroad construction unless those improvements should
be brought through Jonesborough, and therefore [the critics] conclude our paper was gotten up for no other purpose than to be the
medium through which the stockholders who must finally locate
our Rail Road may be induced to vote for that line of survey which
may pass through our town." The editors called such comments
"merely gratuitous" and "wide of the mark," for they had always
been in favor of "that route which will cost the least money to
construct . . . and that will afford the facilities of transportation to
the greatest number of the inhabitants of upper East Tennessee
and yield to the owners of stock in said Rail Road the greatest
amount of nett profits." They favored such a route, "be where it
may, either through Jonesborough or away from Jonesboro'."[61]

Several other writers addressed the issue of the route serving
"the greatest good to the greatest number." One issue of the *Rail
Road Journal* provides two views. "Selma" wrote, "If there is any

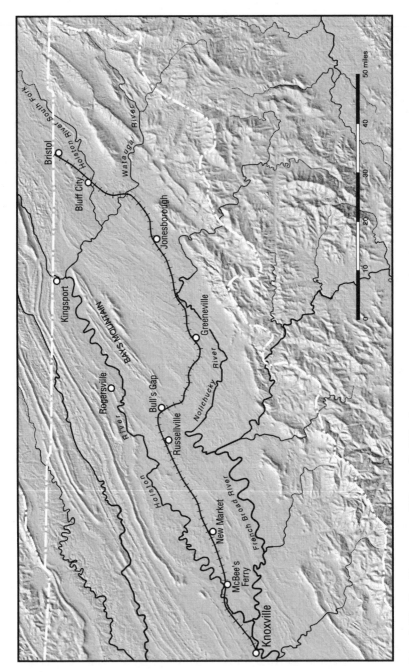

Map 6. The East Tennessee and Virginia Rail Road

benefit to be derived from holding stock in this road, it is but right that those stockholders living in its immediate vicinity should receive that benefit. . . . [They] may be considered as the representatives of the various interests of the several communities through which this road will pass." Furthermore, Selma assumed that most stockholders lived in the wealthier portions of the valleys stretching from the Virginia line to Knoxville. "It requires men of wealth and means to have any considerable quantity of stock, and the men who have accumulated any considerable quantity of property will be found to reside in the richer and more desirable portions of the country." The railroad would pass through these regions because roads are "invariably built so as to embrace the richest scope of country, and thereby secure the largest amount of transportation and travel." County roads "are not built through a barren country, leading by no-town, and connecting no-where and no-place. Who projected and had these roads built? The people living along their routes, because they were necessary to their interest and convenience." Selma had no doubt that the East Tennessee and Virginia Rail Road would incorporate the wealthy areas and communities. "They must have a road leading directly to market, or be within some reasonable distance of them. You cannot persuade them to locate a road in any other manner."[62]

The specific route in any one particular area, Selma argued, depended on the distribution of the stockholders and the features of the land. If the subscribers were spread evenly in a valley, the railroad must go through its center. Even if track mileage and construction costs could be saved by following a straighter line, such savings—"one, two, or three miles in the entire route"—would unjustly favor some residents and violate the principle that "the road is to be built so as to afford the 'greatest good to the greatest number.'"[63] Selma allowed exceptions to be made when one group already had access to some means of communication. "As for example, we on one side say that you, over there, have an excellent McAdamized turnpike, and through its means you have ready access to market. Should you not then, in justice, give us this Railroad more to ourselves, that we may also have a chance to get to market?" The situation seemed even clearer for those living near a river, for "it would be a matter of rank injustice" if they demanded "that a Railroad also should be built along the banks of the stream, and thus deprive others who live fifteen, twenty, or thirty miles to the right or left, and who as earnestly desire, and far more urgently need such a work of internal improvement." With this reasoning, Selma urged the company to follow its original charter and locate the road east of Bays Mountain and the Holston River and west of the Nolichucky.[64]

"A Stockholder" agreed that particular areas were important to the railroad, for "every improvement such as this contemplates local interests in its very inception, and were it not for the existence of interests, which are in some sense local, it would never have a being." Yet the company could not succumb to the wishes of every town that wanted the route to pass through it. While Selma believed that local subscribers deserved to have the route nearby, Stockholder urged the company to consider the interests of "the citizens of New York and San Francisco. Place a weight upon either one of the several links which compose a chain and will not the burden be felt at both ends? The Virginia and Tennessee Road is, or *may be*, a link in the 'Great Rail Way chain' that is to connect the two oceans which bear upon their broad bosoms the freights and fortunes of the civilized world." Unnecessary local costs and inefficiencies would create ripples affecting all parts of the globe. Problems arise, the writer argued, "whenever you veer off the true line to accommodate a town or purchase its good will. Now, how many burden cars, laden with gold dust, ivory, and silks from Japan, China, and California, or how many passenger trains crowded with denizens from the busy marts of commerce would it take by tonnage and fare, to pay for the town? How many years' expense of keeping up, added to the original cost of construction of *one* extra mile, would purchase the town and remove it to the road, if they *must* be united."[65]

Yet Stockholder carefully emphasized that the most direct route did not always win out over significant local interests. Those on the north side of the Holston, in Grainger and Hawkins Counties, had claimed that "that side of the river is the proper side for the location of a Railroad from the Virginia line . . . *because* it is the *shortest* and *cheapest*." But the writer argued that the north side of the Holston produced only 3 tons of iron, as compared to the 5,265 tons produced in the counties to the south and east. "On the *south* of 'the Railroad line' from Lynchburg to Knoxville," he con-

cluded, "lie *heavy* and *important* interests which should be looked
to in the location of your respective roads."[66] Considering both local interests and the most direct route, Lloyd Tilghman formulated
the final route of the railroad by the end of 1850.

Little argument arose over the placement of the route from
Knoxville to Bull's Gap, "there being no question as to the relative
merits," according to Tilghman, of the New Market Valley route as
opposed to any alternative. The difficult problem lay in determin-
ing the northeastern segment of the route. Tilghman and his assistants realized that "by far the most difficult portion of the country
to be examined was to be found between the Watauga, southern
fork of the Holston river, and the Virginia line." They surveyed
three routes, the northern, middle, and southern; the final decision was governed by the company's charter, which required that
"said road shall be located upon the shortest, cheapest, and most
practicable route, compatible with the interests of the people, and
the profits of the road." In deciding upon the southern route,
Tilghman in his report used several of the arguments raised by
Selma and Stockholder. Even though the northern route ran three
miles shorter than the southern one, "in estimating the two routes
as railroad lines, it is found that the equated distance by the
Southern route is even shorter than by the Northern or Middle."
Furthermore, the latter two routes were "hemmed in by heavy
ridges and confined closely to the experimental lines, and in some
cases to maintain the ruling grade and curvature, additional expense will be incurred."[67]

Two of the arguments could have been taken directly from the
Selma and Stockholder articles. When Tilghman asked, "What
position should the road have in order to secure the largest
amount of Freight and Passengers?" he first assumed that upper
East Tennessee was evenly settled, that natural resources were
equally distributed, and that a route down the middle of the region
would be the most equitable. He calculated that with the northern
route, 299 square miles lay north of the line, 1,382 square miles
south of it. For the middle route the ratio was 475 and 1,206
square miles; for the southern route, it was 751 and 930 square
miles. "Surely no one can question that the *Geographical* position
of the Southern route is such as more nearly to comply with one
object of the charter than either of the others." Tilghman went

further and acknowledged that equal distribution did not exist and that "seven-tenths of the wealth and population of the region lies south of the Middle route, taking acre for acre on both sides." Thus, "so far as resources are concerned upon which to depend at home for freight and passengers, there is no comparison between these several routes, and that the true position of the route for the E.T. & Va. R.R. is nearly upon the route designated as the Southern route."[68] Although the planners carefully debated the merits of the different routes, the options had few geographical differences. All focused on a relatively narrow section of upper East Tennessee and ignored the most mountainous portions of the region. Given the influence of this physiography, Tilghman would never have considered placing the route in those mountains. As was the case with the Indian trails and the early roads (see Chapter 2), the railroads followed the path of least resistance.

The engineers decided that the route should run from King's Meadow on the Virginia line (present-day Bristol) to the Holston River at Middletown (now Bluff City). The company would build one bridge 300 feet long over the Holston and another 200 feet long across the Watauga. The line would continue to the southwest and meet a depot in Jonesborough that would be located on the property of A.E. Jackson (who was a member of both the joint stock company and the Board of Directors).[69] Since Jackson lived on the outskirts of town, other residents petitioned the court to relocate the depot next to the courthouse. A group led by Thomas A.R. Nelson, J.F. Deaderick (both members of the joint stock company), and John Neff arranged to have the site of the depot changed, and eventually a 40 foot by 103 foot two-story brick railroad station was constructed.[70] The route continued to Greeneville, Bull's Gap, and then past New Market to Knoxville. Tilghman estimated the total cost for building the East Tennessee and Virginia Rail Road at just over $2 million, with the superstructure and equipment accounting for 60 percent of the total, and grading and masonry making up the rest.[71]

Samuel B. Cunningham, president of the company, broke ground for the railroad on 30 March 1851. Instead of beginning construction at one of the termini, which would have been delayed by work on the connecting railroads, the stockholders decided to start at McBee's Ferry, east of Knoxville.[72] By August, S.B.

Ferguson was supervising 115 workers "with a fine stock of horses, carts, &c."; according to this observer, "the work is finely executed as far as is done." Although the company had surmounted enough of its early financial problems to begin construction, it still teetered on the brink of bankruptcy. "We repeat and emphasize it to every Stockholder," wrote the observer, "that the point we have to fear is your neglect to pay up promptly! Think, we beg of you, what interests you are endangering by your delay. . . . the work stops, and damages to the contractor from the company would be enormous. What you have paid would be lost, your credit gone, not to be retrieved. No basis could be again laid for future hope and action." In 1849, the company had needed shares to be subscribed; now, "not more than one half, perhaps than one third of the amount for the last two calls have been paid in." The plea seemed desperate because, without such financial support, ruin, "certain, irretrievable, and shameful," would result.[73]

Such observations contrasted sharply with those of "Z" (whose article appeared on the same day in the same newspaper). "Z" believed that "there is no ground of discouragement, far less of despair; never in our judgement were the affairs of the company in a more prosperous condition." Stockholders in Jonesborough "are from time to time giving the most substantial and unequivocal evidence of their increasing confidence in the work by the payment of their entire stock in advance, not waiting to pay up in regular calls." "Z" felt optimistic in other areas as well. Whereas a *Greeneville Spy* editorial asserted that no state aid would be forthcoming as long as conditions were "cross and pile" with the railroad, "Z" felt that the contractor was "pushing ahead with full confidence and energy, and is adding almost every day to the number of his hands." Furthermore, "the E. Tennessee delegation will be ready and willing to grant the aid of the State to the work; while in Middle and West Tenn., the same liberal spirit, towards the work, we are informed prevails." The state will see that "we are in earnest about the work; that a large amount of private capital has been invested in the enterprize . . . and that the loan of her credit will ensure the completion of our road and not at all endanger or impair her credit."[74] At the national level, Andrew Johnson had already presented Congress with bills to aid in the construction of the railroad (and to improve the French Broad and

Holston Rivers) and with petitions from Washington County citizens for land grants to help the project.[75]

## THE EAST TENNESSEE AND VIRGINIA RAIL ROAD COMPLETED

By the end of 1851, three miles of the road had been graded and only $15,000 collected from subscriptions. The optimism of "Z" and others seemed to have been mistaken, but their prediction of state aid proved correct. On 15 January 1852, the legislature passed an act allowing for coupon bonds up to $300,000 to be issued for building the railroad's bridges. Before one-third of the bonds could be issued, however, the company had to have forty miles under contract, construction had to be underway, and subscriptions outside the joint stock company had to be sufficient to cover grading and installing culverts. The state government also passed a general act to aid railroads for $8,000 for each mile of road constructed, with the bonds maturing in forty years.[76] The state funding probably triggered renewed interest and confidence in the company. Washington County itself, for example, decided to subscribe. The county court, by an 11 to 8 vote, decided to hold an election "to ascertain if the people of Washington County are willing that the County Court issue bonds of the said County to the East Tennessee & Virginia Railroad Company, to run not less than thirty or more than forty years, for $50,000." On 14 August 1852, the voters decided by a 783 to 271 margin to subscribe.[77] Similarly, Jefferson County citizens subscribed $50,000 of stock in 1853.[78] In November 1854, the joint stock company completed their efforts to find purchasers for the stock in which it had invested in 1849, with conditions "fully & fairly met as pr. agreement with the Board."[79] By 1855, the state had not only invested over two million dollars in internal improvement companies in all parts of Tennessee but had also in particular issued bonds totaling $569,000 for the East Tennessee and Virginia Rail Road.[80]

Such funding, from both the state government and local interests, allowed construction to progress steadily. During the summer of 1855 workers laid track from Knoxville to McBee's Ferry.[81] At the end of October, Samuel B. Cunningham reported to Andrew Johnson that the company was "now ready to commence putting down the Iron rails on that portion of road, Commencing at McBees Ferry, at the termination of the . . . section from Knoxville & extending ten miles East. The Company have in like manner graded, bridged, & ready to put down the necessary timbers for the reception of rails on a second ten miles in connection with the former . . . & terminating near Panther Spring." Four months later, Cunningham wrote again with the news that "our road is now open to N. Market [24 miles from Knoxville] & doing well. We shall make no delay in pushing it immediately to Russelville & to Greenville, as fast as the grading can be let out safely."[82] Railroad construction extended to Russellville, almost fifty miles east of Knoxville, in July 1856, and at the celebration, according to one newspaper, "the people were counted by the acre."[83] After reaching this goal, however, the company stopped laying track and worked instead on grading more of the route. After the East Tennessee and Georgia Railroad had been completed in 1855, rails could be supplied easily at the Knoxville end of the route. With the completion of the Virginia and Tennessee Railroad to Bristol in the fall of 1856, track could best be laid by obtaining rails from the east and setting them down first at the Virginia line and then moving south.[84]

The company resumed laying track in 1857; by June, a total of seventy-eight miles had been laid. Trains ran over two segments, from the Virginia line at Bristol for twenty miles to the west side of the Holston River, and from Bull's Gap southwest to Knoxville fifty-eight miles away. The company ran a stage line between these two sections that, although inconvenient, allowed passengers and merchandise to flow in both directions.[85] Construction on the remaining fifty-two miles continued apace, funded in part by state bonds that now totaled nearly $1.5 million and in part by individuals like Andrew Johnson himself, who owned at least $2,000 of company bonds by 1858.[86] By the end of March 1858, thirty-four more miles had been completed, and trains called at Greeneville. The last of the grading was completed about six weeks later. On 14 May 1858, Samuel B. Cunningham, who had first broken the ground seven years earlier, drove in the last spike of the East Tennessee and Virginia Rail Road.[87] The celebration at Greeneville in June involved "men, women, and children by the thousand; so that by 10 o'clock it was very evident . . . throughout

Fig. 10. Knoxville, 1859. Courtesy of the McClung Historical Collection, Knox County Public Library, Knoxville.

the county that a *great time* was to come off at Greeneville." The
food was spread upon tables "together being about 850 yards in
length . . . , [and] it required some *seven* or *eight* thousand feet of
lumber for the surface of the tables."[88]

After the introductory remarks and the presentation of a ban-
ner to the railroad's president and board of directors, a series of
speeches praised the company's accomplishments, noted the obstacles that had been surmounted, and looked toward a bright future. The celebration provided a final opportunity to reiterate
some of the arguments that had been made in years past. Colonel
R.G. Payne recalled his early visits to East Tennessee, when "he
thought sometimes we had more sharp rocks and uneven surface
in our roads than could be found in any other civilized country on
the face of the earth. For he had almost concluded his very life
would be jolted out of him when riding in stage coaches—so
called."[89] Many speakers echoed John McGaughey's sentiments,
expressed as the last spike was driven: "And our fellow citizens in
upper East Tennessee, after a bondage of 88 years since the germ of
a civil community was first planted upon the banks of the beautiful Watauga, have comparatively speaking, crossed the Jordan to
till the land that can now be made to flow with milk and honey."[90]
The celebration proved to be a great success, and the news quickly
reached all parts of the state. Andrew Johnson wrote to his son
Robert, "I see from the Nashvill union that the Greenevill dinner
went off very well which I was glad to he[a]r—For I had been lead
to think that it would be a failure—I hope that you [and] Charles
contributed your full part in the matte[r] and that you done [it]
willingly."[91]

Upper East Tennessee residents had contributed enough that
by November 1858 the railroad could boast of two engines, six
passenger coaches, eight second-class coaches, four baggage and
mail cars, fifty-five boxcars, thirty-five flatcars, and five dirt cars.
In the previous year, passenger ticket receipts came to $2,723; ex-
ports included over 3.1 million pounds of wheat, 800,000 pounds
of flour, and nearly 180,000 pounds of bacon; and imports from the
east included 180,000 pounds of dry goods, 350,000 pounds of groceries, 48,000 pounds of tobacco, and 11,000 pounds of machinery. For these six months, the railroad had exported a total of
2,184 tons and imported 457 tons of goods. Even when we double

these figures for a twelve-month period, the railroad fell well short of predictions that had been made more than twenty-five years earlier.[92] Nevertheless, many agreed with the federal government when it considered railroads a general benefit "in securing to the producer very nearly the prices of the Atlantic markets, which is greatly in advance of what could have been had on his farm . . . [and] by thus enabling the producer to dispose of his products at the best prices at all times, and to increase rapidly both the settlement and the annual production of the interior States."[93] These effects can be seen by comparing the average price per bushel of corn in Knoxville to prices in national markets. As long as ready access to consumers outside the region was lacking, corn prices in Knoxville ($0.25 in 1840, $0.39 in 1850) were clearly lower than those in either New Orleans ($0.42 in 1840, $0.66 in 1850) or Philadelphia ($0.52 in 1840, $0.63 in 1850). But once the region had been connected to the railroad system, prices in Knoxville in 1859 ($0.78) were comparable with those in New Orleans ($0.79) and Philadelphia ($0.87).[94] Agricultural surpluses could reach distant markets without piling up in Knoxville and depressing prices. Upper East Tennessee was now integrated into national markets, for as Lloyd Tilghman predicted, the railroad formed "one link of the Iron chain, the visible sign of the invisible bonds of commercial interest which must strike their roots into the hearts of the North and South, and strengthen the fastenings that will ever keep the fabric of our Union together."[95] The Knoxville *Register*, writing just before the route's completion, claimed that the railroad formed "not merely the union of Knoxville with Bristol, but the binding together of the North and South with a bond indissoluble."[96] North and South, of course, came apart just as upper East Tennessee strengthened its connections with both regions.

## The Railroad and Self-Perceptions

The construction of the East Tennessee and Virginia Rail Road, with all of the promotion, the repeated calls for support, and the repetitious articles trumpeting the railroad's benefits, gives us one way to trace the origins of the characterizations of Appalachian Mountain residents. Those holding the broader, outward-looking perspective wrote articles and editorials promoting the railroad and depicting nonsupporters—those with inward-oriented views—as being apathetic toward, or even actively against, the qualities of connectedness embodied by the railroad. Within this one indisputably mountainous region, individuals with a regional and national outlook blamed those with a local perspective for ignoring the opportunity to transcend environmental and geographical conditions.

Consider the writer "C," who lamented the lack of support for the railroad but thought it futile to print more facts, because "we could multiply them without number but they would not be read, or if read many would prefer living in barbarism forever to putting forth one animated effort to secure them." The railroad supporters saw themselves as an island of enlightenment in a sea of ignorance. "Were it not for so many noble exceptions of self-sacrificing spirits to be found, who would not abandon the enterprise? Let us not then be driven away by the stupidity and selfishness we are yet to meet."[97] While the editors of the *Rail Road Journal and Family Visitor* agreed with "Z" that the railroad construction was not all "cross and pile," neither was it progressing without problems. Although the work was "not harder than most other employments" and "all was peace and plenty," the editors did report "a few malcontents who perhaps had never in their lives remained six months at regular labor." They also admitted that "a few wished to leave before their month was up, and demanded payment, but it being contrary to the custom of the contractor to receive hands for less than one month, they sued him for settlement, which he resisted very properly." The lesson the editors drew from this incident reveals their opinion of some of the workers: "Such cases are necessary on every road where *such* hands will be found, in order to teach the public the necessity of abiding by some regulations."[98] In this situation, certain upper East Tennessee residents depicted some of their neighbors as shiftless workers, unaccustomed to steady labor and the integrity of a contract.

The terrain set the stage for other images. In the general call for railroads, residents of the most mountainous regions had no chance of being located on the route. With the completion of the line, these people still found it difficult to transport their goods to the tracks. Physical conditions played a central role in shaping the very society that railroad advocates hoped to change. From its inception, the railroad movement expressed a paradoxical view of the land as both generous and miserly. "X" wrote that the "free-man of East Tennessee, as he looks forth on the towering moun-tains which surround him, on the rushing and crystal streams that gush out from their bases and wind along through valleys of the most exuberant fertility, might re-echo the exclamation in still stronger language, and with far deeper tones of patriotic warmth." Yet this land has been, "for ages, shut up from all intercourse with other countries, her immense mineral, manufacturing, and agri-cultural resources undeveloped, and the latent energies of her people compressed by a cordon of mountains on all sides that would have daunted Hannibal himself to overcome." The people could blame nature, but the solution lay in their hands. "We *have* fertile fields; the work shop of the wholesale manufacturer *is not* busy, and the reason of it is, we have not easy communication from place to place."[99] Those who failed to support the railroad would be doomed to the conditions imposed by such an environ-ment. Lloyd Tilghman saw similar environmental conditions at work deadening the region's productive impulses. With early transportation limited by the mountains and river obstructions, "your whole agricultural interest is prostrated and with it every branch of trade in your country." Tilghman concluded, "where there is no inducement to labor, you must not expect people to work."[100]

The proponents of the railroad viewed their own situation and their neighbors in such terms. In their minds the railroad offered revolutionary changes, but people who did not support the con-struction of the East Tennessee and Virginia Rail Road either did not want or failed to understand the improvements that were pos-sible. Perhaps the railroad advocates began to form the idea that even while they sought connections with the rest of the country, others sought, or could not escape from, relative isolation. Within the community of upper East Tennessee, two ways of seeing the world had come into conflict. The railroad supporters, after a long struggle with their unsupportive neighbors, finally overcame the human and geographic limitations of the region and established better communications and economic ties with the rest of the United States. Society in upper East Tennessee would now im-prove, despite the resistance of fellow inhabitants who failed to see the benefits of the railroad. Perhaps new attitudes toward locally oriented neighbors, attitudes that would come to be seen as stereotypes of Appalachian Mountain people, began to form in their minds.

CHAPTER SIX

# The Creation of Popular
# Appalachian Images

THE DOCUMENTARY RECORD clearly indicates the motivations and actions taken by the supporters of the railroad movement. The letters, reports, speeches, and newspaper writings of railroad advocates like Lloyd Tilghman, "Selma," and Samuel B. Cunningham allow us to weigh their opinions and judge the extent of their connections to others. That same documentary record, however, provides only an indirect view of people who did not support the railroad. For a better sense of the outlook and connections of the more locally oriented individuals who lived away from the railroad line—in places like Sams, Rice, and Higgins Creeks—we must turn again to a traveler's account. Like François André Michaux and Francis Asbury half a century earlier, David Hunter Strother explored the highest peaks and most remote areas of upper East Tennessee and northwest North Carolina. His account presents a picture of the mountaineers at midcentury that balances the image presented by the railroad advocates. The account also differs in substantial ways from the images created by local color writers a generation later, images that readers and critics alike commonly accepted as realistic. The most popular of these novelists, Mary Noailles Murfree, never visited the most extreme mountain areas of southern Appalachia that provided the setting for her stories. Instead, she learned about the mountaineers by talking with the residents of the main towns in the larger valleys, like the railroad promoters in Jonesborough who described the "backward" nonsupporters living in the outlying areas. To return to the metaphor of running water, Murfree waded in the mainstream of settlement but remained separate from the rivulets. Had she followed Strother's route, the subsequent image of Appalachia might have been quite different.

## A Remote Mountain Society Observed

David Hunter Strother, a Virginian born in 1816, began contributing stories and drawings to *Harper's New Monthly Magazine* in 1853. He published a total of fifty-five articles over the next quarter century and in the process helped make *Harper's* one of the most popular magazines in the United States. Often using the pseudonym "Porte Crayon," Strother quickly became the magazine's most highly paid contributor and one of the most financially successful writers in the antebellum South.[1] Strother toured the South with his wife and daughter during the winter and spring of 1857 and then made a brief excursion into New England. He published accounts of his travels as "A Winter in the South" and "A Summer in New England," stories that Cecil D. Eby, Jr., describes as "fictionalized narratives, inasmuch as they contain characters— Virginians, of course—through whose eyes the respective areas are seen." On the whole, however, the locations and minor details in the stories lead one to believe that the accounts were authentic. For example, Strother mentions "one Davy Grier, who went mad for love, fled from society, and lived a hermit on the side of this mountain [Bald Mountain]," clearly the same David Greer mentioned in Chapter 4. Eby likewise concludes that "Strother played a significant part in depicting native scenes and people with realism, skill, and understanding."[2]

Strother created in "A Winter in the South" a family belonging to the Virginia gentry to represent his own family's travels from Virginia to New Orleans in 1857. The party included Squire Anthony Broadacre, his wife, his two daughters, his niece, and Robert Larkin, a family friend who, as the only one of the travelers in the story who carried a sketch pad and asked individuals to pose for him, represents the writer-artist Strother himself. Of the many drawings that illustrated the story, several "were prepared by an assistant, David English Henderson, an artist from Jefferson County, who relieved Strother of the tedious landscape and architectural sketches and gave him more time for caricature."[3] The illustrations,

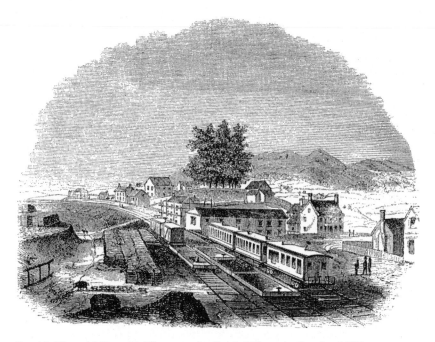

Fig. 11. "Bristol." From "A Winter in the South," *Harper's*, October 1857.

combined with Strother's written descriptions, provide valuable insights into the mountain inhabitants' society and their connections both within and beyond upper East Tennessee.

The Broadacre party reached Tennessee by way of the Virginia and Tennessee Rail Road. Bristol contained "straggling railway tracks, trains of empty and loaded cars, engines puffing and fuming, vast piles of wood, machine-shops, and taverns. There are warehouses full of wheat and corn, great herds of grunting unambitious swine, about to travel in the cars for the first time in their lives." They also noticed "crowds of busy men drinking 'bald-face' and chewing tobacco, speculators in land and pork, insolent stage drivers, gaping country folks, babbling politicians, [and] careless negroes." Two days later the party arrived in Jonesborough, which they described as "generally satisfactory. It had an old-fashioned, substantial air, as if the people who built it intended to live there for the rest of their days. The town is snugly and modestly nestled in a deep hollow, while the adjacent hills are crowned with neat private residences, and several academies of some architectural pretension." At this point the party divided. The women, "who found themselves in comfortable quarters, should remain where they were. To this they the more readily consented as they had a deal of sewing on hand wherewith to occupy their time, and" speaking to the economic connections the region had established, "Jonesborough furnished greater facilities for shopping than they had expected in so remote a locality."[4] The men, on the other hand, decided to explore the nearby mountains; their account provides one picture of society in the most remote portions of the region.

Mr. Jones, a local man, offered to guide the Squire and Larkin to the Roan, Black, and Bald Mountains on the border between Tennessee and North Carolina. Jones was "a tall man, and slender withal, with a keen black eye and dark beard, clothed, externally, in a slouched hat and blanket cloak, which reached nearly to his feet." They encountered few obstacles while traveling, except "the snaky laurel, whose dense evergreen masses often-times obstructed the road." One resident, Grey Briggs, welcomed the travelers to his cabin at the base of Roan Mountain. "The women went to prepare beds and supper forthwith, while the strangers readily accepted the place of honor in front of the wide-mouthed, roaring chimney. In the course of time both horses and riders were fed and made comfortable, and the mountaineer's household gathered around the fire, discoursing of the Roan [Mountain], the corn crops, and the weather."[5]

David Hunter Strother describes such hospitality in more detail when the travelers meet Tom Wilson, who lived at the base of Mount Mitchell on a path "half lost among thickets of dogwood and laurel." When asked if he could guide them to the summit, Wilson mused, "Well, I hain't no might much to do no time; so I s'pose I ken go." He proved to be an expert guide, leading the men on narrow paths carved out of the mountainside and over countless streams. The party became intensely hungry at the top of the mountain, and one member proclaimed, "There's one thing can save us, and I've made up my mind to it. . . . There's Tom Wilson's yaller dog; he's young and fat, and by blood! if we can do no better." But Wilson saved his pet when he recalled "a cabin a little below here, p'raps about a quarter, put up for travelers that come here in the summer to see the sun rise. Now, there might be something thar a

Fig. 12. "Jonesborough." From "A Winter in the South," *Harper's*, October 1857.

Fig. 13. "Distant View of the Roane." From "A Winter in the South," *Harper's*, November 1857.

man could eat." Indeed, the corn and salted bran that Wilson found blunted the travelers' hunger enough to get them back to his cabin by nightfall, where his wife provided a feast for the guests. Strother does not go into "what buckwheat cakes and biscuits, what pork and fried chicken, what stewed pumpkins and cabbage, disappeared from the groaning board, nor . . . the cups of milk, coffee, and persimmon beer that were swallowed during the meal." Afterward, "Mrs. Wilson declared it did her good to see 'em eat—in fact it did every body good; and then, when stuffed until they were nearly blind, and set before the fire to dry, it was a treat to hear the jokes and stories of the day's adventures."[6] The story describes not only the mountaineers' hospitality and openness to strangers but also the abundance of food. The story also suggests that the mountain residents had steady contact with the outside world, for visitors came to the top of Roan Mountain frequently enough for a special cabin to be built there.

Fig. 14. "Tom Wilson." From "A Winter in the South," *Harper's*, November 1857.

The following day the travelers reached the top of Bald Mountain, but they lost their way during the descent. Unfamiliar with the maze of paths and confused by the dense thickets, "they started down the steep mountain side, dodging the limbs of the dwarf oaks, and with whip and rein warily urging their horses over the loose and moss-covered rocks." As night fell, the men forced their way through "deep-washed gullies half filled with ice and snow," although "impenetrable abattis of fallen timber effectually closed the passages between the ravines." Eventually, "a steep stair-way of loose, angular rocks, rendered more slippery and dangerous by a crust of snow, was the only road." Once they managed this descent of the Tumbling Fork, the party "stood upon the brink of a precipice, over which poured a mountain torrent with a clear leap of fifty feet." The travelers abandoned their horses and continued so arduous a trek down the mountain that "it would be a task far beyond the powers of our unskillful pen to describe that trying and hazardous tramp." At length they came to the cabin of a mountaineer named Chandler, and he directed the travelers to see Kan Foster, for "if there's a man in these mountains that can save your horses that man is Kan Foster."[7]

Of medium height and a "keen and wiry build," Kan Foster in his movements suggested "promptness, activity, and resolution in the highest degree. His features, though weather-beaten, were regularly handsome, partly covered with a short black and grizzled beard, and his black eye glittered like a hawk's. His dress consisted of a nondescript hat and a well-worn suit of tawny-colored mountain jeans, made hunting-shirt fashion, and girt about the waist with a leathern belt which bore his knife-sheath." When the travelers arrived at the cabin, he and his wife were in the midst of slaughtering a hog. "At the first signal whoop he sprung to his feet, took the knife out of his mouth, and shouted the welcome 'Come in!' . . . There was a free, frank, hearty hospitality, even in the expression of his face, that warmed like the glow of his blazing chimney." Such hospitality extended to the travelers. "'Friends,' said the mountaineer, 'I rejoice that fortune has led you to the door of my poor cabin. You are at home; the house and all that is in it is at your service.'"[8]

Strother depicted Foster's children and his wife's domestic skills in similarly glowing terms. The children were "endowed with singular beauty," but one in particular was as "slender and graceful as the spotted fawn, with a face whose regular beauty vied with the Greek ideal."[9] The Squire noted that although this family lived far in the mountains, it had "all the graces of civilization." He asked Larkin:

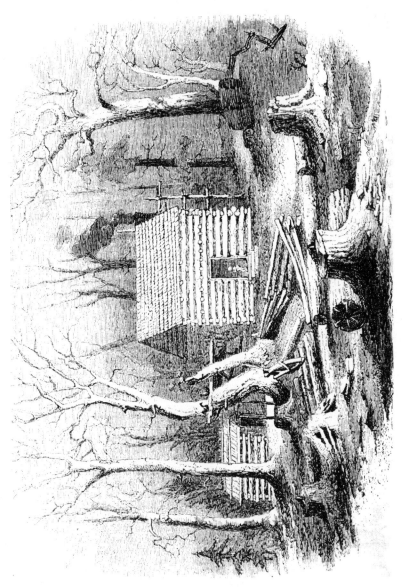

Fig. 15. "Tom Wilson's Cabin." From "A Winter in the South," *Harper's*, November 1857.

Fig. 16. "Descending the Tumbling Fork." From "A Winter in the South,"
*Harper's*, January 1858.

Fig. 17. "Kan Foster." From "A Winter in the South," *Harper's*, January 1858.

Have you observed our good hostess here, how she hurries to
and fro, . . . how she bakes, boils, and stews—striving, with
all grace and cheerfulness, to do honor to her husband's
guests? Have you marked how tidy she keeps her handsome
brood—all clad in home-made of her own weaving, fash-

ioned and patched with her own hand? Or the elder daughter, dilligent and meek, how smilingly she skips to do her mother's bidding . . . Those who have learned so well to perform the duties of daughter, wife, and mother, I say, have been well educated, whether their dwelling is the brownstone palace that rears its carved front on the Fifth Avenue, or the mud-chinked cottage that nestles under the magnificent shadow of the Black Dome.[10]

In certain respects, then, we see that the mountain people could be as "civilized" as anyone in America.

The Fosters also exhibited their geographic and economic connections with other mountain residents. "As the neighbors dropped in one after another, the story of the lost horses was repeated over and over, and the subject discussed in all its bearings." Furthermore, the family operated a mill and "thither came the neighbors from far and near—some mounted and some on foot—bringing their scanty grists tied up in sacks or pillow-cases, and lounging about the premises until the corn was ground." Such connectedness was limited in other respects, however, because the residents seemed naive about some aspects of American society. For example, the mountaineers all marveled at Larkin's sketches "as though he were some great necromancer, performing mysterious feats far beyond the comprehension of the world at large." When the travelers said they had come to see the highest mountains in the United States, one of the neighbors replied, "I've heard there was another mountain higher than these here, somewhar in Kaintuck, or p'raps New York, or some furrin place. My darter read it to me outen a book. It was a fire mountain, and they called it Mount Vesy-vyous." Finally, Larkin acknowledged the family's local orientation when he predicted that the Foster girls would get courted by a local boy and would remain in the region. "In a year or two she will go to school, and pick up a little beau. . . . The growing friendship will be nourished by presents of bird-eggs and pet squirrels; and when they grow up he will woo her with gay ribbons and store-goods from Jonesborough. Then, of course, they'll get married—build a cabin, hardly after the pattern of this one, and live as their fathers have done."[11] The Fosters and their neighbors lived within the community of upper East Tennessee

Fig. 18. "Mary Foster." From "A Winter in the South," *Harper's*, January 1858.

but remained largely separate from people living in Jonesborough and other towns. If we see these mountaineers as the small "rivulets" of settlement, clearly the travelers did not perceive a steady flow into the mainstream of the more open valleys. Although books, schooling, and store-bought goods existed in the Bald

Mountain region, daily life ran its course and could be expected to continue within a local setting.

When Kan Foster and his son returned with the horses after "seven mortal hours with axe and hatchet," the family and neighbors joined in "loud congratulations and well-merited compliments that were showered upon him from all sides." The travelers thanked the Fosters profusely, mounted their horses, and rode back toward town. They crossed the "deep and rocky fords of Indian Creek" and spent one night with Squire Irving at his mansion "on the banks of the 'Chucky' [Nolichucky]." They rejoined the women in Jonesborough and left the next day for points farther south. The entire party was impressed with the town, "hoping, as they bade adieu to Jonesborough, that they had left behind as agreeable impressions as they carried with them." Similarly, they saw the whole region in a favorable light. "East Tennessee is one of the most delightful countries in the world. Possessing a genial climate, a fertile soil, abounding in all those natural resources whose development and use constitute the true wealth of a state, her virgin forests, lovely rivers, and majestic mountains, offer, at the same time, a rich and varied feast to the romantic tourist."[12] Such generalities about the physical environment and its natural resources could easily be found in published works by the mid-nineteenth century. Strother's detailed observations of mountain society, however, provide a much rarer look at one of the most remote portions of Appalachia.

## MARY NOAILLES MURFREE

Such excursions and observations did not always form the basis of the local color movement that dominated American literature from 1870 to 1900. This writing shaped popular notions of Appalachia, but it did not grow out of the kind of personal observations that informed David Hunter Strother. Local color writing, according to Henry Shapiro, "emerged as a response to the existence of a substantial market for descriptive pieces which the readers of the new middle-class monthlies would find interesting." Editors considered the most interesting topics to be ones that provided "a perception of the peculiarity of life in the 'little corners' of America."[13] Many writers wrote such pieces, including Bret Harte and Mark Twain on the west, Sarah Orne Jewett on rural Maine, George Washington Cable on New Orleans, and Joel Chandler Harris on Georgia.[14] Will Wallace Harney, Appalachia's first local colorist, published "A Strange Land and Peculiar People" in *Lippincott's Magazine* in 1873 but was soon eclipsed by Mary Noailles Murfree as the most popular writer of the southern mountains. She published a number of stories in *Atlantic Monthly* from 1878 to 1884 under the pseudonym Charles Egbert Craddock; these were collected into a single volume in 1884, *In the Tennessee Mountains*, which went through seventeen editions in two years and seven more by 1922.[15]

Shapiro argues that the local colorists achieved popularity by convincing the public that the mountain society in their stories did indeed exist. "If the otherness of Appalachia were 'real,' it would form an appropriate subject for description and explication, or the donnée of fiction. It should come as no surprise, then, that the sense of wonder which characterized the earliest sketches of Appalachia rapidly gave way before assertions that the southern mountain region really was a strange land inhabited by a peculiar people." Murfree led the way. "Indeed, the first writer to take for granted the fact of Appalachian otherness, Mary Noailles Murfree, has generally (albeit incorrectly) been credited with the literary 'discovery' of the mountains."[16] Similarly, Durwood Dunn argues that readers and critics alike believed that Murfree "accurately preserved a rare snapshot of Tennessee mountain community before modern industrialism destroyed all such enclaves of local culture."[17] Murfree believed that her stories depicted mountain life truthfully. She told her editors that the stories composing *In the Tennessee Mountains* "all treat of the same subject and locality— the mountaineer and mountains of East Tennessee, and apart from any value which they may possess as fiction they give together a pretty accurate picture of the various phases of life among an interesting, primitive, and little known people in a wild and secluded region."[18] The editors agreed, eventually writing back that the company was "so interested in the freshness of your material and so impressed by your apparent fidelity in the rendering of mountain life that we should like to try the fortune of such a volume."[19] The public was similarly convinced, for northern churches gave home missionaries copies of *In the Tennessee Mountains* to use "as a

Fig. 19. Mary Noailles Murfree. Notman Photo Co., Boston, ca. 1885. Courtesy of the Tennessee State Library and Archives, Nashville.

first mission-study text for those who wished to understand conditions in the region."[20]

Murfree's presentation of the mountain residents and their society can be only briefly summarized here, but her portrayal differs from that of "A Winter in the South" in ways that quickly become apparent. Murfree's mountaineers talk in such a strong dialect that it remains a modern literary convention. One story begins with a mountaineer proclaiming: "I hev hearn tell ez how them thar boys rides thar horses over hyar ter the Settlemint nigh on ter every night in the week ter play kyerds,—'Old Sledge' they calls it; an' thar goin's-on air jes' scandalous,—jes' a-drinkin' of apple-jack, an' a-bettin' of thar money." Strother's mountaineers sometimes speak in dialect; recall that one of Kan Foster's neighbors said, "I've heard there was another mountain higher than these here, somewhar in Kaintuck, or p'raps New York, or some furrin place. My darter read it to me outen a book." In general, however,

Murfree's characters speak in a far more extreme dialect than that spoken by Strother's characters. Murfree and Strother provide similar physical descriptions of the people. The men are generally pictured as tall and lanky, and the women, especially Murfree's young heroines, are "lithe," with the "delicately transparent complexion often seen among the women of these mountains." The writers differ, however, when they speak of the inhabitants' temperament. For Murfree, the mountaineer often had "an expression of settled melancholy on his face . . . , reflected, perhaps, from the indefinable tinge of sadness that rests upon the Alleghany wilds, that hovers about the purpling mountain-tops, that broods over the silent woods, that sounds in the voice of the singing waters." Furthermore, "his listless manner was that of stolidity, not of a studied calm; his brown jeans suit was old and worn and patched; his hat, which had seen many a drenching winter rain and scorching summer sun, had acquired sundry drooping curves undreamed of in its maker's philosophy."[21] While Kan Foster also wore a "well-worn suit of tawny-colored mountain jeans," Strother endows him with energy and action.

To Murfree, the mountain residents' social world seems as forlorn as the individual's clothes. She often speaks of "the vague, hazy reverie which is the habitual mental atmosphere of the quiescent mountaineer." Yet characters who are nonresidents frequently see much to admire: "Their standard of morality and respectability could not be questioned; there had never been a man or a woman of the humble name who had given the others cause for shame; they had lived in this house on their own land for a hundred years; they neither stole nor choused; they paid as they went, and asked no favors; they took no alms,—nay, they gave of their little! As to the artificial distinctions of money and education,—what do the ignorant mountaineers care about money and education!" Rufus Chadd had freed himself from such educational limitations to become a lawyer in a neighboring valley, but he could reflect on "his humble home on the slope of Big Injun Mounting. There he had lived seventeen years in ignorance of the alphabet; he was the first of his name who could write it. From an almost primitive state he had overtaken the civilization of Ephesus and Colbury,—no great achievement, it might seem to a sophisticated imagination; but the mountains were a hundred years behind the progress of those centres." Some mountaineers were so isolated that "to its simple denizens the world beyond was a foreign world, full of strange habitudes and alien complications." Given such conditions, readers probably were not surprised that the men in Murfree's stories spent their days feuding, drinking, and traveling through the woods while the women were spinning and weaving clothes.[22]

Some of the more "uncivilized" characteristics appear in "A Winter in the South." "Why Mr. B. is dragging us to and from through this rocky, half-civilized country," Mrs. Broadacre wondered, "I can not imagine." She was appalled at some of the Squire's table manners, but she wrote, "I am consoled here with the idea that the people won't observe these peculiarities, for they dine without napkins or finger-bowls, and use two-pronged forks with one prong broken off."[23] Mrs. Broadacre, however, applied her comments to the townspeople rather than the mountain residents. The Squire and Robert Larkin did meet individuals that Murfree would describe as "uncivilized," especially distillers and horse thieves, but they describe Kan Foster as living in anything but a "vague, hazy reverie" with an "expression of sad melancholy on his face" and a "listless manner." In short, elements from the two writers' descriptions do match, but Murfree generally depicts the mountaineers in more extreme terms than does Strother.

## THE BASIS FOR MURFREE'S VISION

Murfree developed her image of the mountaineers, her "pretty accurate picture," from her memories of summers spent from the ages of six to twenty-one at the mountain resort of Beersheba Springs. Located 100 miles east of the family home in Murfreesboro, Beersheba Springs served as "the resort of wealth, of fashion and beauty, of Southern family who rode from their distant plantations in luxuriously appointed carriages drawn by splendid blooded horses."[24] From 1856 to 1870, Mary Noailles Murfree spent every May through October in the company of such society. In the process, she met local residents who came into the town. Her sister Fanny remembered occasions when "sad-faced, pallid mountain women in calico or homespun dresses and drooping sun bonnets would come into the big wide hall, and seat themselves in a row on sofas against the wall, or in the swaying cane rockers." As Mary played the piano and sang, "gaunt men slid in silently, and effaced themselves against the wall." After an hour, "they would at some hiatus silently stroll out."[25] At other times, "they would linger for a little conversation with Miss Murfree . . . , [where t]hey willingly expressed their own customs and possessions." The two sisters sometimes left the immediate town and went "foraging among the mountain homes for butter and eggs, chickens, fresh fruits and vegetables, for their table. In this way they met and talked with the women of the region and saw the interiors of their bare little homes."[26]

Such childhood and early adult memories of an easily accessible mountain area formed the basis of Murfree's descriptions of the more remote regions. She wrote to her editor, "I was early familiar with their primitive customs, dialect, and peculiar views of life, for I used to spend much time in the mountains long before I knew of the existence of such a thing as 'literary material'; since then, of course, they have been doubly suggestive."[27] She wrote almost all of her stories while living in Middle Tennessee, and except on one occasion she never again visited the location of her stories. In the fall of 1885, Murfree spent two months in Maryville in the company of mountaineers "more rugged and more independent than those she had known near Beersheba, and their dialect was even more archaic." She usually stayed in "good houses, with prosperous farmers and local officials, but at times the food was pork and potatoes and corn pone."[28] In short, Murfree, the most popular of all local color writers of Appalachia, had little idea of the actual society created by the most remote mountaineers, the subject of her "pretty accurate" stories. Murfree's "knowledge of the mountains," her biographer concludes, "was limited to summers in Beersheba Springs, and to a few short trips into less accessible regions. Beersheba and Maryville are barely in the Smoky Mountains, if at all, and she had known only those mountaineers who came often into contact with residents from the lowlands."[29]

The actual process by which Murfree first conceptualized the mountaineer as different can never be fully explained. Henry Shapiro suggests that to Murfree, "the mountaineers appeared a peculiar people if only for their willingness so to live in a wilderness 'broken by no field or clearing.'"[30] My book offers a different explanation. The mountain residents of upper East Tennessee were never cut off from the larger American society, never so isolated as to develop the characteristics described by the local color writers. Beginning in the Revolutionary War period, people from outside the region regarded the mountaineers as different. At that time few residents saw themselves in such a way, but their perspectives shifted during subsequent decades. The road network, local economy, and movement of individuals and families all indicate the development of varying degrees of connectedness and a growing differentiation between the local and broad perspectives. By the 1840s and 1850s, some mountaineers had begun to see themselves as falling behind the economic growth of other regions. Many of these individuals, living in the more open valleys, pursued and eventually connected themselves to national markets via the railroad. Other residents, like the Higgins, Rice, and Sams families and those whom David Hunter Strother visited, continued to live in the extreme portions of the mountains, far from any railroad connection. Some of these people declined to support the railroad, and the division of opinion helped catalyze growing self-perceptions of difference within upper East Tennessee.

Perhaps the town residents' different views of the mountaineers provided the source material for local colorists such as Murfree. In Beersheba Springs and Maryville she talked with people who, like the residents of Jonesborough, began to consider their more distant mountain neighbors backward. One can imagine a prosperous farmer telling the young Mary Noailles Murfree about the state of his crops, the fair prices he obtained at distant markets, the railroad that made such sales possible, and, conceivably, the destitute mountaineers who had no such access to modern transportation. He himself was advancing toward a bright and prosperous future, while others within his community were mired in a gloomy and primitive past. David Hunter Strother's most telling observation of upper East Tennessee highlights this strange juxtaposition of old and new. "In these days one may see a great many queer sights in Tennessee. He may discern the prints of the deer-skin moccasin and the French kid slipper side by side. Overlooking the mud-chinked cabin of the pioneer, carefully imitated from the handiwork of Daniel Boone, he may see the elegant villa from a design by Downing or Vaux. Strangely contrasting with the simple garb and manner of the olden time, he meets every where the luxury and polish of modern refinement. There are colleges, railroads, piano-fortes, electric telegraphs, and fancy stores."[31] By communicating to Mary Noailles Murfree such distinctions between old and new, the townspeople in effect told the entire nation about the characteristics that distinguished them from their mountain neighbors. Yet the local color writers treated Appalachia as a single entity, devoid of the finer distinctions wrought by geographic, economic, and social factors. The town residents in upper East Tennessee did not realize that despite their real and perceived differences with the mountaineers, the local color writers would paint both groups with the same brush.

# The Implications
# of Connectedness

DURING THE revolutionary and antebellum periods, Jones-borough served as the economic, social, and political center of Washington County and upper East Tennessee. After the Civil War, however, Johnson City, situated only a few miles to the northeast, began to rise in prominence. When construction of the East Tennessee and Virginia Rail Road extended far enough south from Bristol and the Virginia-Tennessee border, Henry Johnson built a brick storehouse at the junction of the railroad and the stage road. This store became the initial railroad depot in 1857 and subsequently the nucleus of a thriving settlement that would eventually be named after its first station agent and postmaster.[1] About a quarter century later, one Johnson City newspaper printed an article titled "A Mountain Girl."[2]

A pen picture of a mountain girl may interest the home readers of The Comet. One half of the world does not know how the other half live; and the ladies of The Comet do not know how their cousin who lives in a "cave" on the steep side of some mountain or knob passes away her time.

She is born in a log hut which is lighted by the open door in the daytime, and by the blazing fire on winter nights. Cracks in the floor, the walls, the ceiling, and a hole out through the wall beside the chimney furnish plenty of air. The house contains but one room and a loft above it. . . . The "baker" (an iron pot with a lid with a rim around it to hold live coals), the frying pan, and the coffee pot stands on

Fig. 20. Main Street, Johnson City, 1883. Courtesy of Archives and Special Collections, Sherrod Library, East Tennessee State University, Johnson City.

the hearth for half an hour before each meal and cook the breakfast, dinner, and supper of coffee, fried meat, and biscuit. . . . On the lofty "fireboard" or mantle piece are the ornamental possessions of the household, the canned peaches, and the lythographed pictures taken from seed catalogues placed inside empty glass jars. . . . The washstand is a post outside of the door holding a tin wash pan. A towel hangs by the door and a comb is placed near a small looking glass on the wall. . . . The view from the front door embraces several fields and is bounded by the dark woods of the "knobs" on the opposite side of the road and branch. Such is the birthplace of our heroine.

Her earliest memory will be of her cradle, made of six unpainted boards. . . . She will early learn that it is useless for her to cry as her mother is too busy to pay attention to her. She will also learn to amuse herself. She will find her own toys. If she has one doll in all her girlhood she will be unusually fortunate. None will trouble themselves to furnish her playthings. . . . At the district school she is a better and more successful student than her brothers. She will learn to read a little (enough to read her Testament, perhaps), to write a letter, and to cipher less. She will attend Sunday school about every other summer from harvest till the big campmeetings are held; for the campmeetings will take all the teachers away, and dissolve the school. When there is an appointment in her neighborhood, if the weather is good, and the preacher comes, she will hear a sermon—perhaps six or eight times a year. . . .

During all these years she has learned very thoroughly another lesson, that she is only a girl. She will keep the flies off the table while her brother eats, and will afterwards eat her dinner off of his soiled plates. She will never expect to eat at the first table. . . . She will, when married, wait upon her husband as a servant. . . . Her husband is idle more than half his time, but she is always busy. He never works very hard except in harvest, and he lounges about the house in all the rainy and cold weather, but she never has time to rest. He looks stout and healthy, but she looks pale, then overworked. . . . She never dreams of being a companion to her husband or an instructor of her children. The courtesies common elsewhere to which her valley and lowland sisters are so accustomed as to accept, without noticing them, would greatly embarass the mountain girl.

This article, written expressly for the *Comet* and not adapted from another newspaper, provides an important view of the mountaineers from within the region.

The piece creates a profound sense of difference within the population of upper East Tennessee. "The ladies" who read the *Comet* shared a common culture in Johnson City and contemplated the "mountain girl's" home, furnishings, childhood, education, and family life with horror and disbelief. Upper East Tennessee in 1884 did not exhibit a single common society whose members knew and understood one another. Instead, two worlds existed in the Tennessee mountains: one centered on the larger towns and more open valleys, where the people frequently interacted with the rest of the United States, and the other focused on the steep mountains and narrow hollows of the Unaka Range, where the inhabitants dealt primarily with their immediate neighbors. By the late 1800s the two societies had diverged to such a degree that "courtesies common elsewhere to which her valley and lowland sisters are so accustomed as to accept, without noticing them, would greatly embarass the mountain girl." Although the two groups coexisted within the same community of upper East Tennessee, "one half of the world does not know how the other half live." As a result, people in towns like Johnson City could unhesitatingly characterize the mountaineers as backward. We might find it difficult to believe that such divergence could exist in a region with so homogeneous a population, yet these perceptions reflected the complex interactions between different peoples within this specific Appalachian mountain setting.

One hundred years earlier, the inhabitants of upper East Tennessee did not see themselves as different from one another or from those living outside the region. Threats of Indian, British, and Loyalist attacks during the revolutionary period created webs of relationships that united the residents. This cohesiveness fostered a localist perspective and prompted individuals to depend on their immediate neighbors for physical, material, and psychological support. Although outsiders like Patrick Ferguson often described the overmountain men as different, the bonds of mutuality formed during the war and surrounding the state of Franklin crisis fed self-perceptions of commonality, not difference, among the inhabitants. Yet developments in the late eighteenth century set into motion events by which these people came to grow apart physically and perceptually. The geography of upper East Tennessee shaped in important ways the transportation and communication connections that were established, or were not established, locally. A network of roads linked the more accessible sites along rivers and in the broad valleys to the major transportation routes that crossed the area. A more extreme physiographic setting rendered some settlements less accessible. Individuals linked to the road network developed an outward-looking view, but others who had more difficulty moving about the region were less geographically and emotionally connected and therefore developed a more inward-turning perspective.

The two outlooks diverged further as the region's economy grew during the first third of the nineteenth century. Upper East Tennessee's agricultural, mercantile, and manufacturing interests helped many inhabitants form stronger connections to far-flung markets. Yet this growth paled in comparison to the economic juggernaut of Middle Tennessee. Some inhabitants with a regional and national viewpoint, such as the merchant and diarist David A. Deaderick, began to perceive their region as falling behind and redoubled their efforts to reverse the trend. These individuals strove against the environmental factors of geography, topography, and soil fertility in the effort to extend their connections to other peoples and places. At about the same time, a smaller group of people sought not external connections but land and more intimate ties with a much more narrow range of people. The Sams, Rice, Higgins, and other families struggled over marginal roads into the southern and eastern fringes of the region, settled on land poor in terms of soil fertility but rich in natural resources, and remained in these locales more persistently than their neighbors elsewhere in Washington County. Their very location within the most rugged portions of the area encouraged them to focus their attention on their own immediate affairs and rendered them relatively isolated from other places in upper East Tennessee. Within the region, therefore, we see that individuals began to separate themselves from others. This process fostered self-perceptions of difference.

The sense of difference crystallized when the better-connected inhabitants tried to overcome mountain geography, bad roads, soil infertility, and other economic disadvantages by campaigning for the East Tennessee and Virginia Rail Road. With the railroad, farmers could reach new markets in a more timely fashion, manufacturers could distribute their goods more easily, landowners would see their property values rise, and such prosperity would bring status, comfort, and refinement to the region. Who could oppose such goals? They seemed so sensible, reasonable, desirable, and attainable that the railroad advocates came to see people who did not support their efforts as being ignorant and backward. The battle to fund and construct the East Tennessee and Virginia Rail Road thus produced clear differences within the inhabitants of upper East Tennessee. Those who constantly pushed outward and made more extensive connections arrayed themselves against individuals who focused their energies on their immediate concerns and daily lives.

This sense of difference, articulated by the inhabitants themselves living within the mountain region, in turn led to potent and enduring images of Appalachia. The article in the *Comet* offers a telling illustration of the differences that the inhabitants of Johnson City, a town in the open valleys located on the railroad line, attributed to their neighbors. Recall that the readers "do not know how their cousin who lives in a 'cave' on the steep side of some mountain or knob passes away her time" and that the mountain girl would have no inkling about "the courtesies common elsewhere to which her valley and lowland sisters are so accustomed." This article appeared in 1884, the same year Mary Noailles Murfree published her extraordinarily popular collection of short stories, *In the Tennessee Mountains*. After a childhood full of summers spent talking with people in well-connected mountain towns, Murfree internalized a picture of the mountaineer that when put into print would fix in the American mind a distinctive and enduring image of the mountaineer. The consequences shape the ways in which we continue to perceive, and misperceive, Appalachia and America.

# Notes

*Note:* Publication information for works cited will be found in the bibliography beginning on page 218.

## PREFACE

1. *Forty-eight Hours,* transcript of "Another America," aired 14 Dec. 1989 (New York: CBS News, 1989), 2.

2. John Solomon Otto, "'Hillbilly Culture': The Appalachian Mountain Folk in History and Popular Culture," *Southern Quarterly* 24 (1986): 28.

## INTRODUCTION: THE FRAMEWORK FOR CONNECTEDNESS

1. Fox, "The Southern Mountaineers," 390, 392.

2. Harney, "A Strange Land and Peculiar People," 429-38. For a thorough treatment of local color writers such as Fox, see Shapiro, *Appalachia on Our Mind.* Americans have a long history of perceiving southern Appalachia and its residents as being different; for examples from primary sources dating back to the colonial period, see Higgs and Manning, *Voices from the Hills.* Cratis D. Williams provides the first modern treatment of the subject in "The Southern Mountaineer in Fact and Fiction." On the persistence of such images, see John Solomon Otto, "'Hillbilly Culture,'" 25-34.

3. Batteau, *The Invention of Appalachia.* Quoted passages appear on pp. 1, 37.

4. Shapiro, *Appalachia on Our Mind,* xiv.

5. Ibid., x, xvi, xiv (quotations from pp. x, xiv).

6. Ibid., 76-77 (quoted passage on p. 77).

7. Ibid., xiv., 81, xi.

8. Fox, "The Southern Mountaineers," 392.

9. Hayes, "The Southern Appalachians," 323, 319; Raitz and Ulack, *Appalachia: A Regional Geography,* 45-49.

10. Richard D. Brown shows a fine sensitivity to the various ways in which different people may be connected. While many eighteenth- and nineteenth-century New England farmers lived insular lives that reflected generations of

local experience, others tapped into print and word-of-mouth information networks that linked them to Americans both near and far. "Close observation of farmers' lives reveals an interplay between routine, quotidian local events and the occasions where information from the world beyond the town and country entered their experience, giving the lie to the image of timeless inertia that makes outsiders' visions of rustic life so appealing and romantic." The same may be said about visions of life in Appalachia. Brown's analysis of newspapers, postal services, and other informational sources reveals that many rural inhabitants "were not in truth insulated from external affairs either in their consciousness or as a matter of practical fact, nor were they content to dwell wholly within a local sphere. All of the farmers considered here were assisted by their neighbors and by society more broadly in learning about the world beyond their neighborhoods." See Brown, *Knowledge Is Power*, chap. 6; quotations from pp. 133, 157. Information systems of print culture provide important measures by which we may judge connectedness in upper East Tennessee. In the following chapters, newspapers provide examples of how writers characterize the region for nonresidents (as Patrick Ferguson did in 1780), communicate scientific farming methods to local residents (as Thomas Emmerson did in the 1830s), or create local perceptions of difference within the population (as supporters of railroads did in the 1850s).

11. Hillery, "Definitions of Community," 117. For a recent overview of historians' work on community, see Hoover, "Community Studies," 297-305.

12. Bell and Newby, *Community Studies*, 31.

13. Bender, *Community and Social Change*, 6-7. For example, a community of scholars may be connected principally by their interests and by electronic mail.

14. Almgren, "Community," 244.

15. For a brief overview, see Almgren, "Community"; for different examples of this approach, see Bell and Newby, *The Sociology of Community*; for a recent contribution to this topic, see Bell, "The Fruit of Difference," 65-82.

16. Tönnies, *Community and Society*, 33-34. These two forms of social organization can be confused because the Gesellschaft "superficially resembles the Gemeinschaft in so far as the individuals live and dwell together peacefully. However, in the Gemeinschaft they remain essentially united in spite of all separating factors, whereas in the Gesellschaft they are essentially separated in spite of all uniting factors" (64-65). Further confusion may arise because I use the term "community" in a much broader sense than does Tönnies. In an attempt at clarity, when referring to Tönnies's ideas I will use his German terms ("gemeinschaft" and "gesellschaft") rather than the English translations.

17. Almgren, "Community," 244.

18. Bender, *Community and Social Change*, 45-51.

19. Gross, *The Minutemen and Their World*; Heyrman, *Commerce and Culture*; Carr, Menard, and Walsh, *Robert Cole's World*.

20. Lasch, *The True and Only Heaven*, 142.

21. Bender, *Community and Social Change*, 33.

22. Tönnies, *Community and Society*, 232.

23. Williams, "The Southern Mountaineer in Fact and Fiction." Martha H. Pipes has published an edited and abridged version of the dissertation in four successive issues of *Appalachian Journal*. The quoted passages appear in *Appalachian Journal* 3 (Winter 1975): 13, 19-20.

24. See the Pipes edition, 23, 18-19.

25. Eller, "The Search for Community," 3-4. One example of an earlier account comes from Jack Weller, who writes that "the community is actually unnecessary to his [the mountaineer's] life except on a very impersonal level; he uses what he needs from the community, ignores the rest, and finds no reason for further community support." See Weller, *Yesterday's People*, 88.

26. See, for example, Kephart, *Our Southern Highlanders*, and Campbell, *The Southern Highlander*.

27. Wilhelm, "Appalachian Isolation," 83.

28. Eller, *Miners, Millhands*, 16. Rodger Cunningham also cites Wilhelm's study when referring to isolation in this sense, but his treatment is very brief. See his *Apples on the Flood*, 100.

29. Hahn, *The Roots of Southern Populism*, 49.

30. Ibid., 38. For migration, see pp. 43, 57, and 68. For absentee landlords, pp. 23 and 66; for the market connections of plantation owners and small farmers, p. 27; for storekeepers and merchants, pp. 32, 38, and 39. Perhaps Hahn would be better served by changing the first quotation mentioned above to "a society that had a logic and resiliency rooted, not only in geographic *circumstances*, but in a complex of social relations," for he clearly demonstrates how the environmental setting discouraged the cotton plantation culture during the 1850s.

31. Dunn, *Cades Cove*, 89. For early settlement, see pp. 4, 5-6.

32. Ibid., 99, 102, 115.

33. Ibid., 115, 143, 85, 145.

34. Ibid., 146, 147.

35. Waller, *Feud*, 106.

36. Ibid., 23, 20-21. Such isolation has persisted even into the twentieth century, according to Dwight Billings, Kathleen Blee, and Louis Swanson. Having reexamined James Brown's ethnographic study of "Beech Creek" in Kentucky, they say that Brown "documented the social patterns of an extremely isolated group of subsistence farm families still living a relatively precapitalist life on the eve of World War II." See Billings, Blee, and Swanson, "Culture, Family, and Community," 155.

37. Waller, *Feud*, 52.

38. MacMaster, "The Cattle Trade," 127-49.

39. Moore, "Economic Development," 222-34; the quoted passage appears on pp. 232-233.

40. Blethen and Wood, "A Trader," 150-65; I have quoted from p. 165.

41. Blethen and Wood, "The Appalachian Frontier," 5.

42. Ibid., 7-8. My agreement with their conclusions should not be surprising because they cite my earlier article, "How Isolated Was Appalachia?" 336-49, in their review of the recent literature. That article served as the starting point for this book.

43. McKinney, "Preindustrial Jackson County," 8.

44. Inscoe, *Mountain Masters*, 36, 37, 52.

45. Ibid., 53.

46. Ibid. As my book will show, these sorts of individuals in upper East Tennessee served as the basis for general images of Appalachia.

47. Mann, "Mountains, Land," 411-34; the quoted passages appear on pp. 430, 411.

48. Hofstra, "Land, Ethnicity," 421-48; the quoted passage appears on p. 421. Robert D. Mitchell first analyzed the region in *Commercialism and Frontier*.

49. Hofstra and Mitchell, "Town and Country," 619-46. For Millwood, see pp. 643-44.

50. Billings, Pudup, and Waller, "Taking Exception," 18.

51. Mann, "Diversity," 132-62.

52. McKinney, "Economy and Community," 163-84; the quoted passage appears on p. 170.

53. Fox, "The Southern Mountaineers," 387.


## 1. Perceptions and Self-Perceptions in the Revolutionary Era

1. *Virginia Gazette* (Richmond, Virginia), 11 Nov. 1780.

2. Clinton, *An Historical Detail*, vol. 2, pt. 2, chap. 4.

3. Vance and Henry, "King's Mountain Expedition," 83-84. *Sic* will not be used elsewhere because quotations have been copied directly.

4. Draper, *King's Mountain*, chaps. 3-5, appendix; Higginbotham, *The War of American Independence*, chap. 14.

5. Cornwallis to Clinton, 29 Dec. 1780, reprinted in Samuel Cole Williams, "The Battle of King's Mountain," 59, n. 17.

6. Nathanael Greene to George Washington, 7 Dec. 1780, reprinted in *State Records of North Carolina*, ed. Walter Clark (Goldsboro, N.C.: Nash Brothers, 1898), vol. 15, p. 174. Hereafter cited as *SRNC*.

7. Corlew, *Tennessee*, 43-51; "An Act for erecting the District of Washington into a County, by the Name of Washington County," *SRNC*, vol. 24, 141-42.

8. Washington County, Court of Pleas and Quarter Sessions, Minute Book (hereafter cited as Wash CPQS), book 1778-85. Page numbers given below are those of the typed transcript. The 1778 population estimate appears in *Goodspeed's History of Tennessee*, 891.

9. 25 Aug. 1778, Wash CPQS, book 1778-85, p. 11.

10. Ibid., 26 Aug. 1778, pp. 12-13.

11. Ibid., 24 Feb. 1779, pp. 27-28.

12. Ibid., 23 Feb. 1779, p. 26.

13. Ibid.

14. Ibid., 28 May 1782, p. 75.

15. Ibid., 22 May 1780, p. 46 for both cases.

16. Other sources argue that a far larger Loyalist threat existed in Washington County. Lyman C. Draper corresponded with Major John Sevier, Jr., and transcribed the following notes during the Autumn of 1844: "Jacob Dykes and Jacob Holley killed Robt. Caldwell, a great Whig and bitter enemy to Tories, and Dykes threatened Col. [John] Sevier's life. A party of five men, calling themselves Regulators, caught Dykes on Big Limestone Creek in Washington County and hanged him; Holley evaded them. . . . These Regulators were indicted, tried, and condemned for murder, but through Col. Sevier's influence were pardoned. In '79 Cols. Sevier and Jno. Carter were elected to the Legislature, but so troublesome were the Tories that they did not dare leave their families and the country, and did not attend—'79 was a troublesome Tory year in the western waters." If Major John Sevier, Jr., remembered accurately, he reveals another way in which Loyalists fostered internal connections; leaders like Sevier and Carter remained in the county with the other inhabitants instead of separating themselves by attending the state legislature in eastern North Carolina. These notes appear in the Draper Manuscript Collection, State Historical Society of Wisconsin, 32S222.

17. Much of the information that follows can be found in Williams, *Tennessee*, especially pp. 24-31, 35-70, 182-94, and 199-212.

18. John Stuart to Henry Clinton, 15 March 1776, quoted in Williams, *Tennessee*, 25-26.

19. Ibid., 35-70.

20. According to Lyman C. Draper, Major James Sevier recalled in 1844 that "[John] Sevier was himself at Watauga Fort—Col. John Carter and family, James Robertson and family, Andrew Greer and family and his son Joseph Greer, Samuel Sherill and family and others" all lived within the fort during the siege. See Draper Collection, 32S142. For the Indians' ability to foster a sense of community among the settlers of South Carolina, see Klein, *Unification of a Slave State*, 92.

21. Draper Collection, 32S147-49.

22. Draper, *King's Mountain*, chap. 9; Bass, "The Last Campaign," 16-19; William Campbell's report, 7 Oct. 1780, in Berkley, "Colonel Isaac Shelby," 128-29.

23. I will analyze this road network in much greater detail in the next chapter.

24. James Sevier to Lyman C. Draper, 19 Aug. 1839, Draper Collection, 11DD165. James Sevier refers to his father's campaign against the Chickamauga Indians during the autumn of 1782. Details of this affair appear in Williams, *Tennessee*, 205-12. Other examples of these different forms of connectedness postdate the battle of King's Mountain. For the mountaineers' participation in the battles of Boyd's Creek (16 Dec. 1780) and Guilford Courthouse (15 March 1781), and for their role in further negotiations with and attacks against different groups of Indians, see Williams, *Tennessee*, 180-204.

25. Ferguson to Lord Cornwallis, 29 Aug. 1780, Cornwallis Papers, Public Records Office, London, collection 30/11, file 63, pp. 81-82.

26. Cornwallis, however, doubted the value of recruiting such militia. He writes, "Ferguson is to move into Tryon County with some militia, whom he says he is sure he can depend upon for doing their duty and fighting well; but I am sorry to say that his own experience, as well as that of every other officer, is totally against him." Cornwallis to Clinton, 29 Aug. 1780, *Correspondence of Charles, First Marquis Cornwallis*, vol. 1, pp. 58-59. Cornwallis proved to be correct, for the British never roused as much support as they had hoped, especially after the defeat at King's Mountain.

27. Ferguson to Cornwallis, 14 Sept. 1780, Cornwallis Papers, file 64, pp. 60-61, and 19 Sept. 1780, file 64, pp. 80-81.

28. Ibid., 3 Oct. 1780, file 3, pp. 176-77.

29. Ibid., 28 Sept. 1780, file 64, pp. 120-21. The decoded phrases appear above the letters and numbers in this copy.

30. *Virginia Gazette*, 30 Dec. 1780.

31. Ferguson to Cornwallis, 30 Sept. 1780, Cornwallis Papers, file 64, pp. 128-29.

32. Ibid., 6 Oct. 1780, file 3, pp. 191-92.

33. Ferguson to Timpany, Sir Henry Clinton Papers, vol. 125, folder 15, William L. Clements Library, University of Michigan. In a postscript, Ferguson added, "Here we are. Kings of King Mountain—altho there is indeed another throne or ridge opposite to us where Gen'l Sumpter and your humble servant may like the two kings of Brentford reign vis-à-vis in daylight—but at night we shine [?]."

34. One word of caution is in order. The analysis of nuances in language emphasizes what is not said as well as what is said. When Ferguson calls the enemy barbarians, it is duly noted. When he does not place any distinct label on his foes, it is also noted. Negative evidence offers only an unstable foundation for an argument, but sometimes it is the only material available to the historian. Few British soldiers left accounts about King's Mountain, and hardly any mention the character of their opponents.

35. Ferguson to Clinton, 6 July; 16, 18, and 27 Sept.; 9 and 12 Oct.; 7, 15, 16, 22, and 25 Nov.; and the letters cited below. All are located in the Clinton Papers in the volumes for 1779.

36. Ferguson to Clinton [?], 13 March 1779, Clinton Papers, vol. 54, no. 1.

37. Ferguson to Captain André, 30 Oct. 1779, Clinton Papers, vol. 73, no. 23.

38. Ferguson to Clinton, 12 Oct. 1779, Clinton Papers, vol. 71, no. 27.

39. Ibid.

40. Ferguson to Cornwallis, 1 Oct. 1780, Cornwallis Papers, file 3, pp. 160-61.

41. "Memoir of Captain Alexander Chesney, July, 1780," in Williams, "The Battle of King's Mountain," 59.

42. *Scots Magazine*, Jan. 1781, reprinted in *SRNC*, vol. 15, p. 183.

43. "Colonel Campbell's orders for the day," ibid., 11 Oct. 1780, p. 115.

44. Ibid., 14 Oct. 1780, p. 119.

45. Dykeman, *With Fire and Sword*, 74.

46. Draper, *King's Mountain*, 334, from manuscript pension statements and letters.

47. Ibid., 437, 448, 444, and 447.

48. The best recent work on the Revolutionary War as fought in the southern backcountry, especially in the Carolinas, can be found in Hoffman, "The 'Disaffected,'" 273-316; Hoffman, Tate, and Albert, *An Uncivil War*; Pancake, *This Destructive War*; Escott and Crow, "The Social Order," 373-402; Clodfelter, "Between Virtue and Necessity," 169-75; and Klein, *Unification of a Slave State*, especially chap. 3.

49. Greene to the President of Congress, 28 Dec. 1780, in Pancake, *This Destructive War*, 73; Greene to Robert Howe, 29 Dec. 1780, in Hoffman, "'The Disaffected,'" 294. William R. Davie, Greene's commissary, recalled that "the troops of both armies took what they wanted without ceremony or accountability, and used it without measure or economy; an indifference common to all armies in similar situations, produced by the impression, that perhaps the next day these resources may be in the hands of the Enemy." Quoted in Crow, "Liberty Men and Loyalists," 163.

50. Hoffman, "'The Disaffected,'" 300.

51. Escott and Crow, "The Social Order," 389. While many of Escott's and Crow's larger arguments are convincing when applied to the North Carolina backcountry, they must be reexamined before applying them to upper East Tennessee. They argue that the backcountry displayed a rigid hierarchical social structure and that "the upper class to a significant degree remained estranged from the society it ruled" (379). Such patterns remain elusive in upper East Tennessee during this period. Furthermore, Escott and Crow, in "The Social Order," argue for a preexisting condition of disconnectedness in the North Carolina backcountry. "Largely indifferent to courthouse and statehouse controversies unless directly threatened, these small farmers typically had little contact with towns, merchants, or established authorities for months at a time and lived in rural independence" (381). They also state that "the mountains and ridges of these western counties [Surry, Wilkes, and Yadkin] separated individuals and families into valleys and settlements that were . . . wholly separate from the world of the towns" (381). I argue in this book that in upper East Tennessee at least, such rural independence and separation did not exist to the degree that Escott and Crow claim for the North Carolina backcountry.

52. Ekirch, "Whig Authority," 109. Reinforcing the importance of disconnectedness from the government, Rachel N. Klein, in *Unification of a Slave State*, argues that in South Carolina during the mid-1770s, political connections linked backcountry settlers with coastal inhabitants. "Recognizing both the ambition and local authority of backcountry men of influence, lowcountry whigs sought to win support by offering access to political and military positions. . . . Coastal whigs were able to win inland support precisely because they recognized and helped to fulfill the political and military ambitions of leading frontiersmen" (88-89). The fragmentation of such government as it occurred in North Carolina would lead to critical disconnections for western settlers.

53. Pancake, *This Destructive War*, 85-88, quotation from p. 88. For more on

Cunningham, see Klein, *Unification of a Slave State*, 97-98. For two examples of Tory plundering among many, see Crow, "Liberty Men and Loyalists," 158-59, and Hoffman, "'The Disaffected,'" 293. Other British actions and policies drove civilians away from their ranks as surely as did this violence. In June 1780, Sir Henry Clinton announced that all paroled prisoners, with some exceptions, could be forced to join the British military. Two months later, Cornwallis declared that those who resisted Clinton's orders could lose their property. See Klein, *Unification of a Slave State*, 101.

54. Cited in Ekirch, "Whig Authority," 110.

55. Cited in Klein, *Unification of a Slave State*, 101. Such disconnections may have begun years earlier, for North Carolina governor Josiah Martin notified the earl of Dartmouth on 12 Jan. 1776 that "the difficulty of communication which becomes daily greater and greater, will totally cut me off from all intercourse with the Interior parts of it [North Carolina] hereafter until I am able by force to lay it open." Cited in Ekirch, "Whig Authority," 105.

56. Cited in Escott and Crow, "The Social Order," 396. Mark A. Clodfelter notes that Nathanael Greene tried to convince many Whig officials to follow a similar parole policy. Greene, for example, successfully "encouraged the governor [John Martin of Georgia] to permit those Tories who had fled from Georgia to return without penalty." See Clodfelter, "Between Virtue and Necessity," 172.

57. Pancake, *This Destructive War*, 186.

58. The following summary of events concerning the state of Franklin is drawn primarily from Cannon, "Four Interpretations," 3-18; Gerson, *Franklin*; and especially Williams, *Lost State of Franklin*.

59. Williams, *Lost State of Franklin*, 108.

60. Anthony Bledsoe to Richard Caswell, 26 March 1787, SRNC, vol. 22, p. 677.

61. Quoted in Gerson, *Franklin*, 48.

62. Legislature of the State of Franklin to Alexander Martin, 22 March 1785, SRNC, vol. 22, p. 637.

63. David Campbell to Richard Caswell, 30 Nov. 1786, ibid., p. 652.

64. John Sevier to Evan Shelby, 11 Feb. 1787, in Sevier and Madden, *Sevier Family History*, 71.

65. Legislature of the State of Franklin to Alexander Martin, 22 March 1785, SRNC, vol. 22, p. 638.

66. Ibid., 639.

67. Ibid., 639-40.

68. Alexander Martin to Washington, Sullivan, and Greene Counties, "A Manifesto," 25 April 1785, ibid., 643.

69. John Sevier to Richard Caswell, 28 Oct. 1786, ibid., 660. Travel between Franklin and New Bern, the capital of North Carolina, took between twelve and fifteen days; Williams, *Lost State of Franklin*, 38.

70. David Campbell to Richard Caswell, 30 Nov. 1786, ibid., 652.

71. "Petition of the Inhabitants of the Western Country, to North Carolina General Assembly," Dec. 1787, ibid., 706.

72. Richard Caswell to John Sevier, 24 April 1787, *SRNC*, vol. 20, pp. 681-82.

73. Richard Caswell to John Sevier, 23 Feb. 1787, *SRNC*, vol. 22, p. 673.

74. Evan Shelby to Richard Caswell, 4 May 1787, ibid., 681.

75. The following description is taken from "Affidavit of Sheriff Pugh," 20 Sept. 1787, ibid., 689-91.

76. The following description is taken from "Oath of David Deaderick," 25 Oct. 1788, ibid., 699-700. The insults described below are copied as they appear in *SRNC*.

77. Andrew Caldwell also swore to the accuracy of Deaderick's deposition; "Oath of Andrew Caldwell," 25 Oct. 1788, ibid., 701. In July of that year, Governor Samuel Johnston had ordered Sevier's arrest on the charge of "high Treason in levying Troops to oppose the Laws & Government of this State and has with an armed force put to death several good Citizens." Samuel Johnston to Judge Campbell, 22 July 1788, *SRNC*, vol. 21, 484. As already mentioned in the summary of events, Sevier eventually escaped but soon abandoned the Franklin cause and swore allegiance to North Carolina.

78. Wyatt-Brown, *Southern Honor*, 353-54.

79. Franklin, *The Militant South*, 12-13.

80. Williams, *Lost State of Franklin*, 75-99, for the Treaties of Dumplin, Hopewell, and Coyatee. Excerpts of the Treaty of Dumplin Creek appear in Sevier and Madden, *Sevier Family History*, 63. John Sevier, Jr., describes the summer of 1788 in Draper Collection, 32S210. During those campaigns, he said, "My father had to remain on the frontiers the whole summer, going from fort to fort with what men that could be spared from the garrisons. Many valuable lives were lost in that war."

81. James Robertson to John Sevier, 1 Aug. 1787, reprinted in Williams, *Lost State of Franklin*, 167.

82. Ibid., 168 (for the Nashville region) and 187 (for Georgia).

83. John Sevier to Don Diego de Gardoqui, 12 Sept. 1788, in Corbitt and Corbitt, "Papers from the Spanish Archives," 103. For the most current and complete treatment of Spain's role in this topic, see Weber, *The Spanish Frontier*, chap. 10.

84. James Madison to Thomas Jefferson, 12 Aug. 1786, in Boyd, *The Papers of Thomas Jefferson*, vol. 10, p. 233.

85. Thomas Jefferson to James Madison, 30 Jan. 1787, in Boyd, *The Papers of Thomas Jefferson*, vol. 11, p. 93.

86. Don Diego de Gardoqui to John Sevier, 18 April 1788, in Henderson, "The Spanish Conspiracy," 233.

87. John Sevier to Don Diego de Gardoqui, 12 Sept. 1788, in Sevier and Madden, *Sevier Family History*, 95.

88. Samuel Cole Williams, who also reproduces this letter, argues that the document "should be read in the light of the fact that the original of it does not exist. A copy of it, translated into Spanish, is preserved in the Gardoqui manuscripts; and this translation was made by Spanish officials who were interested in placing upon the original the construction that would be the more likely to

bring favorable action from the home government in behalf of the plan which Gardoqui had formulated and sponsored." Sevier, he argues, "was intent on procuring prompt aid; to that end he went as far in statement and implication as his ultimate purpose would admit. He proposed an alliance of friendly sovereignties, not an incorporation." Williams, *Lost State of Franklin*, 232, 234.

## 2. THE EARLY ROADS

1. Fink, "Jacob Brown of Nolichucky," 237-43.
2. Sevier and Madden, *Sevier Family History*, 26-34.
3. Deaderick, "Journal of Events," 122, n. 1. On the Shenandoah Valley and the Great Wagon Road, see Mitchell, *Commercialism and Frontier*.
4. This road appears on Marshall Wilson, "Map of Early Settlements of East Tennessee, previously a part of North Carolina and of the Territory of the U.S. South of the River Ohio, Series 1—To End of Year 1776," n.d., in the McClung Collection, Lawson-McGhee Library, Knoxville, Tenn.
5. Myer, "Indian Trails of the Southeast," 801-2, and Wilson, "Map of Early Settlements."
6. *Goodspeed's History of Tennessee*; Henley, "Maj. Charles Robertson, and Some of His Descendants," 22-23.
7. Clark, *State Records of North Carolina*, vol. 24, p. 451.
8. 7 Aug. 1784, Washington County, Court of Please and Quarter Sessions, Minute Book, book 1778-85. Unfortunately, we cannot determine whether or not the court obtained such depositions.
9. Browning, "Washington County Court," 2.
10. In 1796, the Tennessee legislature created Carter County out of Washington, citing how the people "labored under considerable difficulties and inconveniences in attending courts, general musters, elections, and other public duties." Carter County itself fractured about thirty years later. Those living in the tip of the county wanted the county seat, then in Elizabethton, moved to a more central location. Some residents had to travel forty or fifty miles, crossing the "very rapid and difficult" Doe River eight times; others had to "pass five or six miles on foot over steep and difficult mountains." The county seat remained in Elizabethton, but in 1836 Johnson County was formed with the seat in Mountain City. Merritt, *Early History*, 30, 42-43.
11. For land area, see *Rand McNally Commercial Atlas*, 522. The 1778 population estimate appears in *Goodspeed's History of Tennessee*, 891. The 1791 figure comes from *Washington County, Tennessee, Records*, vol. 1, "Washington County List of Taxables, 1778-1801," vi-vii. The 1800 figures can be found in U.S. Bureau of the Census, *Census of the United States*, 1800.
12. 23 Feb. 1779, Wash CPQS, book 1778-85. References to local "hands" responsible for the roads near their homes are scattered throughout the court's minute book.
13. The secondary sources used to locate the roads include: *Goodspeed's History of Tennessee*; Kozsuch, *Historical Reminiscences*; Williams, *History of*

*Johnson City;* Watauga Association of Genealogists, *History of Washington County, Tennessee, 1988;* and Sevier and Madden, *Sevier Family History.*

14. Maps used include a reproduction of an 1828 map of Washington County; Samuel, "Washington County, Tennessee, Post Offices, 1796-1900"; Hyder, Kozsuch, and Park, "Early Carter County, Tennessee"; a hand-drawn map in the Samuel Cole Williams Collection, box 4, acc. no. 85-13, Tennessee State Library and Archives, Nashville; topographical maps produced by the United States Geological Survey; and the maps mentioned above in notes 4 and 5.

15. For the road to Sullivan County, John Russell, Benjamin Cobb, and George Russell had marked a route "most convenient for a public road from Choate's ford . . . to the Court house." This road subsequently came under the care of James Allison and Benjamin Cobb, who were appointed overseers six months later. One of the earliest roads, a 1778 route from Greasy Cove to Jacob Brown's settlement on the Nolichucky, was extended to Jonesborough no later than 1782, when the court ordered Christopher Taylor to plot a route from the courthouse to the Nolichucky. Earlier, Taylor and Sevier had marked off a road from Jonesborough to Sevier's mill six miles away on Big Limestone Creek. Roads such as this last one surely continued further down the valley to Greeneville during the period. This development is made explicit in 1784 when the court ordered a road from Jonesborough westward to the county line, "where the same may intersect the road leading from Greene Court house." See 24 Aug. 1780 and 27 Feb. 1781 for Choate's; 26 Nov. 1778 and 8 Nov. 1782 for Jacob Brown; 30 May 1781 for Sevier's mill; 1 Nov. 1784 for Greeneville; all in Wash CPQS, book 1778-85. Sevier's mill appears in Sevier and Madden, *Sevier Family History,* 34.

16. The very first road ordered by the county court linked Gocher's ford on the Holston to James English, who lived near the Path. Nearly three years later, Joseph Bullar, Alexander Moore, and James Allison surveyed a road between Jonesborough and English's mill on Horse Creek, the stream that flows alongside Christian's War Road. By the end of the war, overseers like William Ellis maintained roads such as the one between Bean's ford of the Watauga and William Dale, who lived "along the Great Road." Bean's ford had already become an important transportation point, with its stop along the Choate's ford–Big Limestone Creek road and its direct link to Jonesborough. See 26 May 1778 for Gocher's ford; 27 Feb. 1781 for English's mill; 3 Feb. 1783 for Dale; 24 Aug. 1780, 27 Feb. 1781, and 30 May 1781 for Bean's ford; all in Wash CPQS, book 1778-85.

17. See 25 Nov. 1779, 4 Feb. 1783, 5 Feb. 1784, and 4 Aug. 1783 for roads running through Robert Young's land east of Jonesborough in what is now Johnson City; and 4, 11 Nov. 1782, 4 Feb. 1783, 4 Aug. 1783, 4 Nov. 1783, and 5 Feb. 1784 for roads to James Stuart's plantation on the Doe River and to nearby areas: all in Wash CPQS, book 1778-85.

18. Clark, *State Records of North Carolina,* 135; 25 Nov. 1779, Wash CPQS, book 1778-85.

19. A map of these new roads must be particularly sketchy because the chaos brought on by the movement to create a state of Franklin in upper East Tennessee destroyed the 1785 and 1786 Washington County court records.

Two sets of records were kept during 1787 and early 1788, one by those maintaining allegiance to North Carolina and another by those seeking independence. Since the former set of minute books alone survives, we have only an
incomplete description of the road network. By the end of 1788, however,
Washington County was once again united under the North Carolina government and keeping one set of records. For a summary, see Williams, *Lost State of
Franklin*.

20. North of Jonesborough, roads were once again ordered connecting Bean's
ford of the Watauga to Choate's ford on the Holston, as well as roads following
the course of both those rivers. Running east from Jonesborough, new roads
followed earlier routes through present-day Johnson City to the Elizabethton/
Sycamore Shoals region, including James Stuart's property between the Doe
and Watauga Rivers. Familiar territory was also covered by roads running directly south of Jonesborough to the Nolichucky River, between Limestone and
Greasy Coves along North Indian Creek, and through the mountains to Burke
County. Finally, a direct line westward from Jonesborough to Greeneville was
requested at the end of 1784, perhaps to facilitate communication between the
two population centers within the new state of Franklin. These roads, taken
together with the requests for overseers, attest to the court's steady interest in
the transportation network. For the northern roads, see 9 May 1787 and court
sessions for Aug. 1788, Nov. 1788, and Nov. 1789. For the eastern sections, see
6 Aug. 1787, 14 May 1788, and Feb. 1789 sessions. For the southern region, see
court sessions for Feb., Aug., and Nov. 1789. All records in Wash CPQS, book
1787-98. The road to Greene County appears in the Nov. 1784 session, Wash
CPQS, book 1778-85.

21. In a flurry of activity during the Feb. and May 1788 sessions, the court
ordered five roads linking Jonesborough first to mills operated by Abednego
Inman and Hugh Campbell on Big Limestone Creek and from there to the
Great War Path and Greene County. See sessions for Feb. and May 1788, Wash
CPQS, book 1787-98. The court requested another road between Jonesborough
and Abednego Inman on 10 Nov. 1789. One could also take other new roads
that were ordered south from Jonesborough to the Nolichucky and turn east,
going upstream to the Embree iron mines at Bumpass Cove, or turn west and go
downstream, following the south bank of the Nolichucky to Greene County.
See sessions for May and Aug. 1788, Feb. 1789, Wash CPQS, book 1787-98.
These roads probably follow a slightly earlier route along the south side of the
Nolichucky from Sevier's ford to Greene County; see 4 Aug. 1784, Wash CPQS,
book 1778-85. Roads such as these provided alternative ways of reaching settlements and markets west of Washington County.

22. Such new locations include roads from Jonesborough to Charles
Robertson on Cherokee Creek and to the head of Clark's Creek; see May 1788
sessions, Wash CPQS, book 1787-98. I will discuss the residents' interest in the
Tennessee-Ohio-Mississippi river system in the next chapter.

23. The watershed between the two streams served as an end point for two
other roads. The court also opened a new route from Sycamore Shoals to Greasy
Cove, which gave the Watauga settlements another means of reaching Greene

County (along the Nolichucky) and of connecting with the road over the mountains to Burke County. See 8 Aug. 1787 and Feb. 1789 sessions for Doe River; 7 Nov. 1787, Feb. and May 1788 sessions, and Aug. 1789 for Gap Creek; Nov. 1788 sessions for Greasy Cove; all found in Wash CPQS, book 1787-98.

24. 5 Feb. 1787, 6 Aug. 1787, May 1788 sessions, Wash CPQS, book 1787-98.

25. Asbury, *Journal and Letters*, vol. 1, p. 631.

26. The court also tried to improve access to the North Carolina piedmont, for it ordered roads to Wilkes and Burke counties through the northeastern tip of Tennessee. The wording in the orders indicates that settlement was sparse in these areas. Roads in the older parts of the county were often defined by human reference points, such as when the court ordered twelve men to "lay off a Road from Mathew Talbots sen. to Robert Young sen." Roads in these newer and more remote areas were described instead by their geographical features or artificial end points. The court "ordered that John Baker near the head of the Brushy fork of Cove Creek be the overseer to mark and cut out a pack Horse road from the Wilkes Line near the head of the said fork the Best way to the Beaver Dam Creek on the way over the Stone Mountain" and "Benjamin Ward be an overseer of the road from the Burke line near the head of the Devils fork of Catawba river the best way" to Baker's road. Therefore, both the wording of the new road orders and the placement of the routes on a map together connote a sense of remoteness and sparse settlement for the easternmost portions of Washington County. See 5 Feb. 1784 and Aug. 1789 sessions, Wash CPQS, books 1778-85 and 1787-98.

27. 7 May 1787 and Feb. and May 1789 sessions for roads from Sycamore Shoals north to Indian Creek; 11 Nov. 1789 for Jonesborough toward Ross's ironworks on the north fork of the Holston; 15 May 1788 for the southeastern route from Greasy Cove to Cane Creek; all in Wash CPQS, book 1787-98.

28. The two roads to the east are found in the Aug. 1790 sessions; for the other roads, see 26 May 1794 (Jump Hill to Telford), 19 Feb. 1795 (Cherokee Creek to Greeneville; Little Limestone and Nolichucky to Greene County), and 18 May 1796 (Jonesborough to Buffalo Mountain), all in Wash CPQS, book 1787-98.

29. The mountains surrounding the Nolichucky River and Greasy Cove, the entire length of the Watauga River, and the principal streams like Gap Creek, Big and Little Limestone Creek, Clark's Creek, and Boone's Creek all became more accessible. These roads appear in nearly every session. See Wash CPQS, books 1787-98 and 1798-1799.

30. Road from James Stuart's plantation to the head of Indian Creek, 4 June 1783, 4 Nov. 1783, and 5 Feb. 1784, Wash CPQS, book 1778-85.

31. Frank Allison was foreman in "Presentment of Grand Jury," Nov. 1798, Washington County Court Records, Archives of Appalachia, Sherrod Library, East Tennessee State University, Johnson City, Tenn. (hereafter WCCR), box 247, folder 10. On the treetop, see 14 Nov. 1804, Carter CPQS, book 1804-5. For reports by grand juries, see WCCR, box 230, folder 1.

32. Asbury, *Journal and Letters*, vol. 2, 308, p. 517.

33. Asbury, *Journal and Letters*, vol. 1, p. 631; vol 2, pp. 124-25. The second trip (over Yellow Mountain) probably followed a path and not a public road. In this portion of the county, as shown above, the court endorsed few roads. In order to put Asbury's travel experiences through Washington County into perspective, we might compare his observations about his journey between Nashville and Knoxville in Oct. 1800. Although the journey lasted hundreds of miles, it posed few difficulties. "From *Monday* morning [Oct. 27] to *Thursday* afternoon [Oct. 30] we have made one hundred and thirty miles; we have experienced no stoppage by water-courses, and have found the roads of the wilderness, their unevenness excepted, pretty good." Asbury, *Journal and Letters*, vol. 2, p. 260.

34. Michaux, *Travels to the West*, 283 (reprint edition).

35. Ibid., 284-85.

36. The term "local knowledge" had been made popular in a somewhat different sense by Geertz, *Local Knowledge*.

37. "Washington County List of Taxables," 10-45, 73. For offices held, see pp. 248-49 and *Goodspeed's History of Tennessee*, 891, 894-95.

38. Property ownership in prime geographical locations led to social and political prominence in other Appalachian areas as well. For Floyd, Harlan, and Perry Counties in southeast Kentucky, see Pudup, "Social Class and Economic Development," esp. pp. 245-50.

39. "Washington County List of Taxables," 73, 60, 72, 151.

40. 6 Aug. 1787, 8 Aug. 1787, and 14 May 1788, Wash CPQS, book 1787-98.

41. Regarding the Nolichucky, for example: "No boats have ever descended it except in a high time of water when the river was raised above its usual level by the rains," and "The navigation is at all times difficult and dangerous. It requires a rise of about four feet above the ordinary level of the water to enable flat bottom boats to descend at all." Depositions of Samuel Mawk and Adam Broyles, "Bill of Exceptions," 28 Feb. 1852, WCCR, box 118, folder 4, pp. 10, 6-8.

42. Michaux, *Travels to the West*, 247-48; Isaac Weld, *Travels Through the States*, 234 (reprint edition). Weld was a British citizen.

## 3. INTERNAL AND EXTERNAL ECONOMIC CONNECTIONS

1. Sevier, "Executive Journal," 1 April 1796, p. 101.

2. Clark, *State Records of North Carolina*, vol. 24, p. 135.

3. Sevier, "Executive Journal," 7 June 1796, p. 109; *Journal of the Senate of the State of Tennessee*, 4 Aug. 1796, p. 11.

4. Sevier,"Executive Journal," 2 Aug. 1796, p. 117.

5. For general works addressing southern agriculture, see Gray, *History of Agriculture*; North, *The Economic Growth*; Sellers, *The Market Revolution*; and Wright, *The Political Economy*. Sean Wilentz surveys the recent literature in "Society, Politics," 51-71. For specific Appalachian regions, see Inscoe, *Mountain Masters*, chaps. 1-2; McKinney, "Preindustrial Jackson County," 1-10; and Moore, "Economic Development," 222-34.

6. Gump, "Possessions and Patterns," 112-14.

7. Michaux, *Travels to the West*, 280-81. Wheat does not usually grow to such heights, so perhaps Michaux here mistook corn for wheat.

8. Gump, "Possessions and Patterns," 117, note 86, for the flour shipment; 118-25.

9. Michaux, *Travels to the West*, 281.

10. 28 Aug. 1780 and 26 Feb. 1782, Wash CPQS, book 1778-85.

11. Ibid., 5 Nov. 1787 for John Hunter, Jr., and Nov. 1789 sessions for Charles Robertson.

12. For other studies that describe similar economically based social connections, see Schlotterbeck, "The 'Social Economy,'" 3-28, and Mann, "Mountains, Land," 411-34.

13. "Judge Overton's Record of Distilleries, 1795-1802," Jacob McGavock Dickinson Papers, Tennessee State Library and Archives, microfilm roll 836.

14. The county court licensed at least twenty-five tavern and ordinary keepers by 1796; see Gump, "Possessions and Patterns," 171.

15. Ibid., 95.

16. Michaux, *Travels to the West*, 150, 154.

17. Minutes of the Superior Court of the District of Washington, vol. 1, 34, reprinted in Browning, "The Washington County Court," 332. Convicted horse thieves were also executed; see the case of 10 Sept. 1782, Court of Oyer and Terminer, cited in *Goodspeed's History of Tennessee*, 896.

18. 27 Nov. 1780, Wash CPQS, book 1778-85.

19. Evan Shelby to Isaac and John Shelby, 3 Jan. 1771, in Abernethy, *From Frontier to Plantation*, 4.

20. Gump, "Possessions and Patterns," 103, 105, 98. In archaeological excavations up to the year 1813 at the Tipton-Haynes site just east of present-day Johnson City, hog remains constituted the most frequent findings. Ibid., 99-100.

21. William Blount to John Gray Blount, 10 Nov. 1790, in Keith, *John Gray Blount Papers*, vol. 2, 140.

22. Gray, *History of Agriculture*, vol. 2, 840.

23. Michaux, *Travels to the West*, 281.

24. Gray, *History of Agriculture*, vol. 2, 840. For a recent examination of the livestock industry in the Shenandoah Valley, see MacMaster, "The Cattle Trade," 127-49.

25. One can survey the extensive literature on subsistence and market agriculture by consulting Clark, *The Roots of Rural Capitalism*; Henretta, *The Origins of American Capitalism*; Kulikoff, *The Agrarian Origins*; and Merrill, "Cash is Good to Eat," 42-71. For the southern mountain region, see Hahn, *The Roots of Southern Populism*, 29-49; and Inscoe, *Mountain Masters*, 11-58.

26. Sevier, "Executive Journal," 5 Feb. 1794 for the sugar, 26 May 1796 for the debts, and 10 Nov. 1795 for Harrison's and Deaderick's store, pp. 169, 187, 181. Webs of indebtedness that tied local residents together appear in many frontier areas; see, for example, Melvoin, *New England Outpost*, and Faragher, *Sugar Creek*.

27. Steiner and Schweinitz, "Report of the Journey," 450. Michaux, *Travels to the West*, 270. For a specific merchant in a comparable area, see Blethen and Wood, "A Trader," 150-65.

28. *Knoxville Gazette*, 23 March 1793.

29. Ibid., 14 July 1792. The Cowans may also have operated on a national scale, but their advertisement did not mention such connections.

30. Fink, *Jonesborough*, 75, cites this information from Deaderick's 1801 daybook.

31. Nov. 1788 sessions, Wash CPQS, book 1787-98.

32. *Washington Newspaper and Advertiser* (Jonesborough), 9 Dec. 1803.

33. Sevier, "Executive Journal," 1 Aug. 1796, p. 189. Indeed, few could take the complementary step and "let Muhl. Harrison have 100 dollars to pay the waggoners for bringing goods from Richmond" or send "the waggon & horses to Jonesbo[rough] to set out for Richmond." Ibid., 6 Sept. 1796 and 29 Nov. 1796, pp. 190, 192.

34. *Washington Newspaper and Advertiser*, 9 Dec. 1803.

35. H.R. Allen, Day Book–Journal B, Jonesborough, Jan. 1800–April 1802, vol. 287, WCCR. The account numbers for Gaines, Robert Allen, and William Allen are 33, 91, and 139, respectively. One cannot determine whether the latter two customers were relatives of John and Robert Allen; if so, such familial ties may explain this movement between counties.

36. The four most frequent customers—John Kennedy, Dr. William Chester, John Brown, and Thomas Stuart—all owned lots in Jonesborough. The most frequent customer in the unlocated group, Mrs. Rosey Bean, almost certainly was married to Russell Bean, a Washington County resident. I located the customers primarily by using the 1798, 1799, and 1801 Washington County tax lists, in "Washington County List of Taxables."

37. Gump, "Possessions and Patterns," 162, for Smith and Dungan; Sevier, "Executive Journal," 181-82, for Allen. The way in which Sevier paid Allen reveals that upper East Tennessee operated not merely on barter but with exchanged notes using a variety of currencies as well. "Josiah Allen set out for home, paid him off for his work by giving him up his note of £6.19, that I got from J. Lacky. Let him have 2 coats for which he is to wall in a Cellar in Feby. next. Paid Josiah Allen for John Richmond 7 dollars, for James Sevier at Mr. May's store £3.2.9 also cash 4 dollars. John Richmond Dr. to cash paid Jos. Allen 7 dollars." Sevier, "Executive Journal," 3 Jan. 1796, p. 183.

38. Gump, "Possessions and Patterns," 166-69.

39. Ibid., 155 lists John Clark, Joseph Hedrick, Elisha Cooper, Ezekiel Able, and Henry Bolboh as blacksmiths. According to the tax lists, Clark lived in Gann's company in 1801 and Hedrick in what became Carter County. Gump mentions that the silversmith Leroy Taylor lived in Leesburg. Gold- and silversmith William Hilliard took orders in Jonesborough; *Washington Newspaper and Advertiser*, 1 Feb. 1804.

40. Fink, *Jonesborough*, 46-48.

41. *Manumission Intelligencer* (Jonesborough), 27 April 1819.

42. Ibid.

43. Williams, "Early Iron Works," 41.

44. Ibid., 45 for Sevier and King. Sevier wrote on 6 Aug. 1795 that he "put into the hands of Walter King a 300 acre & 640 acre warrant to be laid on lands in Sullivan Opposite the Iron Works on No. side of Holston"; Sevier, "Executive Journal," 179. For Carter, see Delfino, "Antebellum East Tennessee Elites," 105.

45. Fink, *Jonesborough*, 64.

46. Fink, "Bumpass Cove Mines," 51-53. The county court encouraged the industry by granting land "unfit for cultivation" to iron works. Chester, for example, received 3,000 acres; 3 Nov. 1812, Wash CPQS, book 1809-17. J. Peck estimated that "the range of hills producing these ores, extends over a distance of from eight to ten miles in length, and more than a mile in breadth"; *Tennessee Farmer* (Jonesborough), Jan. 1838, p. 175.

47. *Manumission Intelligencer*, 27 April 1819. For ironworks in a neighboring area, see Blethen and Wood, "The Antebellum Iron Industry," 79-87.

48. Deaderick, "Journal of Events," 131-32.

49. Ibid., 133, 136-37.

50. Brantz, "Memoranda," 205; Francis Baily, "Journal of a Tour in Unsettled Parts of North America (1797)," in Williams, *Early Travels*, 412.

51. Morris, *The Tennessee Gazetteer*, 211.

52. See Drew Gilpin Faust's historiographical survey of antebellum southern economy and society in "The Peculiar South Revisited," 78-119. For the cotton economy, see pp. 78-86.

53. Gray, *History of Agriculture*, vol. 2, 687, 892. These statistics, based in part on Levi Woodbury's *Tables and Notes*, challenge claims that cotton declined in importance as a cash crop for Middle Tennessee; see Arnow, *Flowering*, 246-48. Others argue that Middle Tennessee farmers shifted away from cotton and toward corn after the 1830s; see Ash, *Middle Tennessee Society*. Despite the rise in planter production, most farmers concentrated their efforts on their own needs and produced only small amounts of cotton. See Rothstein, "The Antebellum South," 373-82, and Wright, *The Political Economy*.

54. Arnow, *Flowering*, 248-49. Steiner and Schweinitz, "Report of the Journey," 516, say that little wheat was grown, "partly because good mills are rare; partly because so much of it is consumed by worms." They also tell how the first peach pits and apple seeds entered the region; ibid., 512.

55. Arnow, *Flowering*, 222. Davidson County, County Court Minutes, Book A, 1783-1791, microfilmed by the Tennessee State Library and Archives, reel 1597, pp. 8, 19-21, 38, 41, 52, and 66-67 for 1783 to 1785 alone. Royall, *Letters from Alabama*, 93. Yet Steiner and Schweinitz, "Report of the Journey," 516, claim that "in the raising of cattle, likewise, little progress has been made."

56. Michaux, *Travels to the West*, 280, 281.

57. Ibid., 277-78. "West Tennessea" refers to present-day Middle Tennessee.

58. Steiner and Schweinitz, "Report of the Journey," 514.

59. Constable and Constable, "Daniel and William Constable Journal," 193.

60. Steiner and Schweinitz, "Report of the Journey," 516. County court records show the establishment of only a few water gristmills during the first decade of settlement; see Davidson County Court Minutes, Book A, 3, 107, 203, 404, 413.

61. Brantz, "Memoranda," 285-86.

62. Arnow, *Flowering*, 234.

63. Michaux, *Travels to the West*, 251-52. Yet Steiner and Schweinitz thought such a water route enabled prices to be kept lower. "The merchants receive their goods from Pittsburg, whence they are taken down the Ohio and transshipped up the Cumberland River. The easy freightage by water is cause for the fact that European goods, the long distance from the seaports notwithstanding, are to be had here at cheap rates." Steiner and Schweinitz, "Report of the Journey," 508. Clearly, what seems expensive to one person may seem affordable to another.

64. Michaux, *Travels to the West*, 184, 252-53.

65. Bacon, "Nashville's Trade," 31-36. Michaux, *Travels to the West*, 252.

66. *Tennessee Gazette*, 18 Feb. 1801.

67. Faux, "Memorable Days in America," 151.

68. Gray, *History of Agriculture*, vol. 2, 870. Gray quotes articles in the Nashville *Review* from 1810.

69. Woodbridge, *History of Nashville, Tenn.*, 302-11.

70. The economic differences between Middle and East Tennessee echo similar relationships that, for example, Steven Hahn, *The Roots of Southern Populism*, finds in antebellum Georgia. As the Black Belt planters in middle Georgia grew even richer in the 1850s, upcountry yeomen resisted the call of commercial agriculture and instead practiced farming that met subsistence needs first and exchanged goods primarily on the local level. Differences in geography and outlook pushed upcountry yeomen ever further behind economically their fellow Georgians in the Black Belt, despite the spread of cotton cultivation and an improved transportation system that included the Western and Atlantic Railroad. See Hahn, *The Roots of Southern Populism*, 29-49.

71. Michaux, *Travels to the West*, 282.

72. Deaderick, "Journal of Events," 132. Farmers, he noticed in 1827, were "decidedly improving on their former practices. Clover is used much more extensively, manuring is seen more in its important light. And some, though very few, are beginning to experiment with lime as manure." Without such changes, Deaderick concluded, "the country must be deserted or the lands *turned out* and more cleared." Ibid., 131.

73. This region, excluding Sullivan County, generally voted Whig from 1835 to 1841. See Bergeron, *Antebellum Politics*, 21, table 2.4.

74. Fink, *Jonesborough*, 252-54; an obituary for Emmerson appears in *Tennessee Farmer*, Aug. 1837, p. 128. Mason Lyon and J. Franklin Deaderick continued to publish the newspaper for one year after Emmerson's death.

75. *Knoxville Enquirer*, 3 Nov. 1824, cited in Fink, "Some Phases," 37, n. 15, mentions the proceedings of the Washington County Agricultural Society; *Tennessee Farmer*, Dec. 1834, p. 1.

76. Brown, *Knowledge Is Power*, 157.

77. *Tennessee Farmer*, July 1836, p. 305.

78. The range of sources shows that the region was not isolated with regard to information. The Jan. 1834 issue, for example, contains articles from the *Genessee Farmer* and *A Treatise on Agriculture* (both New York), the *Maine Farmer*, the *Talahassee Advertiser*, and the *Vermont Free Press*. Newspaper notices arrived from the *Jackson Truth Teller* (Tennessee), the *Independent Yeoman*, the *Tennessee Beacon*, the *North Carolina Standard*, and Tennessee newspapers in Clarksville, Boyd's Creek, and Columbia.

79. *Tennessee Farmer*, June 1835 and Dec. 1834.

80. Ibid., Jan. 1834, pp. 20-21.

81. Ibid., Nov. 1835, pp. 190-91, 180.

82. "History of Navigation on the Tennessee River System," House Doc., No. 254, 75th Cong., 1st sess., 1937, p. 119; Adam Broyles deposition, Bill of Exceptions, *Henderson Clark* vs. *Montgomery Stuart*, 28 Feb. 1852, WCCR, box 118, folder 4. Several depositions in this case claim the Nolichucky, even in the 1850s, was unnavigable except going downstream during an occasional flood.

83. Folmsbee, *Sectionalism and Internal Improvements*, 26-33.

84. Ibid., p. 81, for the board; p. iii for the quoted statement.

85. Solomon and Catharine Beals to David and Elizabeth Stanfield (Grant County, Indiana), 27 Dec. 1837, and Hannah Beals to David and Elizabeth Stanfield, 6 Feb. 1840, Samuel Cole Williams Papers, box 4, folder 21, Tennessee State Library and Archives.

86. George W. and Rebecca Moore (Greene Co.) to William and James Moore, 2 March 1843, Moore Family Small Collection, V-K-1, box 7, Tennessee State Library and Archives.

87. *Tennessee Whig*, 19 Sept. 1839.

88. Ibid., 27 June 1839, 19 Sept. 1839.

89. Buckwalter, "Effects," 26-30.

90. *Tennessee Farmer*, May 1838, p. 258.

91. Ibid., Nov. 1835, p. 178.

92. The latest work to address this issue is McWhiney, *Cracker Culture*. In 1825, David A. Deaderick wrote, "Drunkenness at public meetings has become much less common than at the period referred to [1811-13]. Yet this evil is at *present*, perhaps the most common, and most to be depricated of any equal enormity amongst us." Deaderick, "Journal of Events," 126.

93. *Tennessee Farmer*, April 1838, p. 241, and Nov. 1835, p. 178.

94. "A Friend of Agriculture" to *Washington Republican and Farmers Journal*, reprinted in *Tennessee Farmer*, Jan. 1834, p. 18.

95. Deaderick, "Journal of Events," 128.

96. Ibid., 130, 133.

97. Ibid.

98. Ibid., 130.

## 4. POPULATION PERSISTENCE IN WASHINGTON COUNTY

1. Fox, "The Southern Mountaineers," 387.

2. Frost, "Our Contemporary Ancestors," 315.

3. Campbell, *The Southern Highlander*, 250.

4. Michaux, *Travels to the West*, 193-94 (reprint edition).

5. Parkerson, "How Mobile?" 99.

6. Jones, *Village and Seaport*, 107-8, 106.

7. Smith, "Migration," 476, 478. For the Massachusetts and Virginia data, Smith cites G.C. Villaflor and K.L. Sokoloff, "Migration in Colonial America," 539-70.

8. Shy, "Migration and Persistence," 225.

9. Beeman, *Evolution*, 67, 162.

10. Kenzer, *Kinship and Neighborhood*, 164, table 3A.

11. Soltow, "Progress and Mobility," 408.

12. Barron, *Those Who Stayed Behind*, 79, table 5.1.

13. Dunn, *Cades Cove*, 17, 69, 179.

14. Paludan, *Victims*, 6, 9.

15. McKenzie, *One South or Many?* table 2.2 on p. 75, quoted statement on p. 77.

16. The 1778 estimate appears in *Goodspeed's History of Tennessee*, 891. The 1800 and 1840 figures appear in U.S. Bureau of the Census, Census of the United States, 1800, 1840.

17. These tax lists are contained in Washington County, Trustee's Office, Tax Books, microfilmed by the Tennessee State Library and Archives, Nashville, Tennessee, rolls 639 and 640. The records on roll 639 were transcribed by Mary H. McCown and Nancy J. Stickley, "Washington County List of Taxables," WPA Project 65-44-258.

18. For District 1, see Henley 1790, Gann 1797, Greer 1806, Waddell 1814, and Gray 1824. For District 7/18, see Greasy Cove 1792, Longmire 1797, Odell 1806, Brown 1814, and Haines 1824. For District 13, see Shipley 1790 and 1797, Rector 1805, Barnes 1814, and Hartsell 1824.

19. Walsh, "The Historian as Census Taker" and "Staying Put or Getting Out," 242-60; and 44 (1987), 89-103.

20. Barron, *Those Who Stayed Behind*, 81.

21. McKenzie, *One South or Many?* 75. From 1850 to 1860 in Grainger, Greene, and Johnson Counties, McKenzie shows that farm owners heading free farm households persisted at a rate of 61.5 percent, while the landless stayed at a rate of only 48.5 percent. For heads of households in those same counties in 1860, tenants formed between 16.7 percent and 39.7 percent of the population. See table 2.2 on p. 75 and table 1.3 on p. 25.

22. Parkerson, "How Mobile?" 105, 109, n. 19.

23. Fox, "The Southern Mountaineers," 390.

24. John Gregg in Harrison County, Indiana Territory, to cousin, 27 Dec. 1813, in LaSalle Collection, Indiana Division of the Indiana State Library, Indianapolis. I thank Gregory A. Parrott of Lincoln Trail College for providing a copy of this letter.

25. Benjamin Hyder in Park County, Indiana, to Michael Hyder in Elizabethton, Carter County, Tennessee, 12 Dec. 1830, in Hyder Family Small Collection, Box 10:1, Tennessee State Library and Archives.

26. Hannah Beals in Rheatown, Washington County, to David and Elizabeth Stanfield in Grant County, Indiana, 6 Feb. 1940, in Samuel Cole Williams Papers, Box 4, Tennessee State Library and Archives.

27. Consider the 1790 figures for District 13. The number of individuals from that list drops from twenty-three in 1797 to just a single person in 1805 and to two in 1814, a drop far greater than in any other district during any other time period. But when we examine the rest of Washington County in 1814, we find sixteen more people from the 1790 list, bringing the persistence rate up to 39.1 percent. Similarly, when the 1797 list is considered, eighteen additional people are found in other districts for 1814. Thirty-seven former residents of the District 13 region were found elsewhere in the county in 1814; twenty-six of these individuals lived in the Copas militia company. It seems plausible that a portion of Shipley's company (the District 13 region in 1790 and 1797) came under Copas's control by 1805.

28. The evidence for District 7/18—more surnames in the district than in the rest of the county combined—suggests that this most mountainous district was more self-contained than other portions of the county. At the end of this chapter I consider the role that such evidence may play in the characterizations of Appalachia.

29. *Journal of the Proceedings*, 29 Sept. 1794, p. 33.

30. Fink, "Bumpass Cove Mines," 51. Swingle's property appears on Tax Books, Captain Odell's company, 1806, roll 639.

31. 3 Nov. 1812, Wash CPQS, book 1809-17, p. 100. The court's earlier instructions appear on 26 May 1794, Wash CPQS, book 1787-98, pp. 241-42. Chester's purchase appears in Fink, "Bumpass Cove Mines," p. 51. Such vast tracts of land provided the wood necessary for making charcoal, which in turn played an essential role in the iron-making process.

32. Fink, "Bumpass Cove Mines," 50, 52-54. "Elijah Embree boated corn up the [Nolichucky] river one season in a keel or flat bottom boat but he abandoned the upward navigation as unprofitable. He was a man of great energy and perseverance and would not have abandoned it if he had found it practical or profitable." Reuben Rogers deposition, 28 Feb. 1852, in *Henderson Clark* vs. *Montgomery Stuart*, Bill of Exceptions, p. 15, in WCCR, box 118:4, "1850 Circuit Court-Civil," Archives of Appalachia.

33. The county court appointed an overseer for "the road from Col. Dillards to James Stuarts esqr and the working hands from me Stuarts up to the Greesey Cove & above to work thereon." James Stuart lived about ten miles northeast of Greasy Cove; the road mentioned by the court must have followed North Indian Creek. See 6 Feb. 1782, Wash CPQS, book 1778-85. James Stuart is placed on a hand-drawn map located in the Samuel Cole Williams Collection, box 4, acc. no. 85-13. Internal evidence from the court minutes supports this location.

34. 26 Nov. 1778, Wash CPQS, book 1778-85.

35. Aug. 1810, Wash CPQS, book 1809-17. Jump Hill is located opposite Bumpass Cove on the north side of the Nolichucky. The Red Bank Ford (or Fort) is found at Greasy Cove, according to Sevier and Madden, *Sevier Family History*, 35.

36. Deaderick, "Journal of Events," 133.

37. Simeon Broyles, Sr., appears on the 1845 Scholastic Population list for School District 3, which names Cassi Creek as one of its boundaries. The list is located in Washington County Court Records, box 267:4, "Education," Archives of Appalachia. My discussion of school districts below draws on this archival source material. For Clark and Glaze, see Watauga Association of Genealogists, *History of Washington County*, 170, 344. Since Winkle joined Glaze on the list for School District 2, Winkle presumably lived nearby.

38. For Longmire, see Frazier, *Tennessee Postoffices*, 791. School District 19, which contains Edwards, is also called "Longmire's District." Love's general location is identified on the hand-drawn map in the Samuel Cole Williams collection, mentioned in a previous footnote. His property appears in this area in "Washington County Tennessee Deeds," abstracted by Loraine B. Rae, *Watauga Association of Genealogists Bulletin* 10:2 (1981), 83; 11:2 (1982), 32; and 12:2 (1983), 93. Tilson lived in School District 16, as did Thomas Brown, who was Flag Pond's postmaster the following summer; see *Tennessee Postoffices*, 789. Flag Pond sits at the intersection of the three creeks.

39. The 1792 Greasy Cove tax lists appear in McCown, *Washington County, Tennessee, Records*, 88-89; Edmond Sams's purchase appears in Rae, "Washington County Tennessee Deeds," 11:1 (1982), 5; Webb's grant appears in *North Carolina Land Grants*, 8.

40. This portion of the diary is reprinted in Alderman, *Greasy Cove*, 7.

41. Two large tracts of land, presumably for the ironworks, were taxed at very low rates in 1845. William S. Erwin's 5,640 acres were worth $20, and John M. Seehorn's 5,000 acres were valued at $100.

42. For Erwin's transfers to Jacob C. and Mary Sams, which includes the background information on James Sams, see Washington County Register's Office, Deed Books, vol. 31, pp. 320-23, and vol. 32, pp. 367-69, microfilmed by the Tennessee State Library and Archives, reels 203 and 204, respectively. For Josiah B. Sams's obligations, see reel 204, vol. 32, pp. 269-71.

43. See the deeds mentioned in note 39 as well as Deed Books, reel 204, vol. 32, pp. 92, 313, 315; vol. 33, p. 371; and vol. 34, p. 185. A deed of 3 Feb. 1851 places Jacob C. Sams precisely in the Sams Gap region, "on the headwaters of South Indian Creek" with property straddling the Walnut Mountain road. Walnut Mountain is located directly southwest of Sams Gap in North Carolina. See vol. 32, p. 313.

44. The agreement between Spencer Rice and Jacob C. Sams on 1 Dec. 1856 appears in Deed Books, vol. 36, pp. 298-300.

45. James Higgins sold fifty acres to John Edwards in 1851; Deed Books, vol. 33, pp. 371-72. Several earlier deeds refer to the Edwards fork of Indian Creek, so perhaps John Edwards lived near family members who were already

settled. Ellis Higgins sold land bordering the North Carolina state line to David Profit of Yancey County, North Carolina. Profit owned land and may have lived on land which adjoined this new tract; vol. 37, pp. 356-57.

46. Deaderick, "Journal of Events," 127.

47. Deaderick, "Journal of Events," 127, n. 10. The attorney general's statement for *State* vs. *David Greer*, March term, 1825, is found in Washington County Court Records, box 75:13, "1822 Circuit Court-Civil/Criminal." George Tompkins killed Greer in self-defense in 1834, according to Pat Alderman, "Hermit of Big Bald," in *Greasy Cove*. For a discussion of other "hermits" in North Carolina, see Inscoe, *Mountain Masters*, 53-57.

## 5. Railroads in Upper East Tennessee

1. The developments in upper East Tennessee may usefully be compared with mid-nineteenth-century Kentucky as analyzed by Mary Beth Pudup. She writes: "Southeast Kentucky became relatively isolated from changes taking place during the nineteenth century. But isolation did not so much 'retard' or 'arrest' development as establish a particular path of social and economic development for the mountain region. That developmental path was constituted through social relations both within and outside the region." See Pudup, "Social Class and Economic Development," 243. Kenneth W. Noe describes southwest Virginia's efforts at obtaining internal improvements during the 1830s and early 1840s in *Southwest Virginia's Railroad*, 16-18.

2. See Carter on 11 Dec. 1837 and 19 May 1838 in *Congressional Globe*, 25th Cong., 2d sess., vol. 6, pp. 19, 394; 14 March 1836, 24th Cong., 1st sess., vol. 2-3, p. 254.

3. Motion submitted 15 April 1836, *Register of Debates in Congress*, 24th Cong., 1st sess., vol. 12, pp. 3286-87. A strain of environmental determinism can be seen in Carter's conclusion. Nature not only shaped the region's economic potential but also, by its mountains and river obstructions, hindered access to market and thwarted the "independence and happiness of the people."

4. Ibid.

5. "Memorial to the Honorable the Senate and House of Representatives of the United States in Congress assembled," reprinted in *Farmers' Journal*, 15 Jan. 1831.

6. Ibid.

7. Ibid.

8. *Farmers' Journal*, 15 Jan. 1831.

9. Ibid., 14 Nov. 1831.

10. Ibid.

11. "Report of the Committee of Internal Improvements in the House of Representatives in relation to the Lynchburg and New River Rail Road," 3 Dec. 1831, reprinted in *Washington Republican and Farmers Journal*, 8 Nov. 1834.

12. "To the People of Virginia and Tennessee," Abingdon Convention, Virginia *Republican*, reprinted in *Farmers' Journal*, 14 Nov. 1831. For a full discus-

sion of Southwest Virginia's efforts at building a railroad, see Noe, *Southwest Virginia's Railroad*, chap. 1.

13. Ibid.

14. *Farmers' Journal*, 14 Nov. 1831.

15. Chandler, *The Railroads*, 3.

16. Holland, "The Building," 83-84; Folmsbee, "The Beginning of the Railroad Movement," 84-85.

17. Folmsbee, "The Beginning of the Railroad Movement," 81.

18. Ibid., 85, 87-89.

19. Resolution of 14 March 1836, *Congressional Globe*, 24th Cong., 1st sess., 254.

20. Message of 23 Oct. 1836, *Washington Republican and Farmers' Journal*, 5 Nov. 1836.

21. Ibid., 5 Nov. 1836; 10 Dec. 1836.

22. Folmsbee, "The Beginning of the Railroad Movement," 97-98, 100. The railroad dropped all plans for crossing the mountains of upper East Tennessee in Dec. 1840, when the Tennessee legislature voted against funding the project.

23. Holland, "East Tennessee and Georgia," 95.

24. *Tennessee Whig*, 3 Oct. 1839, 5 Dec. 1839; Holland, "East Tennessee and Georgia," 95, 99-100; "East Tennessee and Virginia," 84.

25. McGaughey, "Succinct History"; *Acts of the State of Tennessee*, 195-99.

26. Holland, "East Tennessee and Virginia," 85-86.

27. The figure comes from the *Jonesborough Whig*, 6 April 1849, cited in Fink, "Did You Know."

28. Andrew Johnson to "an Intelligent Gentleman in Jonesborough," letter in the *Nashville Union and American*, 29 May 1853, about a letter originally written 30 March 1849, reprinted in Johnson, *The Papers of Andrew Johnson*, vol. 1, p. 492.

29. McGaughey, "Succinct History." Land ownership can be determined from the tax lists in the Trustee's Office, Washington County Court Records, microfilm reel 640, Tennessee State Library and Archives, Nashville.

30. *Rail Road Journal*, 13 April 1850, 26 Oct. 1850. The 1850 census lists Samuel Greer, age sixty, as an editor and James L. Sparks, age thirty-six, as a printer. The two men shared more than just an affinity for railroads; they (along with their families) lived in the same dwelling house, number 158 on the census taker's route. George E. Grisham, age eighteen and listed under Greer's family, worked as a typesetter. He eventually published the *East Tennessee Union Flag* in Jonesborough from 1865 until his death a decade later. See U.S. Bureau of the Census, *Seventh Census of the United States, 1850*, and various issues of the *Union Flag*, reel JON 101, "Jonesboro Misc. 1844-1922," microfilmed by the Tennessee State Library and Archives, Nashville, Tennessee.

31. For the newspapers' support of railroads in Southwest Virginia, see Noe, *Southwest Virginia's Railroad*, 23.

32. Ibid., 27 April 1850, reprinted from the Greeneville *Spy*.

33. Ibid., 28 Sept. 1850.

34. McGaughey, "Succinct History."

35. *Rail Road Journal*, 5 Oct. 1850. For a comparable case in which wealthy

railroad advocates faced problems of raising money and of local resistance, see the discussion of the Georgia upcountry in Hahn, *The Roots of Southern Populism*, 34-38.

36. Lloyd Tilghman, "To the President, Directors, and Stockholders, E.T. & Va. R.R. Company," 29 April 1850, reprinted in *Rail Road Journal*, 4 May 1850. For biographical information on Tilghman, see ibid., 13 April 1850; Tilghman, *First Annual Report*.

37. *Rail Road Journal*, 4 May 1850.

38. In southwest Virginia, Kenneth W. Noe similarly finds that "townspeople as a group sang the virtues of railroad construction. To them, railroads provided a golden opportunity to increase their profits and their economic hegemony over the rural hinterlands." Noe, *Southwest Virginia's Railroad*, 58.

39. *First Annual Report*, 17-18.

40. Ibid., 56-57.

41. *Rail Road Journal*, 27 April 1850.

42. Ibid., 5 Oct. 1850.

43. *Abingdon Virginian*, reprinted in *Rail Road Journal*, 26 Oct. 1850.

44. *First Annual Report*, 48-49.

45. *Farmers' Journal*, 14 Nov. 1831; *Rail Road Journal*, 5 Oct. 1850.

46. *Rail Road Journal*, 5 Oct. 1850.

47. Ibid., 4 May 1850.

48. *First Annual Report*, 37, 32. The Abingdon Rail Road convention expressed similar views for its section. The route, "the most direct location possible across the Union, connects New Orleans with the Seat of the National Government and the Eastern Cities," thereby "exerting as it must, a great and, as we believe, most beneficent influence on all the great interests of our country." *Abingdon Virginian*, reprinted in *Rail Road Journal and Family Visitor*, 18 Oct. 1851.

49. *First Annual Report*, 51, 53.

50. Letter from Marietta, Cobb County, Georgia, 30 Sept. 1851, printed in *Rail Road Journal and Family Visitor*, 18 Oct. 1851.

51. *Rail Road Journal*, 13 April 1850.

52. *Abingdon Virginian*, reprinted in *Rail Road Journal and Family Visitor*, 18 Oct. 1851.

53. *Rail Road Journal*, 21 Sept. 1850.

54. Ibid., 13 April 1850.

55. Ibid., 5 Oct. 1850.

56. Ibid., 4 May 1850.

57. Ibid., 27 April 1850. For opposition to the railroad in Southwest Virginia, see Noe, *Southwest Virginia's Railroad*, 24 and 27.

58. Holland, "East Tennessee and Virginia," 91.

59. *Nashville Union and American*, 29 May 1853, reprinted in Johnson, *Papers of Andrew Johnson*, vol. 1, pp. 492-93.

60. *Jonesborough Whig*, 6 April 1849, reprinted in Fink, "Did You Know," pt. 3.

61. *Rail Road Journal*, 4 May 1850.

62. *Greeneville Spy*, reprinted in *Rail Road Journal*, 13 April 1850.

63. Ibid.

64. *Greeneville Spy*, reprinted in *Rail Road Journal*, 27 April 1850.

65. *Rail Road Journal*, 13 April 1850.

66. Ibid., 27 April 1850.

67. Tilghman, *First Annual Report*, 22, 4, 14, 13.

68. Ibid., 15-16.

69. Ibid., 19.

70. Fink, "Did You Know," part 7.

71. Tilghman, *First Annual Report*, 22, 32. Wages were included in the grading and masonry budget. Tilghman considered the following estimates, which he used, to be generous: "labour at fifteen dollars per month, corn at fifty cents, Bacon eight cents, and other articles of use and consumption at the same rates"; ibid., 23. Michael and John Clem were paid for specific jobs, such as earth excavation, per cubic yard, deposited within 100 feet (eleven cents); loose rock excavation (thirty cents); solid rock excavation (seventy cents); hauling earth per 100 feet beyond the first 100 (three-quarters of a cent); plank in foundation, per 1,000 feet (fourteen dollars); bridge abutments and piers, per cubic yard (four dollars). They received half of the payment in bank notes and half in 6 percent bonds convertible into company stock when the road was completed. Fink, "Did You Know," pt. 7.

72. McGaughey, "Succinct History." The date of the groundbreaking was misprinted as 1857 instead of 1851.

73. *Rail Road Journal and Family Visitor*, 30 Aug. 1851.

74. Ibid.

75. Notice of 11 Jan. 1851, *Congressional Globe*, 31st Cong., 2d sess., vol. 23, pp. 225, 246. Albert G. Watkins, representing a congressional district just east of Knoxville along the railroad route, also gave notice of a bill granting lands to the state of Tennessee to aid railroad construction; ibid., 229.

76. McGaughey, "Succinct History." The conditions were evidently met fairly quickly, for by the summer of 1852 the first $100,000 of bonds were sold; Holland, "East Tennessee and Virginia," 94.

77. Fink, "Did You Know," pt. 6.

78. McGaughey, "Succinct History."

79. Samuel B. Cunningham to Andrew Johnson, 29 Feb. 1856, in Johnson, *Papers of Andrew Johnson*, vol. 2, p. 379.

80. Andrew Johnson, "Biennial Legislative Message," 8 Oct. 1855, ibid., 329.

81. McGaughey, "Succinct History."

82. Samuel B. Cunningham to Andrew Johnson, 30 Oct. 1855 and 29 Feb. 1856, in Johnson, *Papers of Andrew Johnson*, vol. 2, pp. 345, 379-80.

83. McGaughey, "Succinct History," and *Knoxville Register*, 7 Aug. 1856.

84. McGaughey, "Succinct History."

85. Ibid., *Knoxville Register*, 11 June 1857. "Inconvenient" may be an understatement, for McGaughey wrote that "perhaps the traveler who was compelled to encounter the mud-holes in going from one point to the other will never forget Bull's Gap."

86. Andrew Johnson, "Biennial Message," 6 Oct. 1857, in *Papers of Andrew Johnson*, vol. 2, p. 483; "Bonds Owned by Andrew Johnson on the 1st of Dec. 1858," vol. 3, pp. 198-99.

87. McGaughey, "Succinct History."

88. *Knoxville Register*, 10 June 1858.

89. Ibid.

90. McGaughey, "Succinct History."

91. Andrew Johnson to Robert Johnson, 15 June 1858, in *Papers of Andrew Johnson*, vol. 3, p. 191.

92. Fink, "Did You Know," pt. 9. The number of passenger coaches and box-cars may be inaccurate, because smudges on the newspaper have blurred the figures. Solomon Jacobs predicted in 1831 that the railroad would carry 7,200 tons of exports and 4,617 tons of imports; see text accompanying note 8 above.

93. "Influence of Railroads upon Agriculture," *Census of 1860, Agriculture,* reprinted in Chandler, *The Railroads*, 25. On the dramatic economic changes wrought by the Virginia and Tennessee Railroad in neighboring Southwest Virginia, see Noe, *Southwest Virginia's Railroad*, chaps. 2-3.

94. Buckwalter, "Effects," 33-34.

95. Tilghman, *First Annual Report*, 58-59.

96. *Knoxville Register*, 20 May 1858.

97. *Rail Road Journal and Family Visitor*, 30 Aug. 1851.

98. Ibid.

99. *Rail Road Journal*, 27 April 1850.

100. Tilghman, *First Annual Report*, 44-45.


## 6. THE CREATION OF POPULAR APPALACHIAN IMAGES

1. Eby, *"Porte Crayon,"* 68-73. For Strother's birthdate and the figure of fifty-five articles, see pp. 4, vii.

2. Ibid., 93 and 218 for the quotations. "A Winter in the South" appeared as an unsigned story over seven installments in *Harper's New Monthly Magazine* 15-16 (1857-58). For the Greer quotation, see *Harper's* 16 (Jan. 1858): 168.

3. Eby, *"Porte Crayon,"* 94.

4. "Winter," Oct. 1857, pp. 594 (for Bristol), 606 (for Jonesborough); Nov. 1857, p. 722 (for sewing and shopping).

5. Ibid., Nov. 1857, pp. 723, 724, 725. Throughout the story, Strother uses "Roane" instead of "Roan," the standard spelling today.

6. Ibid., 734 (for the path), 735 (for Wilson agreeing to guide), 738-39 (for "yaller dog" and "a cabin a little below here"), 740 (for "what buckwheat cakes" and Mrs. Wilson's declaration).

7. Ibid., Jan. 1858, pp. 169, 170-71, 171, 172.

8. Ibid., 172-73, 173. Deed records provide evidence supporting the factual basis of this account. On 21 Nov. 1858, G.W. Higgins sold to Thomas Smith 217 acres of land "on the waters of the Ball [Bald] Mountain creek" adjoining the lands of, among other people, one named Kenady Foster. See Deed Books, vol. 37, pp. 80-81.

9. Ibid., 174-75.

10. Ibid., 175-76.

11. Ibid., 178 (for the neighbors), 174 (for both the mill and Larkin as "necromancer"), 179 (for neighbors discussing mountains), 176-77 (for the Foster girls).

12. Ibid., 180, 183; May 1858, pp. 722, 721.

13. Shapiro, *Appalachia on Our Mind*, 8, 15.

14. Nathalia Wright, "Introduction," in Murfree, *In the Tennessee Mountains*, ix-x.

15. Shapiro, *Appalachia on Our Mind*, 3; Wright, "Introduction," xiii. Parks, *Charles Egbert Craddock*, 108, states that the book went through fourteen editions in the first two years, while Shapiro, p. 18, n. 32, states that eighteen editions were published by 1887.

16. Shapiro, *Appalachia on Our Mind*, 17-18, 18.

17. Dunn, "Mary Noailles Murfree," 197.

18. Letter to Houghton, Mifflin and Company, 24 June 1882, reprinted in Parks, *Charles Egbert Craddock*, 103.

19. Letter to Murfree, 5 Dec. 1883, ibid., 107, n. 19.

20. Shapiro, *Appalachia on Our Mind*, 57.

21. Murfree, *In the Tennessee Mountains*, 80 ("A-Playin' of Old Sledge at the Settlemint"); 289 ("The 'Harnt' That Walks Chilhowee"); 90 ("Old Sledge"). Durwood Dunn credits Murfree with having provided accurate descriptions of architecture and physical settings, but he criticizes her for distorting mountain speech and dialect. He concludes, "Murfree failed in many important respects to depict accurately her human fixtures in the Tennessee mountains." Dunn, "Mary Noailles Murfree," 198-201, quoted passage on p. 201.

22. Ibid., 91 ("Old Sledge"); 196-97 ("The Romance of Sunrise Rock"); 163 ("Electioneerin' on Big Injun Mounting"); 36 ("Drifting Down Lost Creek"). Many other characteristics are summarized in Wright, "Introduction," xvii-xxiv.

23. "Winter," Oct. 1857, pp. 603, 604.

24. Quoted from B.S. Bentley, *Beersheba Springs and Chickamauga Trace* (Chattanooga, n.d.), in Parks, *Charles Egbert Craddock*, 14.

25. Quoted from Fanny N.D. Murfree, "Biography of Mary Noailles Murfree," unpublished manuscript, in Parks, *Charles Egbert Craddock*, 54-55.

26. Quoted from E.B. Spence, "Collected Reminiscences of Mary Noailles Murfree" (master's thesis, Peabody College, 1928), in Parks, *Charles Egbert Craddock*, 55, n. 29.

27. Murfree to T.B. Aldrich, 30 Sept. 1884, in Parks, *Charles Egbert Craddock*, 119.

28. Parks, *Charles Egbert Craddock*, 130, 131.

29. Ibid., 177-78. Durwood Dunn, however, cites a 1932 interview where "Murfree's sister Fannie stated that the family took frequent trips to Smoky Mountain resorts during the 1870's." While the frequency of Murfree's visits during the 1870s might be debated, one cannot dispute that her childhood and early adult impressions of the mountain region were formed at Beersheba Springs, far to the west. See Dunn, "Mary Noailles Murfree," 198.

30. Shapiro, *Appalachia on Our Mind*, 20.
31. "Winter," May 1858, 721.

## EPILOGUE: THE IMPLICATIONS OF CONNECTEDNESS

1. Williams, *History of Johnson City*, 21. One contemporary account calls Johnson City "the largest and most enterprising town in Washington County" and estimates its population at 3,000. See *Goodspeed's History of Tennessee*, 902-3, quoted statement on p. 902.

2. *The Comet* [Johnson City], 16 Aug. 1884. In the article that follows, some punctuation and spelling have been regularized for the sake of clarity. I thank Tom Lee for bringing this piece to my attention.

# Selected Bibliography

PRIMARY SOURCES

**Manuscript Collections**

Archives of Appalachia, Sherrod Library, East Tennessee State
University, Johnson City, Tennessee
    Murray Family Papers
    Special Collections
    Vertical Files
    Washington County Court Records
        Circuit Court Records
        County Court Records
        Justice of the Peace Records
        Miscellaneous Records
        Miscellaneous Judicial Documents
Hoskins Library, University of Tennessee, Knoxville, Tennessee
    Special Collections
Public Records Office, London, England
    Cornwallis Papers. Microfilm copy at the University of
        Michigan, Ann Arbor
Tennessee State Library and Archives, Nashville, Tennessee
    Carter County
        Court of Pleas and Quarter Sessions. Minute Book.
            Prepared and typed by the Tennessee Historical Records
            Survey, Works Projects Administration. Microfilm copy
    Davidson County. County Court Minutes
    Hyder Family Small Collection
    Jacob McGavock Dickinson Papers
    Moore Family Small Collection
    Samuel Cole Williams Papers
    Washington County

County Court Clerk's Office. Minute Books
County Court and Quarterly Court. Prepared and typed by
the Tennessee Historical Records Survey, Works
Projects Administration. Microfilm copy
Register's Office. Deed Books. Microfilm copy
Trustee's Office. Tax Books. Microfilm copy
State Historical Society of Wisconsin, Madison, Wisconsin
Draper Manuscript Collection
William L. Clements Library, University of Michigan, Ann Arbor,
Michigan
Sir Henry Clinton Papers

## Published Primary Sources

*Acts of the State of Tennessee*. 27th General Assembly, 1st sess. Jackson: Gates
and Parker, 1848.
Asbury, Francis. *The Journal and Letters of Francis Asbury*. Edited by Elmer E.
Clark, J. Manning Potts, and Jacob S. Payton. 2 vols. Nashville: Abingdon
Press, 1958.
Bartram, William. *The Travels of William Bartram*. Edited by Francis Harper.
New Haven: Yale Univ. Press, 1958.
Blount, John Gray. *John Gray Blount Papers*. Edited by Alice Barnwell Keith. 4
vols. Durham, N.C.: Christian Printing, 1959.
Brantz, Lewis. "Memoranda of a Journey (1795)." In Samuel Cole Williams,
ed., *Early Travels in the Tennessee Country, 1540–1800*, pp. 284–86. Johnson
City, Tenn.: Watauga Press, 1928.
Chesney, Alexander. "Memoir of Captain Alexander Chesney, July, 1780." In
Samuel C. Williams, "The Battle of King's Mountain as seen by the British
Officers." *Tennessee Historical Magazine* 7 (1921): 54–61.
Clinton, Sir Henry. *An Historical Detail of Seven Years' Campaigns in North
America from 1775–1782*. 2 vols. London, 1783. Reprint: *The American Re-
bellion: Sir Henry Clinton's Narrative of His Campaigns, 1775-1787*. Edited
by William B. Willcox. New Haven: Yale Univ. Press, 1954.
*Congressional Globe*. Washington, D.C., 1838.
Constable, Daniel, and Constable, William. "Daniel and William Constable
Journal." In Samuel Cole Williams, "Nashville As Seen By Travellers, 1801–
1821." *Tennessee Historical Magazine* 1 (1930–31): 182-206.
Cornwallis, Charles Cornwallis. *Correspondence of Charles, First Marquis
Cornwallis*. Edited by Charles Ross. 3 vols. London: John Murray, 1859.
Cuming, Fortescue. "Sketches of a Tour to the Western Country . . . " In Reuben
Gold Thwaites, ed., *Early Western Travels, 1748–1846*. Vol. 4. New York:
AMS Press, 1966.
Deaderick, David Anderson. "Journal of Events (1825–1873) of David Ander-
son Deaderick." Edited by Samuel Cole Williams. *East Tennessee Historical
Society Publications* 8 (1936): 121–37.

Faux, William. "Memorable Days in America." In Reuben Gold Thwaites, ed., *Early Western Travels, 1748–1846*. Vol. 11. New York: AMS Press, 1966.

Jefferson, Thomas. *The Papers of Thomas Jefferson*. Edited by Julian P. Boyd. Vols. 10–11. Princeton, N.J.: Princeton Univ. Press, 1954–55.

Johnson, Andrew. *The Papers of Andrew Johnson*. Edited by Leroy P. Graf and Ralph W. Haskins. Vols. 1–3. Knoxville: Univ. of Tennessee Press, 1967–70.

*Journal of the Proceedings of the Legislative Council of the Territory of the United States of America, South of the River Ohio*. Knoxville: George Roulstone, 1794. Reprint. Nashville: McKennie and Brown, 1852.

*Journal of the Senate of the State of Tennessee*. Knoxville: George Roulstone, 1796. Reprint. Nashville: McKennie and Brown, 1852.

McGaughey, John. "A Succinct History of the East Tennessee and Virginia Railroad." *Knoxville Register*, 27 May 1858.

Michaux, François André. *Travels to the West of the Alleghany Mountains . . .* London, 1802. Reprinted in Reuben Gold Thwaites, ed., *Early Western Travels, 1748–1846*. Vol. 3. New York: AMS Press, 1966.

Morris, Eastin, comp. *The Tennessee Gazetteer*. Nashville: W. Hunt, 1834. Reprint. Edited by Robert M. McBride and Owen Meredith. Nashville: Gazetteer Press, 1971.

Murfree, Mary Noailles. *In the Tennessee Mountains*. New York: Houghton, Mifflin, 1884. Reprint. Knoxville: Univ. of Tennessee Press, 1970.

*North Carolina Land Grants in Tennessee, 1778–1791*. Compiled by Betty Goff Cook Cartwright and Lillian Johnson Gardiner. Memphis: I.C. Harper, 1958.

"Papers from the Spanish Archives Relating to Tennessee and the Old Southwest, 1783–1800.' Translated and edited by D.C. Corbitt and Roberta Corbitt. *East Tennessee Historical Society Publications* 15 (1943): 89-103.

*Register of Debates in Congress*. Washington, D.C.: Gales and Seaton, 1836.

Royall, Anne Newport. *Letters from Alabama, 1817–1822*. New York: 1830. Reprint. University: Univ. of Alabama Press, 1969.

*Scots Magazine*. January 1781. Reprinted in *State Records of North Carolina*. Edited by Walter Clark. Vol. 15. Goldsboro, N.C.: Nash Brothers, 1898.

Sevier, John. "Executive Journal of Governor John Sevier." Edited by Samuel Cole Williams. *East Tennessee Historical Society Publications* 1 (1929): 95–153.

———. "Journal of John Sevier." Edited by John H. DeWitt. *Tennessee Historical Magazine* 5–6 (1919–20): 156–94, 232–64, 18–68.

Shelby, Isaac. "King's Mountain Narrative." Reprinted in Lyman C. Draper, *King's Mountain and Its Heroes: History of the Battle of King's Mountain*. Cincinnati: Peter G. Thomson, 1881.

*State Records of North Carolina*. Edited by Walter Clark. Vols. 11–26. Goldsboro, N.C.: Nash Brothers, 1895–1906.

Steiner, Abraham, and Frederick C. de Schweinitz. "Report of the Journey to the Cherokees and the Cumberland Settlements (1799)." In Samuel Cole Williams, ed., *Early Travels in the Tennessee Country, 1540–1800*, pp. 448–525. Johnson City, Tenn.: Watauga Press, 1928.

[Strother, David Hunter]. "A Winter in the South." *Harper's New Monthly Magazine* 15–16 (1857–58).

Tilghman, Lloyd. *First Annual Report of the Chief Engineer to the President and Directors of the East Tennessee and Virginia Rail Road Company.* Jonesborough: Rail Road Journal, 1850.

United States Bureau of the Census, *Census of the United States,* 1800, 1830, 1840, 1850.

Vance, David, and Robert Henry. "King's Mountain Expedition." *Historical Papers.* Ser. 3, pp. 24–35, 78–89. Durham: Trinity College Historical Society, Duke University, 1899.

"Washington County, Tennessee, Deeds." Abstracted by Laraine B. Rae. *Watauga Association of Genealogists Bulletin* 10–12 (1981–83): 63-87, 4-15, 17-35, 3-17, 88-106.

*Washington County, Tennessee, Records.* Compiled by Mary H. McCown, Nancy E. Jones Stickley, and Inez E. Burns. Johnson City, Tenn.: Privately printed, 1964.

Weld, Isaac. *Travels Through the States of North America [1795–1797].* London, 1807. Reprint. New York: Augustus M. Kelley, 1970.

Woodbury, Levi. "On Cultivation and Manufacture of Cotton, Also Foreign Trade." U.S. House, Exec. Doc. 24-246. Washington, D.C.: Government Printing Office, 1836. Serial Set 289.

## Newspapers

*Comet* (Johnson City)
*Farmers' Journal* (Jonesborough)
*Knoxville Enquirer*
*Knoxville Gazette*
*Knoxville Register*
*Manumission Intelligencer* (Jonesborough)
*Rail Road Journal* (Jonesborough)
*Rail Road Journal and Family Visitor* (Jonesborough)
*Tennessee Farmer* (Jonesborough)
*Tennessee Gazette* (Nashville)
*Tennessee Whig* (Elizabethton)
*Virginia Gazette* (Richmond)
*Washington Newspaper and Advertiser* (Jonesborough)
*Washington Republican and Farmers' Journal* (Jonesborough)

## Maps

Archives of Appalachia, Sherrod Library, East Tennessee State University, Johnson City, Tennessee
Hyder, Nat E., Mildred Kozsuch, and Alan Park. "Early Carter County, Tennessee."

Samuel, P.T. "Washington County, Tennessee, Post Offices, 1796–1900."
    Washington County, 1828. Reprint.
Map Division, William L. Clements Library, University of Michigan, Ann Arbor.
    United States Coast Survey, 1864. "Part of Tennessee, North and
        South Carolina, Kentucky, Virginia, Georgia, and Alabama."
Map Room, Harlan Hatcher Graduate Library, University of Michigan, Ann
Arbor.
    United States Geological Survey. Topographical Maps.
McClung Collection, Lawson-McGhee Library, Knoxville, Tennessee.
    Wilson, Marshall. "Map of Early Settlements of East Tennessee,
        previously a part of North Carolina and of the Territory of the U.S.
        South of the River Ohio, Series 1—To End of Year 1776."
Tennessee State Library and Archives, Nashville, Tennessee.
    Manuscript map. Samuel Cole Williams Collection. Box 4.
    Washington County, 1836. Civil District Boundaries.


SECONDARY SOURCES

Abernethy, Thomas Perkins. From Frontier to Plantation: A Study in Frontier
    Democracy. Chapel Hill: Univ. of North Carolina Press, 1932.
Alderman, Pat. Greasy Cove in Unicoi County: Authentic Folklore. Johnson City,
    Tennessee: Overmountain Press, 1975.
Almgren, Gunnar. "Community." The Encyclopedia of Sociology. Edited by Edgar
    F. Borgatta and Marie L. Borgatta. New York: Macmillan, 1992.
Appalachia in the Making: The Mountain South in the Nineteenth Century. Edited
    by Mary Beth Pudup, Dwight B. Billings, and Altina L. Waller. Chapel
    Hill: Univ. of North Carolina Press, 1995.
Arnow, Harriet Simpson. Flowering on the Cumberland. New York: Macmillan,
    1963.
Ash, Stephen V. Middle Tennessee Society Transformed, 1860–1870: War and
    Peace in the Upper South. Baton Rouge: Louisiana State Univ. Press, 1988.
Bacon, H. Phillip. "Nashville's Trade at the Beginning of the Nineteenth Cen-
    tury." Tennessee Historical Quarterly 15 (1956): 30–36.
Barron, Hal S. Those Who Stayed Behind: Rural Society in Nineteenth-Century
    New England. Cambridge: Cambridge Univ. Press, 1984.
Bass, Robert D. "The Last Campaign of Major Patrick Ferguson." South Caro-
    lina Historical Association Proceedings, 1968. Columbia: South Carolina His-
    torical Association, 1969.
Batteau, Allen W. The Invention of Appalachia. Tucson: Univ. of Arizona Press, 1990.
Beeman, Richard. The Evolution of the Southern Backcountry: A Case Study of
    Lunenburg County, Virginia, 1746–1832. Philadelphia: Univ. of Pennsylva-
    nia Press, 1984.
Bell, Colin, and Howard Newby. Community Studies: An Introduction to the So-
    ciology of the Local Community. New York: Praeger, 1971.
Bell, Colin, and Howard Newby, eds. The Sociology of Community: A Selection of
    Readings. London: Frank Cass, 1974.

Bell, Michael M. "The Fruit of Difference: The Rural-Urban Continuum as a System of Identity." *Rural Sociology* 57 (Spring 1992): 65–82.

Bender, Thomas. *Community and Social Change in America*. Baltimore: Johns Hopkins Univ. Press, 1978.

Bergeron, Paul H. *Antebellum Politics in Tennessee*. Lexington: Univ. Press of Kentucky, 1982.

Berkley, Henry J. "Colonel Isaac Shelby and other Maryland Heroes of the Battle of King's Mountain, October 7th, 1780." *Maryland Historical Magazine* 27 (1932): 128–139.

Billings, Dwight, Kathleen Blee, and Louis Swanson. "Culture, Family, and Community in Preindustrial Appalachia." *Appalachian Journal* 13 (1986): 154–70.

Billings, Dwight B., Mary Beth Pudup, and Altina L. Waller, "Taking Exception with Exceptionalism: The Emergence and Transformation of Historical Studies of Appalachia." In Mary Beth Pudup, Dwight B. Billings, and Altina L. Waller, eds., *Appalachia in the Making: The Mountain South in the Nineteenth Century*, pp. 1–24. Chapel Hill: Univ. of North Carolina Press, 1995.

Blethen, Tyler, and Curtis Wood. "The Appalachian Frontier and the Southern Frontier: A Comparative Perspective." Paper presented at the Appalachian Studies Conference, Helen, Georgia, 23-25 March 1990.

Blethen, Tyler, and Curtis Wood. "A Trader on the Western Carolina Frontier." In Robert D. Mitchell, ed., *Appalachian Frontiers: Settlement, Society, and Development in the Preindustrial Era*, pp. 150–65. Lexington: Univ. Press of Kentucky, 1991.

Brown, Richard D. *Knowledge Is Power: The Diffusion of Information in Early America, 1700–1865*. New York: Oxford Univ. Press, 1989.

Browning, Howard M. "The Washington County Court, 1778–1789: A Study in Frontier Administration." *Tennessee Historical Quarterly* 1 (1942): 328–43.

Browning, Howard Miller. "Washington County Court: The Government of a Tennessee Frontier Community, 1778–1790." M.A. thesis, Vanderbilt University, 1938.

Buckwalter, Donald W. "Effects of Early Nineteenth Century Transportation Disadvantage on the Agriculture of East Tennessee." *Southeastern Geographer* 27 (1987): 18–37.

Campbell, John C. *The Southern Highlander and His Homeland*. New York: Russell Sage Foundation, 1921.

Cannon, Walter Faw. "Four Interpretations of the History of the State of Franklin." *East Tennessee Historical Society Publications* 22 (1950): 3–18.

Carr, Lois Green, Russell R. Menard, and Lorena S. Walsh. *Robert Cole's World: Agriculture and Society in Early Maryland*. Chapel Hill: Univ. of North Carolina Press, 1991.

Caudill, Harry M. *Night Comes to the Cumberlands: A Biography of a Depressed Area*. Boston: Little, Brown, 1962.

Chandler, Alfred D., Jr. *The Railroads: The Nation's First Big Business*. New York: Harcourt, Brace, and World, 1965.

Clark, Christopher. *The Roots of Rural Capitalism: Western Massachusetts, 1780–1860*. Ithaca: Cornell Univ. Press, 1990.

Clodfelter, Mark A. "Between Virtue and Necessity: Nathanael Greene and the Conduct of Civil-Military Relations in the South, 1780–1782." *Military Affairs* 52 (Oct. 1988): 169–75.

Corlew, Robert E. *Tennessee: A Short History*. 2d ed. Knoxville: Univ. of Tennessee Press, 1981.

Crow, Jeffery J. "Liberty Men and Loyalists: Disorder and Disaffection in the North Carolina Backcountry." In Ronald Hoffman, Thad Tate, and Peter Albert, eds., *An Uncivil War: The Southern Backcountry during the American Revolution*. Charlottesville: Univ. of Virginia Press, 1985.

Cunningham, Rodger. *Apples on the Flood: The Southern Mountain Experience*. Knoxville: Univ. of Tennessee Press, 1987.

Delfino, Susanna. "Antebellum East Tennessee Elites and Industrialization: The Examples of the Iron Industry and Internal Improvements." *East Tennessee Historical Society Publications* 56/57 (1984–85): 102–19.

Draper, Lyman C. *King's Mountain and Its Heroes: History of the Battle of King's Mountain*. Cincinnati: Peter G. Thomson, 1881.

Dunn, Durwood. *Cades Cove: The Life and Death of a Southern Appalachian Community, 1818–1900*. Knoxville: Univ. of Tennessee Press, 1988.

———. "Mary Noailles Murfree: A Reappraisal." *Appalachian Journal* 7 (1979): 197–204

Dykeman, Wilma. *With Fire and Sword: The Battle of King's Mountain, 1780*. Washington, D.C.: National Park Service, 1978.

Eby, Cecil D., Jr. *"Porte Crayon": The Life of David Hunter Strother*. Chapel Hill: Univ. of North Carolina Press, 1960.

Ekirch, A. Roger. "Whig Authority and Public Order in Backcountry North Carolina, 1776–1783." In Ronald Hoffman, Thad Tate, and Peter Albert, eds., *An Uncivil War: The Southern Backcountry during the American Revolution*. Charlottesville: Univ. of Virginia Press, 1985.

Eller, Ronald D. *Miners, Millhands, and Mountaineers: Industrialization of the Appalachian South, 1880–1930*. Knoxville: Univ. of Tennessee Press, 1982.

———. "The Search for Community in Appalachia." In Carl Ross, ed., *Contemporary Appalachia: In Search of a Useable Past*. Boone, N.C.: Appalachian Consortium Press, 1987.

Escott, Paul D., and Jeffery J. Crow. "The Social Order and Violent Disorder: An Analysis of North Carolina in the Revolution and the Civil War." *Journal of Southern History* 52 (1986): 373–402.

Faragher, John Mack. *Sugar Creek: Life on the Illinois Prairie*. New Haven: Yale Univ. Press, 1986.

Faust, Drew Gilpin. "The Peculiar South Revisited: White Society, Culture, and Politics in the Antebellum Period, 1800–1860." In John B. Boles and Evelyn Thomas Nolen, eds., *Interpreting Southern History: Historiographic Essays in Honor of Sanford W. Higginbotham*, pp. 78–119. Baton Rouge: Louisiana State Univ. Press, 1987.

Fink, Miriam. "Some Phases of the Social and Economic History of Jonesboro, Tennessee, Prior to the Civil War." M.A. thesis, Univ. of Tennessee, 1934.

Fink, Paul. "Bumpass Cove Mines and Embreeville." *East Tennessee Historical Society Publications* 16 (1944): 48–64.

———. "Did You Know How the Railroad Came to Washington County?" *Jonesborough Herald and Tribune*, undated. In Vertical Files, Archives of Appalachia, Sherrod Library, East Tennessee State University, Johnson City, Tennessee.

———. "Jacob Brown of Nolichucky." *Tennessee Historical Quarterly* 21 (1962): 235–50.

———. *Jonesborough: The First Century of Tennessee's First Town*. Johnson City, Tenn.: Overmountain Press, 1989. Originally published as Report No. TN-JONO-1-72-138-2. Johnson City: Upper East Tennessee Office, Tennessee State Planning Commission, 1972.

Fischer, David Hackett. *Albion's Seed: Four British Folkways in America*. New York: Oxford Univ. Press, 1989.

Folmsbee, S.J. "The Beginning of the Railroad Movement in East Tennessee." *East Tennessee Historical Society Publications* 5 (1933): 81–104.

Folmsbee, Stanley John. *Sectionalism and Internal Improvements in Tennessee, 1796–1845*. Knoxville: East Tennessee Historical Society, 1939.

Fox, John, Jr. "The Southern Mountaineers." *Scribner's Magazine* 29 (1901): 387–99, 556–70.

Franklin, John Hope. *The Militant South, 1800–1861*. Cambridge< Mass.: Harvard Univ. Press, 1956.

Frazier, D.R., comp. *Tennessee Postoffices and Postmaster Appointments, 1789–1984*. N.p., 1984.

Frost, William Goodell. "Our Contemporary Ancestors in the Southern Mountains." *Atlantic* 83 (1899): 311–19.

Geertz, Clifford. *Local Knowledge: Further Essays in Interpretive Anthropology*. New York: Basic Books, 1983.

Gerson, Noel B. *Franklin: America's "Lost State."* New York: Crowell-Collier Press, 1968.

*Goodspeed's History of Tennessee*. Chicago: Goodspeed Publishing, 1887.

Gray, Lewis Cecil. *History of Agriculture in the Southern United States to 1860*. 2 vols. Washington, D.C.: Carnegie Institution of Washington, 1933.

Gross, Robert. *The Minutemen and Their World*. New York: Hill and Wang, 1976.

Gump, Lucy Kennerly. "Possessions and Patterns of Living in Washington County: The Twenty Years Before Tennessee Statehood." M.A. thesis, East Tennessee State Univ., 1989.

Hahn, Steven. *The Roots of Southern Populism: Yeoman Farmers and the Transformation of the Georgia Upcountry, 1850–1890*. New York: Oxford Univ. Press, 1983.

Harney, Will Wallace. "A Strange Land and Peculiar People." *Lippincott's Magazine* 12 (Oct. 1873): 429–38.

Hayes, C. Willard. "The Southern Appalachians." *National Geographic Monographs* 1 (1895): 305–36.

Henderson, Archibald. "The Spanish Conspiracy in Tennessee." *Tennessee Historical Magazine* 3 (Dec. 1917): 229–43.

Henley, Mrs. Charles Fairfax. "Maj. Charles Robertson, and Some of His Descendants." *American Historical Magazine* 3 (1898): 21–28.

Henretta, James A. *The Origins of American Capitalism: Collected Essays.* Boston: Northeastern Univ. Press, 1991.

Heyrman, Christine Leigh. *Commerce and Culture: The Maritime Communities of Colonial Massachusetts, 1690–1750.* New York: Norton, 1984.

Higginbotham, Don. *The War of American Independence: Military Attitudes, Policies, and Practice, 1763–1789.* New York: Macmillan, 1971.

Higgs, Robert J., and Ambrose N. Manning, eds. *Voices from the Hills: Selected Readings of Southern Appalachia.* New York: Ungar, 1975.

Hillery, George A., Jr. "Definitions of Community: Areas of Agreement." *Rural Sociology* 20 (1955): 111-23.

"History of Navigation on the Tennessee River System." House Doc. No. 254. 75th Cong., 1st. Sess., 1937.

*History of Washington County, Tennessee, 1988.* Compiled by the Watauga Association of Genealogists—Upper East Tennessee. Johnson City, Tenn.: n.p., 1988.

Hoffman, Ronald. "The 'Disaffected' in the Revolutionary South." In Alfred F. Young, ed., *The American Revolution: Explorations in the History of American Radicalism,* pp. 273–316. DeKalb: Northern Illinois Univ. Press, 1976.

Hoffman, Ronald, Thad Tate, and Peter Albert, eds. *An Uncivil War: The Southern Backcountry during the American Revolution.* Charlottesville: Univ. of Virginia Press, 1985.

Hofstra, Warren R. "Land, Ethnicity, and Community at the Opequon Settlement, Virginia, 1730–1800." *Virginia Magazine of History and Biography* 98 (July 1990): 421–48.

Hofstra, Warren R., and Robert D. Mitchell. "Town and Country in Backcountry Virginia: Winchester and the Shenandoah Valley, 1730–1800." *Journal of Southern History* 59 (Nov. 1993): 619–46.

Holland, James W. "The Building of the East Tennessee and Virginia Railroad." *East Tennessee Historical Society Publications* 4 (1932): 83–101.

———. "The East Tennessee and Georgia Railroad, 1836–1860." *East Tennessee Historical Society Publications* 3 (1931): 89–107.

Hoover, Dwight W. "Community Studies." In Mary K. Cayton, Elliot Gorn, and Peter Williams, eds., *Encyclopedia of American Social History,* pp. 297–305. New York: Scribners, 1993.

Hsiung, David C. "How Isolated Was Appalachia? Upper East Tennessee, 1780–1835." *Appalachian Journal* 16 (1989): 336–49.

Inscoe, John C. *Mountain Masters, Slavery, and the Sectional Crisis in Western North Carolina.* Knoxville: Univ. of Tennessee Press, 1989.

Jones, Douglas Lamar. *Village and Seaport: Migration and Society in Eighteenth-Century Massachusetts.* Hanover, N.H.: Univ. Press of New England, 1981.

Kenzer, Robert C. *Kinship and Neighborhood in a Southern Community: Orange County, North Carolina, 1849–1881.* Knoxville: Univ. of Tennessee Press, 1987.

Kephart, Horace. *Our Southern Highlanders*. New York: Macmillan, 1922. Reprint. Knoxville: Univ. of Tennessee Press, 1976.

Klein, Rachel N. *Unification of a Slave State: The Rise of the Planter Class in the South Carolina Backcountry, 1760–1808*. Chapel Hill: Univ. of North Carolina Press, 1990.

Kozsuch, Mildred, ed. *Historical Reminiscences of Carter County, Tennessee*. Johnson City, Tenn.: Overmountain Press, 1985.

Kulikoff, Allan. *The Agrarian Origins of American Capitalism*. Charlottesville: Univ. Press of Virginia, 1992.

Lasch, Christopher. *The True and Only Heaven: Progress and its Critics*. New York: W.W. Norton, 1991.

MacMaster, Richard K. "The Cattle Trade in Western Virginia, 1760–1830." In Robert D. Mitchell, ed., *Appalachian Frontiers: Settlement, Society, and Development in the Preindustrial Era*, pp. 127–49. Lexington: Univ. Press of Kentucky, 1991.

McKee, James. "Alfred E. Jackson: A Profile of an East Tennessee Entrepreneur, Railway Promoter, and Soldier. Part 1." *East Tennessee Historical Society Publications* 49 (1977): 9–36.

McKenzie, Robert Tracy. *One South or Many? Plantation Belt and Upcountry in Civil War–Era Tennessee*. Cambridge: Cambridge Univ. Press, 1994.

McKinney, Gordon B. "Preindustrial Jackson County and Economic Development." Paper presented at the Appalachian Studies Conference, Morgantown, West Virginia, 17-19 March 1989.

———. "Economy and Community in Western North Carolina, 1860–1865." In Mary Beth Pudup, Dwight B. Billings, and Altina L. Waller, eds., *Appalachia in the Making: The Mountain South in the Nineteenth Century*, pp. 163–84. Chapel Hill: Univ. of North Carolina Press, 1995.

McWhiney, Grady. *Cracker Culture: Celtic Ways in the Old South*. Tuscaloosa: Univ. of Alabama Press, 1988.

Mann, Ralph. "Diversity in the Antebellum Appalachian South: Four Farm Communities in Tazewell County, Virginia." In Mary Beth Pudup, Dwight B. Billings, and Altina L. Waller, eds., *Appalachia in the Making: The Mountain South in the Nineteenth Century*, pp. 132–62. Chapel Hill: Univ. of North Carolina Press, 1995.

———. "Mountains, Land, and Kin Networks: Burkes Garden, Virginia, in the 1840s and 1850s." *Journal of Southern History* 58 (Aug. 1992): 411–34.

Melvoin, Richard I. *New England Outpost: War and Society in Colonial Deerfield*. New York: W.W. Norton, 1989.

Merrill, Michael. "Cast is Good to Eat: Self-Sufficiency and Exchange in the Rural Economy of the United States." *Radical History Review* 4 (1977): 42–71.

Merritt, Frank. *Early History of Carter County, 1760–1861*. Knoxville: East Tennessee Historical Society, 1950.

Mitchell, Robert D. *Commercialism and Frontier: Perspectives on the Early Shenandoah Valley*. Charlottesville: Univ. of Virginia Press, 1977.

Mitchell, Robert D., ed. *Appalachian Frontiers: Settlement, Society, & Development in the Preindustrial Era*. Lexington: Univ. Press of Kentucky, 1991.

Moore, John Trotwood, and Austin P. Foster. *Tennessee: The Volunteer State,*
    *1769–1923.* 4 vols. Chicago: S.J. Clarke, 1923.
Moore, Tyrel G. "Economic Development in Appalachian Kentucky, 1800–
    1860." In Robert D. Mitchell, ed., *Appalachian Frontiers: Settlement, Society,*
    *and Development in the Preindustrial Era,* pp. 222–34. Lexington: Univ. Press
    of Kentucky, 1991.
Myer, William Edward. "Indian Trails of the Southeast." *Forty-second Annual*
    *Report, Bureau of American Ethnology. Smithsonian Institution.* Washington,
    D.C.: Government Printing Office, 1928.
Noe, Kenneth W. *Southwest Virginia's Railroad: Modernization and the Sectional*
    *Crisis.* Urbana: Univ. of Illinois Press, 1994.
North, Douglass C. *The Economic Growth of the United States, 1790–1860.*
    Englewood Cliffs, N.J.: Prentice-Hall, 1961
Otto, John Solomon. "'Hillbilly Culture': The Appalachian Mountain Folk in
    History and Popular Culture." *Southern Quarterly* 24 (1986): 25–34.
Paludan, Phillip Shaw. *Victims: A True Story of the Civil War.* Knoxville: Univ.
    of Tennessee Press, 1981.
Pancake, John S. *This Destructive War: The British Campaign in the Carolinas,*
    *1780–1782.* University: Univ. of Alabama Press, 1985.
Parkerson, Donald H. "How Mobile Were Nineteenth-Century Americans?"
    *Historical Methods* 15 (1982): 99–109.
Parks, Edd Winfield. *Charles Egbert Craddock (Mary Noailles Murfree).* Chapel
    Hill: Univ. of North Carolina Press, 1941.
Paullin, Charles O. *Atlas of the Historical Geography of the United States.* Edited
    by John K. Wright. Washington, D.C.: Carnegie Institution of Washington
    and American Geographical Society of New York, 1932.
Pudup, Mary Beth. "Social Class and Economic Development in Southeast
    Kentucky, 1820–1880." In Robert D. Mitchell, ed., *Appalachian Frontiers:*
    *Settlement, Society, and Development in the Preindustrial Era,* pp. 235–60.
    Lexington: Univ. Press of Kentucky, 1991.
Raitz, Karl, and Richard Ulack. *Appalachia, A Regional Geography: Land, People,*
    *and Development.* Boulder, Colo.: Westview Press, 1984.
*Rand McNally Commercial Atlas and Marketing Guide.* Chicago: Rand McNally, 1987.
Rothstein, Morton. "The Antebellum South as a Dual Economy: A Tentative
    Hypothesis." *Agricultural History* 41 (1967): 373–82.
Schlotterbeck, John T. "The 'Social Economy' of an Upper South Community:
    Orange and Greene Counties, Virginia, 1815–1860." In Orville Vernon
    Burton and Robert C. McMath, Jr., eds., *Class, Conflict, and Consensus:*
    *Antebellum Southern Community Studies,* pp. 3–28. Westport, Conn.: Green-
    wood Press, 1982.
Sellers, Charles. *The Market Revolution: Jacksonian America, 1815–1846.* New
    York: Oxford Univ. Press, 1991.
Sevier, Cora Bales, and Nancy S. Madden. *Sevier Family History, with the Col-*
    *lected Letters of Gen. John Sevier . . .* Washington, D.C.: Kaufmann Printing,
    1961.
Shapiro, Henry D. *Appalachia on Our Mind: The Southern Mountains and Moun-*

taineers in the American Consciousness, 1870–1920. Chapel Hill: Univ. of North Carolina Press, 1978.

Shy, John. "Migration and Persistence in Revolutionary America." In Elise Marienstras and Barbara Karsky, eds., Autre Temps, Autre Espace: Etudes sur l'Amérique Pré-industrielle. Nancy, France: Presses Universitaires de Nancy, 1986.

Smith, Daniel Scott. "Migration of American Colonial Militiamen: A Comparative Note." Social Science History 7 (1983): 475–80.

Soltow, Lee. "Progress and Mobility Among Ohio Propertyholders, 1810–1825." Social Science History 7 (1983): 405–26.

Taylor, George Rogers, and Irene D. Neu. The American Railroad Network, 1861–1890. Cambridge, Mass.: Harvard Univ. Press, 1956.

Thorndale, William, and William Dollarhide. Map Guide to the United States Federal Censuses, 1790–1920. Baltimore: Genealogical Publishing, 1987.

Tönnies, Ferdinand. Community and Society (Gemeinschaft und Gesellschaft). Translated and edited by Charles P. Loomis. New York: Harper and Row, 1957.

Villaflor, G.C., and K.L. Sokoloff. "Migration in Colonial America: Evidence from the Militia Muster Rolls." Social Science History 6 (1982): 539–70.

Waller, Altina L. Feud: Hatfields, McCoys, and Social Change in Appalachia, 1860–1900. Chapel Hill: Univ. of North Carolina Press, 1988.

Walsh, Lorena S. "The Historian as Census Taker: Individual Reconstitution and the Reconstruction of Censuses for a Colonial Chesapeake County." William and Mary Quarterly 38 (1981): 242–60.

———. "Staying Put or Getting Out: Findings for Charles County, Maryland, 1650–1720." William and Mary Quarterly 44 (1987): 89–103.

Weber, David J. The Spanish Frontier in North America. New Haven: Yale Univ. Press, 1992.

Weller, Jack. Yesterday's People: Life in Contemporary Appalachia. Lexington: Univ. of Kentucky Press, 1965.

Wilentz, Sean. "Society, Politics, and the Market Revolution, 1815–1848." In Eric Foner, ed., The New American History, pp. 51–71. Philadelphia: Temple Univ. Press, 1990.

Wilhelm, Gene, Jr. "Appalachian Isolation: Fact or Fiction?" In J.W. Williamson, ed., An Appalachian Symposium: Essays Written in Honor of Cratis D. Williams, pp. 77–91. Boone, N.C.: Appalachian State Univ. Press, 1977.

Williams, Cratis D. "The Southern Mountaineer in Fact and Fiction." Ph.D. diss., New York University, 1961.

———. "The Southern Mountaineer in Fact and Fiction." Edited by Martha H. Pipes. Part I. Appalachian Journal 3 (1975): 8-41.

Williams, Samuel Cole. "The Battle of King's Mountain: As Seen by the British Officers." Tennessee Historical Magazine 7 (April 1921): 51-66.

———. "Early Iron Works in the Tennessee Country." Tennessee Historical Quarterly 6 (1947): 39–46.

———. History of Johnson City and Its Environs. Johnson City, Tenn.: Watauga Press, 1940.

————. *History of the Lost State of Franklin*. Rev. ed. New York: Press of the Pioneers, 1933.

————. *Tennessee During the Revolutionary War*. Nashville: Tennessee Historical Commission, 1944.

Woodbridge, John, ed. *History of Nashville, Tenn*. Nashville: Methodist Episcopal Church, South, 1890.

Wright, Gavin. *The Political Economy of the Cotton South: Households, Markets, and Wealth in the Nineteenth Century*. New York: W.W. Norton, 1978.

Wright, Nathalia. "Introduction." In Mary Noailles Murfree, *In the Tennessee Mountains*. New York: Houghton, Mifflin, 1884. Reprint. Knoxville: Univ. of Tennessee Press, 1970.

Wyatt-Brown, Bertram. *Southern Honor: Ethics and Behavior in the Old South*. New York: Oxford Univ. Press, 1982.

# Index